Falaise
The Flawed Victory

The Destruction of Panzergruppe West August 1944

Anthony Tucker-Jones

Pen & Sword

MILITARY

An imprint of
Pen & Sword Books Ltd
Yorkshire - Philadelphia

First published in Great Britain in 2008 by
PEN & SWORD MILITARY
An imprint of
Pen & Sword Books Ltd
Yorkshire – Philadelphia

Paperback edition 2018

ISBN 978 1 52673 852 3

Typeset in 11/13 Ehrhardt by Concept, Huddersfield, West Yorkshire

Printed and bound by CPI Group (UK) Ltd, Croydon, CR0 4YY

Pen & Sword Books Ltd incorporates the Imprints of Aviation, Atlas, Family
History, Fiction, Maritime, Military, Discovery, Politics, History, Archaeology,
Select, Wharncliffe Local History, Wharncliffe True Crime, Military Classics,
Wharncliffe Transport, Leo Cooper, The Praetorian Press, Remember When,
Seaforth Publishing and Frontline Publishing.

For a complete list of Pen & Sword titles please contact

PEN & SWORD BOOKS LTD
47 Church Street, Barnsley, South Yorkshire, S70 2AS, England
E-mail: enquiries@pen-and-sword.co.uk
Website: www.pen-and-sword.co.uk

Or

PEN & SWORD BOOKS
1950 Lawrence Rd, Havertown, PA 19083, USA
E-mail: Uspen-and-sword@casematepublishers.com
Website: www.penandswordbooks.com

Contents

Preface to the paperback edition

When this book was first published my aim had been to offer a completely different approach to what is after all a very well-known battle. This was done by following the fate of the panzer divisions involved individually from start to finish. My central focus was Hitler's Panzergruppe West, the command formation that in theory was supposed to throw the Allies back into the sea following the D-Day landings. It was to direct the powerful armoured counterattacks planned by Rommel. Its efforts though were stymied from the start in part by a confused chain of command, a lack of supporting infantry divisions and the Allies' command of the air and sea. While the panzers struggled to launch any meaningful strategic counterattacks, one of their finest moments though was undoubtedly the desperate defence at Caen.

Over the years the approach to the Normandy campaign has always been, why did the allies with their overwhelming resources take so long to breakout? There was an obsession over proposed deadlines – which persistently ignored the old military mantra that the plan never survives contact. Much that could go wrong did go wrong. Most notably initial key objectives were not secured, the great storm in the English Channel wrecked the Allies' build-up and grounded their fighter bombers at a key moment in the battle. The destruction wrought by the Germans on Cherbourg denied the Allies of a much-needed port at which to land their supplies. Likewise the German defence of Caen proved an especially tough nut to crack and became the linchpin of the whole battle. It was the flexibility and swift responses of ad hoc German battle groups that so often outfought the Allies.

Ironically in terms of other campaigns fought during the Second World War, Normandy's three-month duration was actually quite swift. In North Africa the British took from May 1941 until October 1942 to decisively defeat Rommel in Libya and then from November 1942 until May 1943 to finally crush the remaining German and Italian forces trapped in Tunisia. Similarly the war in Italy was an equally hard slog that dragged on from September 1943 until the very end of the war. Whereas by September 1944 the Allies had almost reached the Rhine. It was the swift German recovery from their defeat at Falaise and the worsening weather that conspired to cheat the allies of a much quicker victory in the West.

This book is titled *Falaise: The Flawed Victory* not so much as a criticism of Allied strategy, but because, while the Germans lost most of their tanks, crucially the bulk of the crews escaped to fight again. The surviving German infantry were useful but it was the panzertruppen who were most valuable. This amongst the numerous other setbacks suffered by the Allies is the one that stands out the most. Without these crews the re-equipped panzer divisions could never have been able to launch Hitler's surprise Christmas Ardennes offensive or indeed his spring offensive in Hungary.

The Allies achieved a very decisive victory but in an ideal world they would have completely sealed the Falaise pocket and then created a bigger encirclement before the fleeing German armies reached the Seine. Instead the Germans were able to fight a successful rearguard action and get away over the river. The escape of the German armies at Rouen and from southern France proved a major embarrassment to the Allies. It should be noted the Germans also committed countless errors during the Normandy campaign. All of which helped hasten their defeat.

The fascination in the Normandy campaign endures as does the appetite for new studies on the subject. The reissue of *Falaise: The Flawed Victory* in paperback offered an opportunity to rewrite and update, but I decided to leave it largely as it is, warts and all. On the whole I would like to think it has stood the test of time and I hope readers continue to enjoy its uniquely German panzer-division perspective. Certainly it continues to highlight how Hitler was the architect of his own destruction in the Battle for Normandy, by leaving his panzers desperately trying to seal a rapidly leaking dam in such a piecemeal fashion.

Preface and acknowledgements

In the hot, dusty summer of 1944 Hitler's panzers fought desperately, first to throw the Allies back into the sea and then to extricate themselves from encirclement in the Normandy countryside. For two and a half bloody months the Germans held the Allies at bay following Operation Overlord and the D-Day landings, but when they were finally trapped in the Falaise pocket it became a corridor of death.

General Dwight Eisenhower, Allied Supreme Commander, conjuring an image of Dante's *Inferno*, remarked:

> The battlefield of Falaise was unquestionably one of the greatest 'killing grounds' of any of the war areas. Roads, highways and fields were so choked with destroyed equipment and dead men and animals that passage through the area was extremely difficult. Forty-eight hours after the closing of the gap I was conducted through it on foot, to encounter scenes that could be described only by Dante. It was literally possible to walk for hundreds of yards at a time, stepping on nothing but dead and decaying flesh.

The final defeat of the German Army in the Falaise pocket on 20 August 1944 is rightly seen as the culmination of the hard-fought Normandy campaign. The destruction of the Wehrmacht, especially the vital panzer divisions in the West, seemed assured. Some likened it to Hitler's crushing defeats at Stalingrad and in Tunisia.

Eisenhower's view of Falaise though was tainted with an air of regret:

> In the wider sweep directed against the crossings of the Seine behind the German Army, the rapidly advancing Americans were also forced to halt to avoid overrunning their objectives and firing into friendly troops. The Germans again seized the opportunity to escape with a greater portion of his strength than would have been the case if the exact situation could have been completely foreseen.

Respected American military historian Steven Zaloga is on record as saying: 'Controversy over the Falaise Gap has been a staple of popular histories of the war, many of the accounts being sensationalist clap-trap'. That the Battle for Normandy did not go exactly to plan and that the pinching off of the Falaise pocket was not achieved with the finesse that the Allies may have liked should not detract from the fact that the desired result was achieved.

That the victory was subsequently seen as flawed is not so much a result of the numbers of Germans escaping the trap, after all they left all their heavy equipment behind, but due to their quite remarkable recovery abilities. The escape of small, experienced cadres from each of the panzer divisions seemed to matter little at the time, especially with the Germans retreating pell-mell back across the River Seine. What equipment they did salvage from the chaos of the Normandy countryside lay discarded on the dockside at Rouen and elsewhere.

Nonetheless, it was not long before the shortcomings of Falaise and the failure to conduct a wider encirclement of the Germans up against the Seine became apparent. The reconstituted panzer divisions were soon to cause havoc in Alsace, the Ardennes, the Eifel, the Low Countries, the Hurtgen Forest, the Saar, the Rhineland and the Rhur; more specifically at Aachen, Arnhem, Arnswalde, Balaton, Bastogne, Celles, Cologne, Geilenkirchen, Hunxe, Metz, Nijmegen, Oosterbeek, Remagen, Rimlingen and St Vith. Essentially they were involved everywhere that the Germans sought to impede the Allies slow but steady advance across Western Europe toward Hitler's crumbling Reich.

In particular the escape of II SS Panzer Corps was to have dire consequences. Just three weeks after the liquidation of the Falaise pocket on 17 September 1944 Montgomery launched Operation Market Garden, intended to take the Allies over the Rhine and into the Nazi industrial heartland of the Ruhr. Tragically, this operation was to be thwarted in spectacular fashion, especially as the British airborne spearhead landed amidst the recuperating 9th SS and 10th SS Panzer Divisions at Arnhem. Although the SS were extremely under strength, when the Allied ground forces were unable to reach the paras the outcome was inevitable.

Yet worse was to come. All those panzer divisions destroyed in the Falaise pocket were rebuilt and, remarkably, just four months later took part in Hitler's audacious Ardennes counteroffensive. This was launched on 16 December 1944, spearheaded by the 1st SS and 12th SS Panzer Divisions, both veterans of Normandy. Although the offensive was stopped in its tracks, it showed how the defeat at Falaise had singularly failed to completely crush the panzers on the Western Front.

Just two months before the end of the war, the severely-mauled panzer units of the 6th SS Panzer Army then took part in Hitler's final massive counter-offensive on the Eastern Front. Although the Soviets' Operation Bagration, timed to coincide with D-Day, had torn the heart out of the panzers on the Eastern Front, following the Ardennes offensive 6th SS Panzer Army was still able to move east to take part in this major counteroffensive in Hungary. The few panzer units left in the West even launched a small counterattack eastwards from the Ruhr pocket in March 1945, in a desperate attempt to escape the encircling Allies.

What shines out, irrespective of the rights or wrongs of Nazi Germany, is the sheer professionalism exhibited by the Wehrmacht and Waffen-SS even when continued resistance seemed a futile exercise. The genesis of this book occurred in 1984 following writing an article to mark the 40th anniversary of D-Day and interviewing one of the directors of the then brand new Portsmouth D-Day Museum.

Of the plethora of books that were published that year, one in particular, Max Hastings' *Overlord: D-Day and the Battle for Normandy*, caused a storm of controversy for lauding the Germans' feat of arms. 'The glory of German arms in Normandy – and it was glory,' he wrote, 'in however evil a cause – was won by the officers and men at divisional level and below who held the line against the Allies under intolerable conditions for more than two months'. Over twenty years on Hastings' reputation as a military historian remains untarnished and he remains unrepentant: 'In *Overlord*, I argued that Hitler's army was the outstanding fighting force of the Second World War ... Since I wrote *Overlord*, however, my own thinking has changed – not about the battlefield performance of the combatants, but about its significance. Moral and social issues are at stake, more important than any narrow military judgement'. Indeed German military professionalism is one thing, but the Nazi regime passed beyond the pale.

I remember walking Gold and Omaha beaches thinking how had the Allies gained and then enlarged such a precarious toehold. The American cemetery behind Omaha provides stark testimony to the bloody battle for Normandy. Driving west through Arromanches, Bayeux and Carentan then north up the Cotentin Peninsula, I wondered why the Germans had allowed their forces to become trapped in Cherbourg and then outflanked at St Lô despite clinging on so resolutely in the Caen area. How had they got it so wrong in Normandy but bounced back, dragging the war on for another eight months.

Much heated debate has raged about the effectiveness and employment of the panzer divisions in Normandy, though it was the numerically superior German infantry divisions that bore the brunt of the fighting. The failure of the panzers to launch a decisive counterstroke has been blamed on a muddled chain of command, inertia, Hitler's intransigence and the Allies superiority on the ground and in the air.

The reality is that from the very start there were insufficient German armoured formations in Normandy and although they rose to almost a dozen they were largely committed in a piecemeal manner, trying to plug an increasingly leaking dam. Remarkably, never once did they waver despite losing all strategic initiative in the face of Hitler's stubborn refusal to yield ground until it was too late.

In the intervening years much has been written about Overlord and the liberation of France. This particular volume is designed to examine the individual experiences and fate of each of the panzer divisions that fought there under the direction of both Panzergruppe West and 7th Army. In terms of narrative it follows each unit chronologically as it joined the battle, before coming together in the Falaise salient. It is notable that no single volume provides an overview of the subsequent fate of those panzer divisions involved in Normandy and this study also offers to rectify this in some small way.

Many organisations and people were kind enough to assist me during the researching of this book, notably Barnstaple Library and Record Office. Individuals who offered me their time and wisdom were many, but in particular I would like to single out John Blackman, for assistance with the photographic research; David Fletcher, for his sage guidance on the merits of Allied armour; Rupert Harding, who above and beyond the call of duty helped with reference material and had faith in the broad scope of this project; Tim Newark and Pat Ware, who kindly encouraged and supported the initial research on Falaise and Villers-Bocage; and lastly, Philip Sidnell for his sterling editorial work with both the text and photographs. Special thanks are due to Leo Cooper and Pen and Sword Books for assistance with key maps.

Finally, I must thank my wife Amelia and daughter Henrietta, who have endured with such patience and fortitude my passion for military history and the necessary solitude of a writer. For their unfailing indulgence I dedicate this book to them with my heartfelt thanks and love.

Anthony Tucker-Jones
Barnstaple, Devon
2007

Dramatis Personae – Senior German Commanders

Adolf Hitler
Commander-in-Chief, Oberkommando der Wehrmacht (OKW – the Armed Forces
High Command)

Generalfeldmarschall Wilhelm Keitel
Chief of Staff OKW

Generaloberst Alfred Jodl
Chief of Operations Staff OKW

Generalfeldmarschall Gerd von Rundstedt
Commander-in-Chief West or Oberbefelshaber West (OB West) (until 2 July 1944)

Generalfeldmarschall Günther von Kluge
Replaced von Rundstedt, as C-in-C West and Rommel as commander Army Group
B (until 18 August 1944)

Generalfeldmarschall Walther Model
Replaced von Kluge as C-in-C West and commander Army Group B

General Günther Blumentritt
Chief of Staff to C-in-C West

Generalfeldmarschall Erwin Rommel
Commander Army Group B (until 17 July 1944 when wounded)

General Friedrich Dollmann
Commander 7th Army (until 28 June suicide/heart attack)

General Geyr von Schweppenburg
Commander Panzergruppe West (until 6 July 1944)

General der Panzertruppen Heinrich Eberbach
Replaced Schweppenburg as commander Panzergruppe West/5th Panzer Army
(until 9 August) then Panzergruppe Eberbach, also succeeded Hausser as commander 7th Army (until 31 August when captured)

SS-Obergruppenführer Josef 'Sepp' Dietrich
Commander I SS Panzer Corps, replaced Eberbach as commander Panzergruppe
West/5th Panzer Army

SS-Obergruppenführer Hermann Priess
Replaced Dietrich as commander I SS Panzer Corps

SS-Obergruppenführer Paul Hausser
Commander II SS Panzer Corps, then succeeded Dollmann as commander
7th Army (until 20 August 1944 when wounded)

SS-Obergruppenführer Wilhelm 'Willi' Bittrich
Replaced Hausser as commander II SS Panzer Corps

General der Fallschirmtruppen Eugen Meindl
Commander II Parachute Corps

General der Flakartillerie Wolfgang Pickert
Commander III Flak Corps

General der Artillerie Wilhelm Fahrmbacher
Commander XXV (25th) Corps in Brittany, interim commander (12–18 June
1944) LXXXIV (84th) Corps following Marcks' demise

General der Panzertruppen Hans von Funck
Commander XLVII (47th) Panzer Corps

General der Panzertruppen Walter Krüger
Commander LVIII (58th) Panzer Corps

General der Infanterie Erich Straube
Commander LXXIV (74th) Corps

General der Panzertruppen Adolf Kuntzen
Commander LXXXI (81st) Corps

General der Artillerie Erich Marcks
Commander LXXXIV (84th) Corps (until 12 June 1944 killed in action)

Generalleutenant Dietrich von Choltitz
Replaced Marcks as commander LXXXIV Corps (until 28 July) then Commandant
Paris (until 25 August 1944 when captured)

Generalleutenant Otto Elfeldt
Replaced von Choltitz as commander LXXXIV Corps (until 20 August 1944 when
captured)

General der Infanterie Hans von Obstfelder
Commander LXXXVI (86th) Corps

Principal German Armoured Fighting Vehicles Deployed in Normandy

Tanks
PzKpfw IV Ausf H and Ausf J Medium Tank
PzKpfw V Panther Ausf A and Ausf G Heavy Medium Tank
PzKpfw VI Tiger I Ausf E Heavy Tank
PzKpfw VI Tiger II Ausf B Heavy Tank

Assault Guns
Sturmgeschütz III Ausf G Assault Gun
Jagdpanzer IV Tank Destroyer
Jagdpanther Heavy Tank Destroyer

Self-propelled Guns
Hummel Heavy Howitzer
Wespe Light Field Howitzer
Marder III Anti-tank Gun

Principal Allied Armoured Fighting Vehicles deployed in Normandy

Tanks
M4 Sherman Medium Tank
Sherman Firefly Medium Tank
M5 Light Tank
Cromwell Cruiser Tank
Churchill Infantry Tank

Tank Destroyers
M10 Wolverine Gun Motor Carriage
M18 Gun Motor Carriage
M36 Gun Motor Carriage

Self-propelled Guns
M7B1 Howitzer Motor Carriage
Sexton 25pdr Tracked

For comparative analysis of the merits of German and Allied armour see pp. 16–19.

List of Plates

Maps

List of Maps
1. German Army Groups B & G areas of responsibility June 1944.
2. German Panzer, Infantry and Airborne Divisional dispositions as of 6 June 1944.
3. The Battle for Caen, 6 June–24 July 1944.
4. Containing Epsom, 24–29 June 1944.
5. Charnwood, 7–9 July 1944.
6. Stopping Goodwood, 18–20 July 1944.
7. The Falaise Pocket, 16–20 August 1944.
8. The Allied Breakout and race to the Seine, 1–20 August 1944.

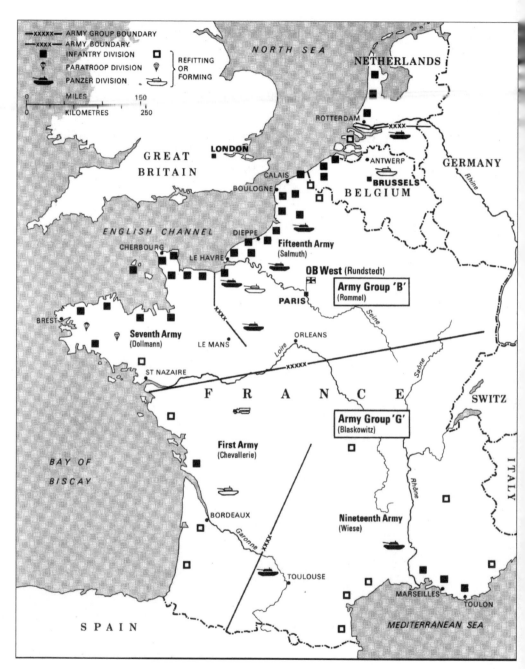

German Army Groups B & G areas of responsibility, June 1944.

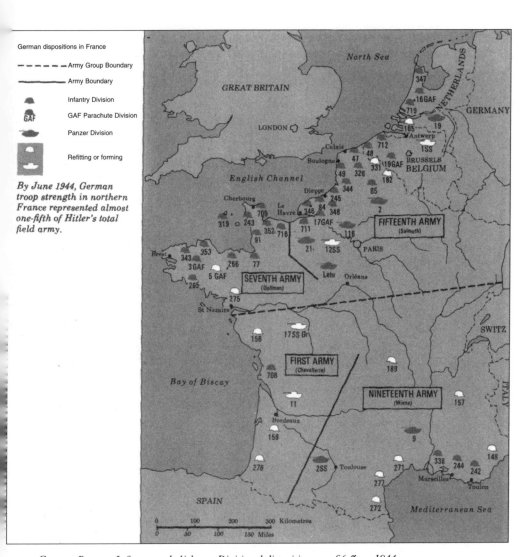

German dispositions in France

- - - - - Army Group Boundary

———— Army Boundary

Infantry Division

GAF Parachute Division

Panzer Division

Refitting or forming

By June 1944, German troop strength in northern France represented almost one-fifth of Hitler's total field army.

German Panzer, Infantry and Airborne Divisional dispositions as of 6 June 1944.

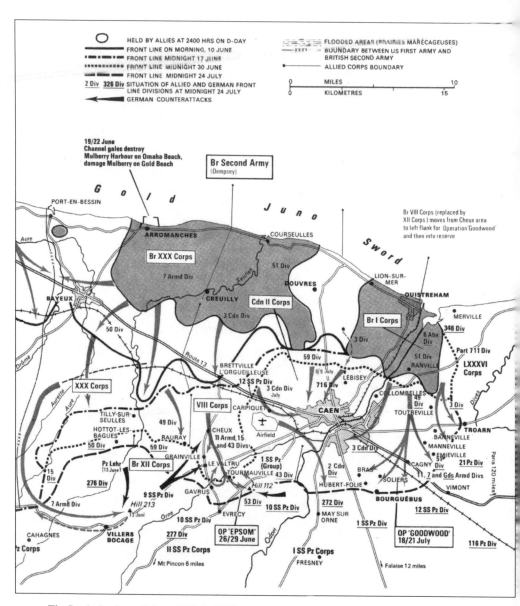

Key:

○ HELD BY ALLIES AT 2400 HRS ON D-DAY
▬▬▬ FRONT LINE ON MORNING, 10 JUNE
▬·▬·▬ FRONT LINE MIDNIGHT 17 JUNE
▪▪▪▪▪ FRONT LINE MIDNIGHT 30 JUNE
▬▬▬ FRONT LINE MIDNIGHT 24 JULY
2 Div | 326 Div SITUATION OF ALLIED AND GERMAN FRONT LINE DIVISIONS AT MIDNIGHT 24 JULY
➤ GERMAN COUNTERATTACKS

▬ ▬ FLOODED AREAS (PRAIRIES MARÉCAGEUSES)
—×××— BOUNDARY BETWEEN US FIRST ARMY AND BRITISH SECOND ARMY
•—• ALLIED CORPS BOUNDARY

MILES 0 10
KILOMETRES 0 15

19/22 June
Channel gales destroy
Mulberry Harbour on Omaha Beach,
damage Mulberry on Gold Beach

Br Second Army
(Dempsey)

Br VIII Corps (replaced by
XII Corps) moves from Cheux area
to left flank for Operation 'Goodwood'
and then into reserve

G o l d
J u n o
S w o r d

PORT-EN-BESSIN
ARROMANCHES
COURSEULLES
Br XXX Corps
51 Div
7 Armd Div
DOUVRES
LION-SUR-MER
OUISTREHAM
BAYEUX
CREUILLY
Cdn II Corps
MERVILLE
346 Div
Br I Corps
3 Div
6 Abn Div
50 Div
3 Cdn Div
51 Div
Part 711 Div
RANVILLE
LXXXVI Corps
Route 13
BRETTVILLE L'ORGUEILLEUSE
59 Div
8/9 July
XXX Corps
12 SS Pz Div
3 Cdn Div July
716 Div
LEBISEY
COLLOMBELLES
3 Div
TILLY-SUR-SEULLES
49 Div
VIII Corps
CARPIQUET
CAEN
49 Div
TOUTREVILLE
TROARN
HOTTOT-LES-BAGUES
CHEUX
11 Armd, 15 and 43 Divs
Airfield
3 Cdn Div
BANNEVILLE
MANNEVILLE
EMIEVILLE
50 Div
59 Div
RAURAY
GRAINVILLE
1 SS Pz (Group)
2 Cdn Div
BRAS
CAGNY
5 Div
21 Pz Div
15 Div
Pz Lehr [13 June]
Br XII Corps
LE VALTRU
TOURMAUVILLE
43 Div
HUBERT-FOLIE
SOLIERS
11, 7 and Gds Armd Divs
VIMONT
276 Div
9 SS Pz Div
GAVRUS
Hill 112
7 Armd Div
Hill 213
13 June
10 SS Pz Div
53 Div
10 SS Pz Div
272 Div
BOURGUÉBUS
12 SS Pz Div
CAHAGNES
VILLERS BOCAGE
277 Div
EVRECY
OP 'EPSOM' 26/29 June
MAY SUR ORNE
1 SS Pz Div
OP 'GOODWOOD' 18/21 July
116 Pz Div
Pz Corps
II SS Pz Corps
Mt Pincon 6 miles
I SS Pz Corps
FRESNEY
Falaise 12 miles
Aure
Aure
Drôme
Seulles
Aurette
Aure
Orne
Odon
Dives
Paris 120 miles

The Battle for Caen, 6 June–24 July 1944.

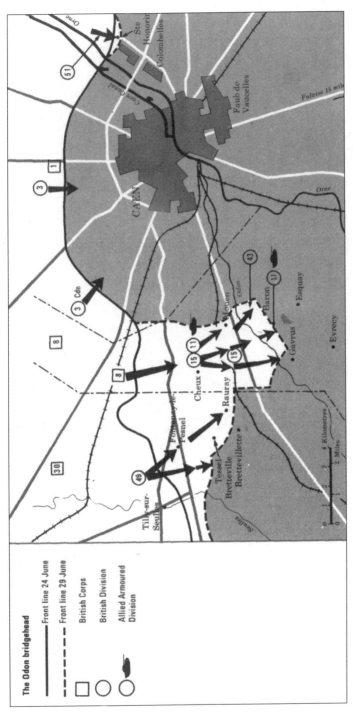

Containing Epsom, 24–29 June 1944.

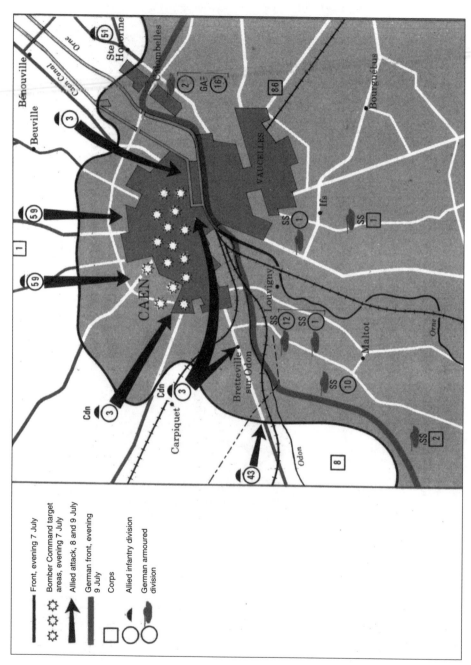

Legend:

Front, evening 7 July

Bomber Command target areas, evening 7 July

Allied attack, 8 and 9 July

German front, evening 9 July

Corps

Allied infantry division

German armoured division

Charnwood, 7–9 July 1944.

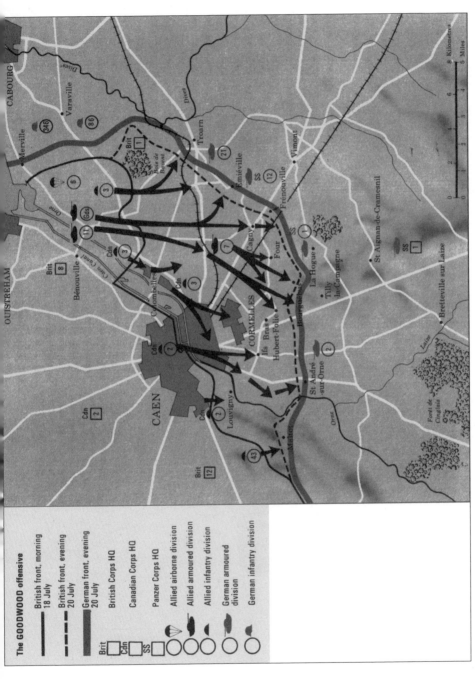

Stopping Goodwood, 18–20 July 1944.

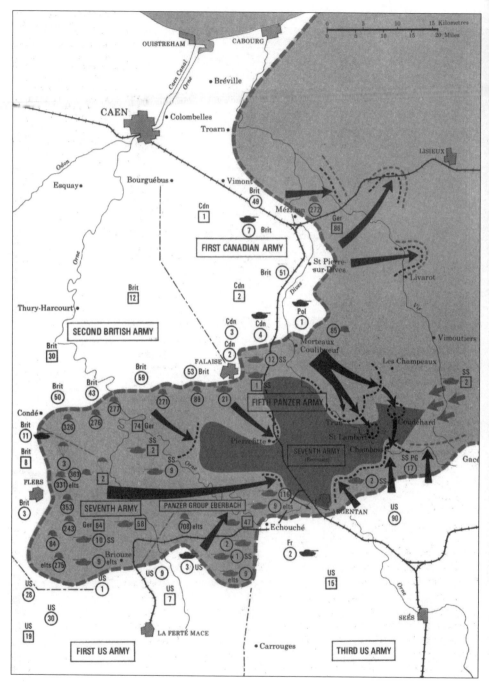

The Falaise Pocket, 16–20 August 1944.

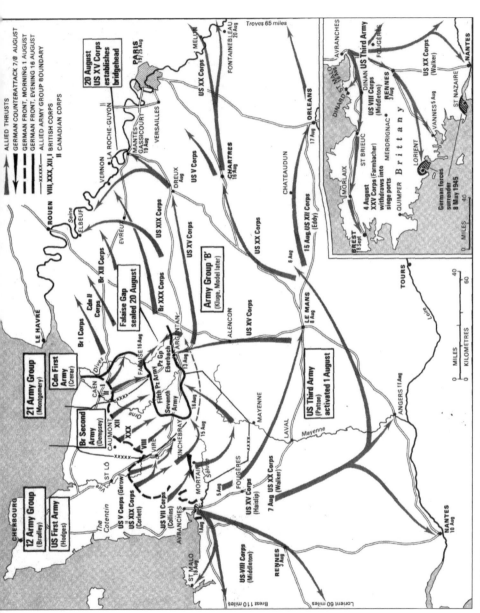

The Allied Breakout and race to the Seine, 1–20 August 1944.

ALLIED THRUSTS
GERMAN COUNTERATTACK 7/8 AUGUST
GERMAN FRONT, MORNING 1 AUGUST
GERMAN FRONT, EVENING 16 AUGUST
VIII,XXX,XII,I BRITISH CORPS ————— ALLIED ARMY GROUP BOUNDARY
II CANADIAN CORPS

20 August US XV Corps establishes bridgehead

PARIS 19/25 Aug

Troyes 65 miles

MELUN

FONTAINEBLEAU 20 Aug

US XX Corps

VERSAILLES

ORLEANS 17 Aug

MANTES-GASSICOURT 19 Aug

LA ROCHE-GUYON

VERNON

US V Corps

DREUX Aug

US XIX Corps

CHARTRES 16 Aug

US XV Corps

ROUEN

Seine

ELBEUF

EVREUX

US XV Corps

CHATEAUDUN

US XX Corps

15 Aug US XII Corps (Eddy)

6 Aug

Army Group 'B' (Kluge, Model later)

LE HAVRE

Br I Corps

Cdn II Corps

Br XII Corps

Falaise Gap sealed 20 August

FALAISE 16 Aug

Br XXX Corps

ALENÇON

US XV Corps

LE MANS 8 Aug

TOURS

Loire

40 MILES

60 KILOMETRES

CAEN

Orne

Fifth Pz Army Pz Gp Eberbach

ARGENTAN

17 Aug

Seventh Army

16 Aug

US Third Army (Patton) activated 1 August

ANGERS 11 Aug

Cdn First Army (Crerar)

21 Army Group (Montgomery)

Br Second Army (Dempsey)

CAUMONT

XXX

XII

VIII

VIRE

TINCHEBRAY

15 Aug

MAYENNE

LAVAL

Mayenne

12 Army Group (Bradley)

US First Army (Hodges)

CHERBOURG

The Cotentin

ST LÔ

US V Corps (Gerow)

US XIX Corps (Corlett)

US VII Corps (Collins)

Vire

XXXXX

MORTAIN

Sélune

FOUGÈRES

7 Aug US XX Corps (Walker)

NANTES 10 Aug

5 Aug

US XV Corps (Haislip)

AVRANCHES

1 Aug

ST MALO 16 Aug

US VIII Corps (Middleton)

REYNES 3 Aug

Brest 110 miles

Lorient 80 miles

0 MILES 40
0 KILOMETRES 60

AVRANCHES 30/31 July

DINARD 15 Aug

DINAN US Third Army

FOUGÈRES

US VIII Corps (Middleton)

4 August XXV Corps (Farmbacher) withdraws into siege ports

ST MALO 14 Aug

ST BRIEUC

MERDRIGNAC*

RENNES 3 Aug

Brittany

MORLAIX

QUIMPER

BREST 5 Sept

VANNES 5 Aug

LORIENT

ST NAZAIRE

German forces surrender 8 May 1945

0 MILES 40

AVRANCHES

US XX Corps (Walker)

NANTES

Chapter 1

Panzergruppe West's Dilemma

Just four days after the monumental D-Day landings in northern France, RAF Typhoons swooped down out of the skies onto a chateau and neighbouring orchard, followed by Mitchell light bombers of the 2nd Tactical Air Force. Surprised German radio operators and staff officers caught in the open scattered in all directions as the ground shook beneath them. When the prolonged raid was finally over a German general lay dead, along with twelve fellow officers; in one fell swoop Hitler's panzer forces in Normandy had been successfully decapitated.

Intent on resisting the D-Day landings, Panzergruppe West became an operational combat command on 8 June 1944 at Chateau La Caine; within two days it had sealed its own fate. Allied signal intercepts from four large radio trucks parked in nearby trees were its undoing, tipping off the Allies' fighter-bombers to its exact location. On the eve of the crucial Battle for Normandy, Panzergruppe West ceased to function.

Invasion where?

In the summer of 1944 the battle-hardened German Heer, or Army, and Waffen-SS stood poised to inflict a bloody reverse on the long-anticipated Allied landings in Northern France. That invasion was imminent was beyond doubt following the Allied landings in the Mediterranean the previous year. The failure of Operation Jubilee, the British and Canadian raid on Dieppe on 19 August 1942, had firmly convinced the Germans that they could contain and defeat an Allied amphibious assault on French soil.

However, the German armed forces, or Wehrmacht, stationed in Northern France, much to the advantage of the Allies, were blighted by strategic indecision, a cumbersome chain of command and a succession of commanders, not to mention the meddling hand of Adolf Hitler. The Allied landings in French Northwest Africa in 1942 and the subsequent defeat of the Germans in Tunisia the following year, led Hitler to believe that the Allies might land in the south of France and in the Bay of Biscay.

Generalfeldmarschall Gerd von Rundstedt, Commander-in-Chief West, or Oberbefehlshaber West (OB West), expected the Allied invasion of France after the 7th, 10th and 3rd SS Panzer Divisions rolled into Vichy France on 11 November 1943 in response to the Allied landings in Africa. The sixty-nine year old von Rundstedt had commanded Army Groups during the conquest of Poland and France and then led Army Group South during the successful overrunning of Ukraine, but had been dismissed by Hitler after being forced to retreat. Back in favour in July 1942 he had been appointed C-in-C West with the responsibility for fortifying France against the expected Allied invasion.

Rundstedt reasoned the Allies would attack the Pas de Calais as this was the shortest crossing point and just four days march from the vital German industrial region of the Ruhr. The massing of the American 3rd Army and the Canadian 1st Army opposite the Pas de Calais convinced von Rundstedt as well as Generalfeldmarschall Erwin Rommel (who took command of Army Group B stretching from the Dutch border to the Loire in February 1944), and Hitler.

The Allies deliberately blinded the Germans along the Channel by knocking out their radars, though this had to be done in such a selective manner as not to alert the Germans as to the true location of the amphibious assault. RAF Typhoon fighter-bombers played a key role in this, striking sites from Ostend to Cherbourg and the Channel Islands. To help foster the illusion that the Pas de Calais was the most likely crossing point, some radars in this area were left alone. Along the coast, out of ninety-two radar sites only eighteen were operational by the time of the invasion, and they were to be further misled by dummy invasion fleets.

The net result was that Oberkommando der Wehrmacht (OKW – the Armed Forces High Command) gave priority to General Hans von Salmuth's 15th Army north of the Seine. This meant Rundstedt's better forces remained in the Pas de Calais area due to the Allies' successful deception efforts, which had a negative effect on General Friedrich Dollmann's 7th Army covering Normandy and Brittany. A phantom Allied 4th Army in Scotland also convinced the Germans of a threat to Norway, pinning down even more troops in Scandinavia.

A team of highly experienced Army Group and Corps-level generals surrounded Rundstedt, including Rommel, Dollmann, von Salmuth, Geyr von Schweppenburg, Josef 'Sepp' Dietrich and Erich Marcks. The key players in terms of the panzer forces were Rommel and Schweppenburg; they had the casting votes on how best to deploy the panzers to counter an Allied invasion, which would ultimately result in bitter acrimony.

Hitler accepted Rundstedt's view though Rommel suspected an attack would take place between Caen and Cherbourg, with a possible second invasion astride the Somme directed toward the port of Le Havre. Following the attack on Dieppe the Germans could not rule out another frontal assault to capture a valuable port. At the time of the Dieppe raid, Dollmann's 7th Army HQ had noted:

> With the reserves afloat were twenty-eight tanks, certainly of the same type as those landed. Now the employment of altogether fifty-eight similar tanks cannot be connected with a brief sabotage operation. Although operational orders have also fallen into our hands, it is not possible to deduce whether it was a question of an operation of local character, or – in case of success – if it would form the initial stage of 'invasion'.

Many senior German officers assessed that if the Allies had achieved a successful lodgement at Dieppe it would have heralded a full-scale invasion: though Rundstedt did not share this view. What the German commanders did not know was where the main weight of the Allied assault or *schwerpunkt* might fall, which meant any initial landings were likely to be considered diversionary.

Hitler did take on Rommel's concerns for Normandy and on 6 May 1944 signalled Rundstedt that he attached great importance to Cherbourg and the Normandy coast. In response the 91st Airlanding Division was sent to the Cotentin Peninsula, the 21st Panzer Division was relocated from Brittany south of Caen and the Panzer Lehr Panzer Division was summoned from Hungary to be positioned south of Chartres. This was bad news for the Allies having selected Normandy for D-Day and Operation Overlord.

Hitler's armoured fist

By June 1944 about one fifth of Hitler's field army was occupying Western Europe; Rundstedt had well over half a million men guarding the European coastline, with some fifty-eight divisions stationed in France and the Low Countries. Scattered across Belgium, France and the Netherlands, these forces included ten panzer divisions and one panzergrenadier division. These represented Hitler's armoured fist.

These forces seemed formidable, particularly for the Allied planners trying to work out the best way to overcome them, Rundstedt though was painfully aware of their shortcomings: 'I had over 3,000 miles [4,800km] of coastline to cover, from the Italian frontier in the south to the German frontier in the north, and only sixty divisions with which to defend it. Most of them were low-grade units, and some of them were skeletons'. This meant, not even allowing for reserves, one division per fifty miles (eighty kilometres), a clear case of overstretch. The Allies had thirty-nine divisions, 8,000 bombers and 284 warships, totalling nearly three million men, to throw at the German defences.

Rundstedt's forces were divided into two Army Groups. Rommel's Army Group B comprised Dollmann's 7th Army, consisting of sixteen divisions stationed in northwestern France, and von Salmuth's 15th Army, consisting of twenty-five divisions stationed in Belgium and northeastern France. Dollmann, a gunner by trade having served with the artillery during the First World War, became commander of 7th Army, an entirely infantry formation in 1939, which he had led into France in May the following year. There he remained with his headquarters in Le Mans, tasked to defend northern France. The infantry divisions of his command were largely ill-equipped, immobile, second-rate units. General Johannes Blaskowitz's Army Group G consisted of General Kurt von der Chevallerie's 1st and General Friedrich Wiese's 19th armies, totalling seventeen divisions, stationed on the Biscay and Riviera coasts respectively.

One key armoured command was the I SS Panzer Corps, this had been created in July 1943 in Berlin Lichterfeld, though it officially came into being at Beverloo, Belgium. SS-Obergruppenführer Sepp Dietrich, former commander of the 1st SS Panzer Division, assumed control, while the SS Panzer Corps of SS-Obergruppenführer Paul Hausser was redesignated II SS Panzer Corps. The latter had been initially created in the Netherlands in July 1942 as the SS Panzer General Kommando.

Dietrich's command had spent much of the summer of 1943 helping seize control of northern Italy following the country's defection to the Allies. His Corps moved to Septeuil, west of Paris in April 1944 where the 1st SS, 12th SS and Panzer Lehr Panzer Divisions as well as the 17th SS Panzergrenadier Division were placed under its direction, forming part of Panzergruppe West.

Most of the panzer divisions deployed in Western Europe were refitting after heavy combat on the Eastern Front. In the north, stationed in 15th Army's area of responsibility, were the 2nd, 19th (scheduled to return to Poland), 21st, 116th, Panzer Lehr, 1st SS and 12 SS Panzer Divisions. To the southeast in 19th Army's area were the 9th and 2nd SS Panzer Divisions; while to the southwest with 1st Army were the 11th Panzer and 17th SS Panzergrenadier Divisions.

Organisation of the Heer and Waffen-SS panzer divisions was similar, with a panzer regiment of two battalions or *abteilungen*, a Sturmgeschütz and/or Panzerjäger *abteilung*. The nominal structure also included two panzer-grenadier regiments (one motorised and one armoured), artillery, engineer, flak, medical and reconnaissance units. In reality the structure and the manpower of the units varied according to local circumstances. In Normandy the German infantry divisions' anti-tank battalions largely consisted of towed weapons, but six Panzerjäger Battalions were also equipped with Marder self-propelled and Sturmgeschütz assault guns.

Reserve panzer units were very sparse in the summer of 1944. In the spring of the previous year just four training Reserve Panzer Divisions, the 155th, 178th, 179th and 273rd, were formed in France. Their task though was to provide replacement cadres for existing units rather than being combat formations in their own right.

Nevertheless, in March 1944, because of the worsening situation on the Eastern Front and in Italy and the expected opening of the second front, OKW began considering using the 155th, 179th and 273rd to constitute three new panzer divisions. For the combat cadres it was decided to employ those divisions used to rescue Army Group South on the Eastern Front, namely the 9th Panzer and 10th and 16th Panzergrenadier Divisions. They were instructed to be combat ready by 1 May 1944, which in reality was a tall order.

General Adolf Kuntzen's LXXXI Corps based in Rouen, on the Seine, north of Paris had the only anti-invasion experience. His HQ was responsible for 302nd Infantry Division, charged with defending Dieppe and the surrounding area, along with the 336th Infantry Division. It had fallen to Kuntzen's corps with the assistance of the 10th Panzer Division to halt the Allies' Dieppe raid. The LXXXI Corps' control of an armoured division had been short-lived and by June 1944 its subordinate units consisted of the 245th and 711th Infantry Divisions and the 17th Luftwaffe Field Division. Kuntzen and his staff would play a very belated and minor role in the Normandy campaign.

Conflict in the High Command

To defeat an Allied invasion, C-in-C West favoured the 'crust-cushion-hammer' concept, the crust being formed by the static sea defences, the cushion by infantry reserves and the hammer by the armoured divisions held further back. Schweppenburg, commander of Panzergruppe West, agreed with Rundstedt in believing the panzer divisions should be kept inland, ready to encircle the Allies as they tried to advance on Paris. His command had been set up with responsibility for training the panzer divisions, but it was also conceived as a headquarters, subordinated to the German 7th Army, to coordinate a panzer counterattack in the event of an invasion in Normandy.

Schweppenburg was a highly experienced panzer corps commander. A First World War veteran, he had served in London in the mid-1930s as the German Military Attaché. He then commanded 3rd Panzer Division for the attack on Poland and promptly fell out with his corps commander, General Heinz Guderian; Schweppenburg had been superior to Guderian, until the latter was put in charge of Hitler's panzer forces in 1938. During the invasion of France in 1940 he had commanded the XXIV Panzer Corps and had subsequently commanded a panzer corps with Guderian's 2nd Panzer Army.

By April 1943 Schweppenburg, commanding the LXXXVI Corps at Dax (located at the end of the Pyrenees), found himself lumbered with the proposed Operation Gisela designed to seize the ports along the northern coast of Spain. He dubbed the plan to seize Bilbao with a division and Madrid with four others as 'folly.' Luckily Hitler opted not to alienate General Francisco Franco's Spain. Schweppenburg was transferred to assume command of Panzergruppe West in October 1943, now notably full of admiration for what Guderian had achieved with the *panzertruppen.*

In contrast Rommel wanted the panzers well forward to deal with the Allies as soon as they waded ashore. He felt any airborne landings in the rear could be easily dealt with by those troops to hand. Rommel had made his name as a panzer leader in France and North Africa and had also orchestrated the successful seizure of northern Italy. He knew only too well how potent Allied air power could be, which is partly why he advocated keeping the panzers near the coast. He did not reckon with the power of the Allies' naval gunfire, which would greatly hamper the panzers even when they did get near the beachhead.

During the Dieppe raid the nearest German armour within striking distance belonged to the 10th Panzer Division, under General Wolfgang Fischer, stationed at Amiens 60 miles (96km) away. The 1st SS Panzer Division, under Sepp Dietrich, was 80 miles (128km) away northwest of Paris. It had fallen to the 302nd Infantry Division under Generalleutnant Conrad Hasse to thwart the seaborne attack.

Ironically, the Germans afterwards noted bombastically: 'Our rapid intervention and the powerful aspect of the panzer division made a great impression on the populace'. Although the 10th Panzer and 1st SS Panzer Divisions had gone on alert at 0625, 10th Panzer did not head north until 0900 and then it was hampered by inadequate maps and worn out vehicles. Its progress was far from proficient and the Luftwaffe was equally slow off the mark to react. Fischer arrived at Dieppe just as the survivors were surrendering at 1308 hours.

While Hitler was understandably impressed by Rommel's proposals, it was Schweppenburg who swayed the day by personally visiting him to argue that the panzers should be held under a centralised command in the forests astride the Seine. Schweppenburg felt the greatest threat would be from an airborne landing. He was also of the view that the Allies should be allowed to penetrate inland before being counterattacked. Hitler backed von Runstedt and Schweppenburg, refusing Rommel's request to deploy the 12th SS at the base of the Cotentin Peninsula and for Panzer Lehr to deploy to Avranches.

The conflict over this issue reached such a tempo that Rommel and Schweppenburg fell out. 'I am an experienced tank commander,' Rommel told Schweppenburg, 'you and I do not see eye to eye on anything. I refuse to work with you any more'. On a personal level, Rommel can only have felt slighted after a subordinate commander whose responsibility was ostensibly to oversee panzer training had undermined his authority. It must have further irked him that even if Panzergruppe West did become an operational command he expected it to come directly under Army Group B's control. In the event this was not to happen.

Field Marshal Bernard Law Montgomery was well aware of these tensions; in April 1944 he had briefed his commanders, commenting:

> Some of us here know Rommel well. He is a determined commander and likes to hurl his armour into battle. But according to what we know of the chain of command, the armoured divisions are being kept directly under Rundstedt and delay may be caused before they are released to Rommel. This fact may help us, and quarrels may arise between the two of them.

This argument between Rundstedt and Schweppenburg on the one hand and Rommel on the other resulted in an unwieldy compromise, with Rommel retaining command of 2nd (beyond the Somme), 21st and 116th Panzer Divisions (beyond the Seine), and the 1st SS and 12th SS Panzer Divisions; and Panzer Lehr remaining under von Rundstedt's authority. The reserves constituted part of Panzergruppe West. The latter attempted to avoid frittering away its panzers by getting OB West to issue an order forbidding the piecemeal diversion of elements of the panzer divisions; once the reality of the invasion set in this order was soon abandoned.

The reserves though could not be deployed without the approval of OKW. Hitler as C-in-C exercised command through his Chief of Staff, Field Marshal Wilhelm Keitel, and Chief of Operations Staff, General Alfred Jodl. This meant that the release of C-in-C West's reserve panzer force was unlikely to happen in a hurry.

Even the forward deployment of a single panzer division caused much debate. General Günther Blumentritt, von Rundstedt's Chief of Staff noted:

> There were prolonged arguments as to where the 21st Panzer Division should be placed. Field Marshal von Rundstedt would have preferred it to the south of St Lô, behind the Cherbourg [Cotentin] Peninsula. But Rommel chose to put it nearer the coast and on the other flank, close to Caen. This meant that it was too near the coast to be really available as a reserve for the sector as a whole.

Rommel's intuition was to prove correct, although the ultimate issue of where the rest of the panzer divisions should be best placed was never really resolved, nor in reality could it be. It is strange, given the lessons the Germans had provided Europe about the power of massed armour, that their panzer divisions should be scattered from Bordeaux to Belgium.

Prior to D-Day it was hard for the Germans to hide their troop and panzer movements along France's roads and railways. In particular Route Nationale 13 followed the Normandy coastline from Cherbourg in the west to Caen in the east. Before, during and after the Normandy campaign, the Allied air forces and Special Forces did all they could to interrupt the Germans' lines of communication. In the run up to D-Day, fighter-bombers and bombers of the British 2nd Tactical Air Force and the US 9th Air Force conducted an offensive against German rolling stock across northern Europe. Carried out during the last week of May, its aim was to hamper Hitler's ability to reinforce his armies in northwest France once Operation Overlord was underway. Between 1 March and 6 June 1944 thirty-six marshalling yards in northern France and Belgium were bombed 139 times.

Attacks on the rail bridges over the Seine and Meuse had commenced on 7 May 1944, also designed to prevent the Germans bringing up reinforcements. The initial attacks on the Seine included Mantes-Gassicourt and Oissel, but from the end of the month onwards ten rail and fourteen road bridges were targeted as a top priority. By D-Day, from Conflans to Rouen all the rail bridges across the Seine were down.

One failing of this campaign was not destroying the bridges over the Loire at Saumar and Tours. Had this been achieved it would have greatly hampered the 2nd SS Panzer Division and 17th SS Panzergrenadier Division's move north to join the battle in Normandy.

Allied light bombers conducted low-level incendiary raids on German targets, in particular airfields and communication centres, they also carried out long-range night-time raids. During the period 1 May–5 June 1944, thirty-six Luftwaffe airfields from the Netherlands to Brittany were targeted. Similarly low-level fighter-bomber sweeps were made over occupied Europe against targets of opportunity. Over the English Channel, daylight aircraft patrols were conducted to prevent the movement of light shipping and coastal convoys.

On the ground, the French resistance also coordinated their efforts with the British Special Operations Executive (SOE) and American Office of Strategic Services (OSS) to hinder the German movement of reinforcements by road and rail toward Normandy once the Allied invasion was underway. In February 1944 General Charles de Gaulle created the French Forces of the Interior (FFI) under General Koenig to unite all the various resistance groups, which would bravely harass German troop movements.

Colonel Passy (Captain André Charles Lucien Dewavrin) headed de Gaulle's Free French Intelligence Service and established a network of spies watching developments along the defences of Hitler's so called Atlantic Wall. Dewavrin, ironically a former Assistant Professor of Fortifications at Saint-Cyr, was not particularly interested in the concrete of the German defences but rather their radar installations. The French resistance set up a transmitter network throughout Normandy, particularly the Caen area, Bayeux, Grandcamp and Ste Mère-Ènglise.

Lost opportunity

Just two days before D-Day Rommel, reassured that the tides would not be suitable for an invasion, departed from his HQ at the Chateau Roche Guyon outside Paris for his home near Ulm on the Danube, leaving his Chief of Staff, Lieutenant General Hans Speidel, in charge. General Dollmann was in Rennes hosting a wargame and Sepp Deitrich was in Brussels.

Sometime after 0100 on 6 June 1944, a bleary-eyed Admiral Hoffman was roused from his bed at the HQ of Chief of Operations Naval Group West in the Bois de Boulogne, Paris. Chief of Staff Hoffman found himself leafing through a series of reports from the remaining naval radar stations. Despite the Allies' best efforts there could be no hiding the vast fleet approaching the Normandy coast and Hoffman turned to his men: 'this can only be the invasion fleet. Signal to the Führer's headquarters the invasion is on'.

Rundstedt recalled:

> At four o'clock in the morning, three hours after I received the first reports of the invasion, I decided that these landings in Normandy had to be dealt with. I asked the Supreme Command in Berlin for authority to commit these two divisions into the battle.
>
> Although Panzer Lehr and the 12th SS Panzer Divisions were under my command, I could not move them until I had received permission from Berlin. Berlin replied that it was still uncertain as to whether or not these first assaults were the main Allied efforts or merely a diversion.

The 1st SS, 12th SS and Panzer Lehr Panzer Divisions and the 17th SS Panzergrenadier Division could not be released without Hitler's express permission. By 0600 von Rundstedt was convinced that the invasion was the real thing and his Chief of Staff, General Blumentritt, requested that the panzer reserves be released to C-in-C West.

Rather surprisingly, the German High Command were not unduly alarmed by all this activity. Most incoming information was to a large extent ignored. Berlin dithered, still half expecting an attack across the Pas de Calais. Jodl was more concerned about the situation in Italy, where Rome had just fallen to the Allies, and the anticipated summer Soviet offensive on the Eastern Front; vague reports from Normandy did not seem that serious.

On hearing the news, Rommel dutifully sped back but did not arrive until the afternoon of D-Day and was unable to exert any influence on the swift commitment of the panzers. It was not until the end of 6 June that the Germans finally began to move their panzer reserves toward the Allied bridgehead. The 2nd Panzer Division moved west from Amiens, while the 9th SS and 10th SS Panzer Divisions, part of the powerful II SS Panzer Corps, would be summoned from the Eastern Front five days later.

Rundstedt later noted with regret:

> I have been criticized because it was said that I delayed too long in committing my Panzer Divisions against the bridgehead. Although Panzer Lehr and the 12th SS Panzer Divisions were under my command I could not move them until I had received permission from Berlin ... They hesitated all that night and the next morning were unable to make up their minds. Finally, at four o'clock in the afternoon on 6 June, twelve hours after I had made my request, I was told that I could use these Panzer Divisions. This meant that a counterattack could not be organised until the morning of 7 June. By then the bridgehead was over thirty hours old and it was too late.

Bitterly commenting on this inertia after the war Rundstedt, perhaps trying to salvage his own reputation, told his captors:

> I was not allowed to use them without getting permission from the Führer in his headquarters on the Eastern Front. What did he know of the battle in Normandy? We rang up every few hours, but he refused until it was too late, until, in fact, you had your anti-tank guns and many tanks ashore. I practically had to ask him whether I was to put a sentry at the front or back of my headquarters.

At 1400 on the 6th Hitler released the 12th SS (allowed to move to Lisieux but not committed) and Panzer Lehr to von Rundstedt. General Dollmann, like Rundstedt, did not hear of this decision until 1600 either. It mattered little, as neither division would be able to intervene on D-Day.

Hauptmann Helmut Ritgen of the Panzer Lehr Division knew a golden opportunity had been lost:

> From 6 June onwards, 21st Panzer had been thrown piecemeal into battle to counter the British airborne landings. This armoured attack towards the shore was halted prematurely when the British paratroopers landed in our rear. On D-Day night the British I Corps had captured a coastal strip six miles [10km] long though not yet very deep. In vain the exhausted German defenders looked for reinforcements but all local reserves had been used up.
>
> C-in-C West had ordered increased readiness to move forward Panzergruppe West, which included 12th SS, Panzer Lehr, and the 17th SS Panzergrenadier Division. 12th SS Panzer was put under command of Army Group B and Kurt Meyer [commander 12th SS Panzergrenadier Regiment 25] led them towards a sector of the 711th Infantry Division east of the Orne. Movement was difficult because of air strikes and too many failures of radio sets.

Panzergruppe West was directed to become a combat command, but not under Rommel's direct authority. When Schweppenburg finally got the order, he claimed he was dismayed at the muddled arrangements:

> The chain of command from Panzergruppe West up was most unfortunate. Panzergruppe West was still under 7th Army. The decision to interpose another staff between Rommel and von Geyr may have been made by OB West because it was aware of the friendly relation between Panzergruppe West and the staff of 7th Army – the latter acting as a 'buffer state'. At a moment when everything depended on rapid action, orders were issued to just two and three-quarters Panzer Divisions by the following headquarters: I SS Panzer Corps, Panzergruppe West, 7th Army at Le Mans, Army Group B, OB West, and OKW.

Clearly the situation was a complete mess and the Germans were to tie themselves in dreadful knots. Schweppenburg's Panzergruppe West staff immediately found themselves involved in resisting the Allied invasion. He recalled:

> On the morning of 7 June I was ordered to take over, with my staff, the sector on both sides of the Orne up to Tilly-sur-Suelles. I moved out immediately. After reaching Argentan, two conditions became evident, both of primary importance to the movement of Panzer forces. Enemy air action had thoroughly and skilfully destroyed those

points along the main arteries where the roads narrowed within the defiles of villages and towns. Owing to the road net and the terrain, it was difficult even in daylight to find a bypass, and then only with considerable delay.

Rommel must have felt equally frustrated that the chain of command for his panzers ran via Schweppenburg to von Rundstedt. He exercised direct control for barely three days.

Pending the arrival of Panzergruppe West, as of 0400 on the 7th June, I SS Panzer Corps assumed command of 12th SS, 21st and Panzer Lehr. Dietrich became responsible for 7th Army's armoured counterattack and was well aware that the burden of this operation would fall on the teenagers of the 12th SS.

Unfortunately the staff of I SS Panzer Corps did nothing to clarify the situation for the divisional commanders. Although the Corps ordered an attack toward Courseulles-sur-Mer, in the event Panzer Lehr drifted toward Bayeux and the 12th SS moved northwest of Caen. At the time the I SS Panzer Corps was just starting its 438-mile (700km) journey from Belgium. Schweppenburg lamented I SS Panzer Corps' dithering:

> It is not known why I SS Panzer Corps wavered, but probably the divergent influence of higher staffs must share the blame. If one has to pass final judgement on the conduct of this Corps, it should be stated that it has missed the psychological moment – and the bus. It was still possible in the morning of 8 June to deal the British a severe blow in the vicinity of Courseulles-sur-Mer. On 10 June enemy concentration along the entire beachhead had progressed so rapidly that the German forces were no longer permitted the same freedom of action that existed forty-eight hours earlier.

Counterattack

On 8 June Schweppenburg found himself in command of the three Panzer Divisions, he was also given the coastal 716th Infantry Division, which he discovered (numbering just 300 men) only existed in the imagination of the higher staffs, as the rest had been swept away during the invasion. The general knew that time was of the essence:

> I had been anxious not to interfere before. After visiting the combat divisions, I made a verbal report by telephone to the commander 7th Army. I informed him that I was prepared to attack at the earliest possible moment and requested a free hand as to the time and place.

The plan was to counterattack along the Caen–Lion-sur-Mer road.

However, 21st Panzer was tied up on the left bank of the Orne and could not be deployed as a divisional formation. The damaged bridge at Thury-Harcourt delayed Panzer Lehr and 12th SS was lacking its panzers.

In the meantime, the Germans' coastal defence had been pierced and the way south was clear for the Allies; during the night of 7 June the British 50th (Northumbrian) Infantry Division took Bayeux and the following day the American 1st Infantry Division captured Tour-en-Bessin and Le Coudrai on the Bayeux–Isigny road.

Schweppenburg and his staff assessed that, despite the success at Bayeux, the British and Canadians would not launch a large-scale attack until thorough preparations had been made. In contrast it was felt the Americans were less likely to be so cautious and therefore possibly constituted a greater threat, especially if they were to push into the gap between Panzergruppe West and 7th Army.

Schweppenburg was dismissive of Rommel's urge to strike the Allies on the beaches with the panzers. This would expose them to concentrated naval gun-fire and fighter-bombers; in addition, the existing forces were insufficient for such a task and vital fuel and ammunition stocks lay too far to the rear to assist rapid deployment.

Panzergruppe West's fears were realised at 1000 hours when the attack was launched. The 12th SS struggled to get south of Creully in the face of heavy naval bombardment; Panzer Lehr, lacking fuel, could only commit a *kampfgruppe* (battle group), while 21st Panzer could offer little help. Air support from the Luftwaffe was non-existent. Crucially, despite this the Germans were able to hold onto the vital roads leading to Caen.

Rommel pitched up at I SS Panzer Corps on 10 June to inform them that XLVII Panzer Corps with two panzer divisions would be committed to their left and that Panzergruppe West would assume control between the Orne and the Vire rivers. Then in the afternoon he visited Schweppenburg's command post. Allied intelligence knew that this HQ had moved northwest of Thury-Harcourt to the Chateau at La Caine about 12 miles (20km) southwest of Caen on the 8th. Rommel narrowly missed the Allied air attack, which Schweppenburg recalls:

> About a half hour later the command post of Panzergruppe West was subjected for several hours to severe bombing and strafing. All personnel of the operations section as well as most of the officers of the forward echelon were killed. The bulk of the vehicles and almost all the technical equipment of the signal battalion were destroyed, in spite of their thorough dispersion. Thus the staff could no longer

function. Although I myself was slightly wounded, I was ordered to assemble and re-form the staff. Since this mission entailed working in Paris, I drove to Rommel and requested a new assignment at the front.

The irony was that Luftwaffe representatives had attended the meeting and not only could they not promise support for the proposed panzer attack toward Creully, they could not even protect Schweppenburg's HQ from air attack. About forty officers and men were killed in the raid, including Generalmajor Ritter von Dawans, Schweppenburg's Chief of Staff. The I SS Panzer Corps was placed under the direct control of Dollmann's 7th Army.

With Schweppenburg wounded and Panzergruppe West's communications severed, the survivors were withdrawn to act as a provisional HQ and at the end of June took over the front from the River Orne to Vire. General Heinrich Eberbach claimed that there was no friction between Panzergruppe West and 7th Army, but this is difficult to believe when both formations were competing for control of the same resources.

It had not taken long for Schweppenburg to realise just how vulnerable the German Army was to Allied combined armed forces; naval gunfire, artillery and aircraft were causing excessive casualties and were a drain on morale. In particular, the panzer divisions were threatened with rapid attrition, especially as replacement units were insufficient. Schweppenburg knew that a readjustment of tactics was needed:

> Our intention was to concentrate the Panzer force beyond the range of naval guns, to disregard any temporary loss of ground, and to hit the enemy with the strongest possible concentration of tanks. These attacks were to be repeated after every gain in elbow-room produced by strategic mobility of the Panzer forces.

Such tactics were to prove highly difficult to implement in the weeks that followed.

Chapter 2

The Road to Falaise – Goodwood, Cobra and Mortain

Like a punch-drunk boxer the Germans for the next two months would successfully block the blows of the Allies without being able to hit back effectively. British and Canadian efforts to barge past Caen would come to nought in the face of the massed panzers, but when the Americans attacked in the west after securing Cherbourg, a weak panzer counterattack simply hastened the unravelling of the Germans' weakening defences.

Strategic ground

At the Wolf's Lair, Rastenburg, East Prussia, Adolf Hitler was convinced that Normandy was not the main invasion. He was aided in this delusion by the Allies' major deception plans, the bombing of Calais and the ongoing disruption of the northern French rail system. The bogus activities of Lieutenant General George S Patton's fictitious forces convinced the Germans that he was going to land north of the Seine and as a result numerous German divisions, especially armoured, remained beyond the river for upto a week after D-Day. The Germans were only to have eight panzer divisions engaged during the first six weeks of the battle, whereas the Allies were expecting at least twice as many.

Following the D-Day landings both the Allies and the Germans knew the strategic ground lay in the east, where the British 2nd Army was fighting around the city of Caen. Just to the southeast lay the open tank country that could facilitate an Allied break-out. Rommel and Schweppenburg appreciated only too well that the strategic ground lay in the Caen–Falaise area.

The geography on the left wing of Panzergruppe West consisted of the restrictive Normandy hedgerow terrain known as the *bocage*. East of the Orne in the Caen–Falaise sector it was largely open and therefore more suited to fluid tank operations. Rommel understood the Allies had to be stopped from reaching this ground at all costs. A series of prominent geographical features south of Caen provided the Germans with an ideal stop line, here the panzers could make a stand.

While the German Navy was in no position to contest control of the English Channel and the Luftwaffe was distracted by the Eastern Front and defence of the Reich, Hitler's panzer forces constituted a very real threat to the mainly-inexperienced American Army and the weary British Army once they were ashore. The smug benefit of hindsight has made the Battle for Normandy appear ultimately a one-sided affair – with the Allies numerical dominance of land, air and sea, how could they possibly lose?

In 1944 no one really knew how things would play out, or indeed could anticipate the unforeseen consequences of the Allied victory at Falaise. In the first few crucial weeks following D-Day the German generals had every reason to believe they could drive the Allies back into the sea if they acted swiftly and decisively.

Qualitative edge

The one major advantage Panzergruppe West had over the Allies was the qualitative edge of its panzers. The Germans realised they could never match the Allied numbers but they ensured that they could outshoot them. The Germans were to deploy in total ten panzer divisions and one panzergrenadier division, numbering approximately 160,000 men equipped with just over 1,800 panzers, in Normandy. In addition to this there were another dozen or so General Headquarters Panzer Formations, mainly of battalion strength with about 460 panzers. This gave an accumulated strength for 7th Army, Panzergruppe West and the various Panzer Corps commands of around 2,260 tanks.

The Americans, British, French, Canadians and Poles were to commit thirteen armoured divisions and numerous independent armoured brigades to the battle. Their accumulated total for the campaign amounted to almost 8,700 tanks. On D-Day alone nearly 1,500 Allied tanks were put ashore. By the time of Operation Goodwood on 18 July, Allied tank strength stood at almost 5,900 and continued to rise, reaching almost 6,760 a week later when Operation Cobra was launched. By the time the Germans commenced their Avranches/Mortain counterattack against the Americans in early August, the American Army could muster almost 4,000 tanks.

On the whole the German armour deployed in Northern France was vastly superior to that of the Allies and easily outgunned their tanks. While the Allies sought to counter the German technological lead on land, sea and air at every single stage of the war, their failure to develop a war-winning battle tank was a glaring omission that even the British Prime Minister, Winston Churchill, sought to hide from the general public lest it affect morale.

The most common type of panzer in Normandy, totalling 748 tanks, was the PzKpfw IV Ausf H and Ausf J, which went into production in 1943 and

1944 respectively. With frontal armour of 80mm and a 7.5cm KwK 40 L/48 anti-tank gun, this provided the backbone of the German panzer divisions. Its gun had a twenty per cent greater muzzle velocity than that of the American-built M4 Sherman's 75mm gun, meaning it could punch through 92mm of armour at 500 yards, while the Sherman could only manage 68mm. Normally the Panzer IV was allocated to the 2nd battalion or II Abteilung of a panzer regiment, although there were a number of exceptions. The I Abteilung of the 9th Panzer Division's Panzer Regiment 33 was equipped with Panzer IVs and both *abteilungen* of 21st Panzer's Panzer Regiment 22 were equipped with it.

The PzKpfw V, or Panther, represented the pinnacle of German tank production, mounting the even more powerful 7.5cm KwK 42 L/70 gun that could penetrate 120mm of armour at 1,094 yards. On the Eastern Front it had proved itself superior to the Soviet T-34, though mechanical teething problems initially rendered it unreliable. The main models deployed in Normandy were the Ausf A and Ausf G. Theoretically each I Abteilung of a panzer regiment was equipped with this tank.

While the PzKpfw VI Tiger I was a formidable weapon with 100mm frontal armour and 8.8cm KwK L/56 gun, only three battalions were deployed in Normandy, with about 126 tanks. The Tiger's technological excellence meant it took twice as long to build as the Panther; however, its gun could easily deal with every single type of Allied tank. The Tiger could tear a Sherman apart, while the latter could not cope with the Tiger's frontal armour. The American 75mm gun could only penetrate the Tiger at close range and while the British 17-pounder gun was much more effective it was not available in significant numbers. Even those Shermans armed with a 76mm gun had to close to 300 yards. The Allied response to a Tiger was to overwhelm it or sneak up behind it!

The Tiger II, or King Tiger/Royal Tiger, was brand new in June 1944, but only equipped one company, totalling about a dozen tanks, in Normandy. In many ways its high fuel consumption, limited operational range, fragile steering and slow turret traverse nullified its powerful main armament, the 8.8cm KwK43 L/71 and very thick armour.

Another common armoured fighting vehicle in Normandy was the Sturm-geschütz or StuG III assault gun, armed with the 7.5cm StuK40 L/48, and to a lesser extent the StuG IV equipped with the same weapon, which was used to equip the tank destroyer battalions of the panzer divisions and in some cases substituted for the Panzer IV. They also equipped the independent Sturm-geschütz Brigades, a number of which were deployed throughout France. Lacking a turret, this assault gun was a very good defensive weapon and ultimately ideally suited for the Normandy countryside.

The Jagdpanzer IV, mounting the same gun as the Panther, was intended as a StuG replacement but was never built in sufficient numbers. It appeared in 1944 and began to replace the Marder self-propelled gun in the panzer divisions' tank destroyer battalions. Only about sixty were deployed in Normandy. Similarly the Jagdpanther, based on the Panther chassis and armed with the 8.8cm Pak 43, were few in number in Normandy, about a dozen at the most.

The main self-propelled anti-tank weapon was the Marder armed with a 7.5cm Pak 40/3, with limited numbers of the Pak 43-armed Hornisse. The principal self-propelled artillery in Normandy comprised the Hummel self-propelled 15cm howitzer based on the Panzer IV chassis, and the Wespe based on the Panzer II, armed with a 10.5cm gun. The Germans also deployed a range of hybrid self-propelled guns based on French tank and ammunition tractor chassis.

The most common Allied tank to fight in Normandy was the American M4 and M4A1 (with cast hull) Sherman. Mechanically reliable, it was handicapped by thin armour and a gun lacking sufficient punch. Its good cross country speed and higher rate of fire could not make up for these two key shortcomings. Tank crew survival was paramount as tanks could be replaced relatively easily but not experienced crews; the Sherman, however, had a nasty habit of burning when hit and if this happened the crew only had a fifty per cent chance of survival.

Despite extensive combat experience with the American and British armies in North Africa, Sicily and Italy, by 1944, for a variety of reasons, the Americans had failed to develop a worthy successor to the Sherman, meaning the Allies had to rely on numbers rather than quality. This crucial failure was to be a key factor in the Germans being able to hold on for so long in Normandy.

The Americans developed tank destroyers based on the Sherman that could penetrate at least 80mm of armour at 1,000 yards, notably the M10 Wolverine armed with a 3-inch gun and the M36 armed with a 90mm gun, though these were not available in sufficient quantities. The 3-inch gun was intended to tackle the Tiger, but being only able to penetrate the frontal armour at 50 yards rendered it all but ineffective against this panzer. Similarly, the M18 Hellcat armed with a powerful 76mm was too few in number.

Two thirds of the tanks used by British, Canadian and Polish armoured units in Normandy were Shermans, the rest being mainly British-built Cromwell and Churchill tanks. The Cromwell cruiser tank was numerically and qualitatively the most significant British tank and, along with the Sherman, formed the main strength of the British armoured divisions. However, even armed with a 75mm gun it was inferior to the late model Panzer IVs and the Panther. Although fast, the narrowness of the hull made up-gunning it very difficult. Similarly, the

British Churchill infantry tank, though heavily armoured, could not take any gun larger than the 75mm.

The heaviest British weapon, the 17-pounder (76.2mm), could open up 120mm of armour at 500 yards and was either towed or mounted in limited numbers of Shermans designated the Firefly VC. Later it was also mounted in the Valentine chassis, creating the unwieldy Archer self-propelled gun, and in the M10 to create the Achilles; these, though, did not enter service until well after the Normandy campaign. The Sherman Firefly was the only Allied tank capable of taking on the Panther and the Tiger on equal terms, but due to the shortage of guns it was only issued one per troop. The net result of all this was that the Allies' tanks were in for a severe mauling at the hands of the panzers.

It is vitally important to remember that at the time the Battle for Normandy was far from a forgone conclusion. The Dieppe failure loomed large in everyone's minds and despite the Allies' considerable planning and preparation there was a very real fear that D-Day might go the same way. The successful landings in North Africa had been against ill-equipped French forces that were in a state of political disarray, while those on Sicily and the Italian mainland had been against the Italian Army which was largely a spent force. Striking Hitler's *Festung Europa* was an entirely different matter, even if the German forces were in some cases second rate, reconstituting or recuperating.

The eastern flank

After the Germans had successfully blunted Montgomery's initial advances, rather than fight a bloody frontal battle for Caen, he decided 2nd Army would launch its main effort to the west, towards Villers-Bocage and Evrecy, then southeast towards Falaise. He committed two veteran divisions, the 51st (Highland) and 7th Armoured ('Desert Rats'), for two main flank attacks. The 51st were to attack through the 6th Airborne Division, east of Orne and the 7th Armoured would attack to the southwest.

The 51st's attack on 11 June was crushed and two days later the assault petered out. The 7th Armoured Division's advance was slow, but a hole in the German line between Villers-Bocage and Caumont was detected. Greeted by joyful locals, the advance elements of 7th Armoured entered Villers-Bocage on 13 June. The scene was set for the Villers-Bocage debacle in which the British spearhead was mauled by a handful of German Tiger tanks and an opportunity to turn the German line thrown away.

Hitler hurried to the HQ in Soissons on 17 June, ironically built to oversee the invasion of Britain, to confer with Rommel and von Rundstedt. His generals wanted their troops withdrawn out of range of the Allied naval guns which were providing devastating fire support against their panzers. Hitler refused, insisting they be concentrated for a counterattack on the junction of the British and American armies.

Fortunately for Hitler, the Allies' momentum faltered as the weather began to deteriorate and on the 19th a violent storm halted all shipping in the English Channel for three days. The Allies' military build-up virtually ground to a halt, delaying 20,000 vehicles and 140,000 tons of stores. In the meantime, distracting Hitler's attention back to the Eastern Front, on 22 June the Russians launched Operation Bagration, which would ultimately smash Army Group Centre in spectacular fashion.

Due to the bad weather the Germans were granted a vital breathing space during which they were able to reorganise their forces and move without Allied air strikes. Some felt that prior to D-Day Schweppenburg overdid night training, but he was in fact exercising great foresight. Allied firepower was greatly curtailing German freedom of movement during daylight hours. The deterioration in the weather would have been an ideal time to launch a counterattack, but the opportunity was lost.

The Allies still had the initiative and if they could maintain it the Germans would remain off balance. Montgomery declared he would tie the panzers down on the eastern flank in the Caen–Caumont sector, destroying them in a series of offensives that would look like an attempted break-out toward Paris, while the Americans mopped up the German forces in the Cotentin Peninsula and took the port of Cherbourg prior to their own break-out attempt.

The Americans knew they were not facing the Germans' top panzers. What tanks the German forces could muster on their western flank were mainly Czech or French models, such as the French-equipped training unit Panzer Ersatz und Ausbildungs Abteilung 100 and Panzer Abteilung 206, which could scrape together about seventy tanks of indifferent quality. Only Panzerjäger Abteilung 243 was equipped with any notable armour, totalling twenty-four self-propelled guns and assault guns. The main garrison units were the 243rd and 709th Infantry Divisions, which had been reinforced by the 3rd Parachute Division and the 77th Infantry Division moved up from Brittany.

Once the Americans reached Barneville-sur-Mer on the west coast of the Cotentin Peninsula on 18 June they set about pushing north and securing Cherbourg. They opened their attack four days later, the defenders resisted until the 26th before surrendering, although pockets of resistance continued for a further two days. By the end of the month the Americans had captured over 39,000 German prisoners and were now ready to strike southward. Both Panzer Abteilung 100 and 206 ceased to exist.

The week-long British Epsom offensive, west of Caen toward Evrecy and Esquay southwest of the city, launched on 25/26 June was intended as a preemptive strike to tie up German armour reinforcements. Barely a week later, the British and Canadians conducted Operation Charnwood, a frontal attempt on Caen, though they only succeeded in taking the northern half of the city.

By late June there were almost eight panzer divisions between Caen and Caumont on a 20 mile (32km) front facing the British 2nd Army. In particular the 2nd, 12th SS, 21st Panzer, Panzer Lehr and the 716th Infantry Divisions were all tied up in the immediate Caen area. Facing the British were approximately 725 German tanks, while on the American front there were only 140. Caen became the bloody fulcrum of the whole battle; here the cream of Panzergruppe West would be ground down in a series of unrelenting British attacks culminating in Operation Goodwood.

The desperately needed German infantry divisions that should have freed up the panzers for a counterstroke remained north of the Seine. Hitler held them back presumably because he still feared an attack across the Pas de Calais. By the end of June it was evident that von Rundstedt's 'crust-cushion-hammer' tactics had failed despite the slowly increasing number of panzer divisions; tied down in the face of Allied firepower and attacks, the panzers could do little more than fire-fight as the situation developed. To make matters worse, by the beginning of July the unrelenting operational commitment of the panzers was taking its toll, 58 per cent of the Panthers and 42 per cent of the Panzer IVs were in the maintenance depots.

General Dollmann, 7th Army's commander, died at his field HQ on 28 June; it is unclear if he had a heart attack or committed suicide, but SS-Obergruppenführer Paul Hausser from the II SS Panzer Corps assumed command. SS-Obergruppenführer Wilhelm 'Willi' Bittrich who had fought in Poland and France, subsequently commanding the 2nd SS and 9th SS Panzer Divisions took charge of the II SS Panzer Corps.

At this point Rommel and von Rundstedt drove the 600 miles (960km) to Berchtesgaden to see Hitler. They tried to prevail upon him to permit their forces to withdraw behind the Seine. In addition, Rommel wanted to strengthen the weakened Panzergruppe West and 7th Army with 15th Army's reserves and those forces tied up with Army Group G, way to the south. To their dismay, Hitler steadfastly refused; instead of heeding the advice of his two highly-experienced generals, he chose to do what he always did when anyone stood up to him.

Lacking friends at court, Rundstedt's days as C-in-C West were numbered. On 3 July Hitler accepted von Rundstedt's offer to stand down on health grounds and on the same day the hapless Schweppenburg was removed as commander of Panzergruppe West. Rundstedt held Hitler's Chief of Staff, Field Marshal Keitel, partly responsible for this state of affairs; indeed Rundstedt was contemptuous of Keitel's skills as a military coordinator. Removing two such senior generals at a critical moment seemed madness and can have done little to reassure Rommel of his future.

At the beginning of July Panzergruppe West's Chief of Staff informed Rommel: 'The morale of the troops is good, but one can't beat the materiel of the enemy with courage alone'. They were outnumbered four to one in tanks in the British sector; in the American sector it was worse, eight to one.

Günther von Kluge was summoned from the Eastern Front to replace von Rundstedt, but he was no more able to stabilise the situation than his predecessor. He did not last long following the failure of the Mortain counter-offensive in mid-August; summoned to Berlin he shot himself. Walter Model was then recalled from the Eastern Front to oversee the final defeat in Normandy.

General Heinrich Eberbach was appointed in Schweppenburg's place. He had commanded Panzer Regiment 35 within the 4th Panzer Division and fought well in Poland, Belgium, France and Russia. At Baranovitch he had gone to the aid of the 3rd Panzer Division and, despite securing victory, for a short time faced charges of disobeying orders. Whilst on the Eastern Front Eberbach had been wounded a number of times and suffered with continuing kidney problems; nonetheless, in August 1943 he was promoted to General der Panzertruppen. By December he was recuperating in Germany, but had then returned to Russia.

In Normandy one of Eberbach's first actions was to see the newly-appointed von Kluge and then Rommel to get appraised of the current situation facing Army Group B, Panzergruppe West and 7th Army. The fighting had so far cost the Germans 87,000 casualties, as well as 417 irreplaceable panzers and assault guns. Afterwards he visited the 12th SS Panzer Division defending Caen on 7 July and ordered elements of the 21st Panzer Division to support the beleaguered 16th Luftwaffe Field Division.

By the first week of July, elements of the 2nd SS Panzer Division were making their presence felt on the American front, supporting elements of the 17th SS Panzergrenadier Division, which had been their since early June. By mid-July the 1st SS, 21st Panzer and Panzer Lehr Panzer Divisions had been withdrawn into reserve, but Montgomery's Operation Goodwood prevented everything except Panzer Lehr from shifting west.

In the meantime, the American Army fought to broaden its bridgehead. Twelve divisions were committed to a series of frontal assaults, culminating in the capture of St Lô on the 18th, despite dogged resistance from Panzer Lehr and II Parachute Corps. By then the Americans had suffered over 62,000 casualties struggling through the bocage. Hausser though was forced to keep his two armoured divisions committed and was unable to withdraw his panzers into reserve.

Shortly afterwards Eberbach demonstrated his tactical and strategic abilities with Panzergruppe West by thwarting Montgomery's Operation Goodwood, launched east of Caen on the 18th. Three British armoured divisions were stopped dead in their tracks, quite literally. The Germans inflicted 5,500 casualties and destroyed over 400 tanks for the loss of over 100 panzers.

Then, to compound the Germans' woes after losing Dollmann, Rundstedt and Schweppenburg, they lost Rommel on 17 July when he was wounded after RAF Typhoons strafed his car on the open road. Rommel was hospitalised with serious head injuries and returned home in August. Implicated in the 20 July Bomb Plot against Hitler, Rommel poisoned himself on 14 October and was buried with full military honours. One can only speculate how things would have progressed in Normandy if he had stayed in charge.

By the 20th Eberbach's command was suffering a serious manpower drain, the Panzergruppe to date had suffered 40,000 casualties but only received 2,300 replacements. Four days later the Americans commenced Operation Cobra on the Germans weak western flank.

The break-out
General Günther Blumentritt, Chief of Staff OB West, later recalled:

> Although most of the German high command regarded the British as more dangerous, which resulted in the concentration of more troops and good panzer divisions near Caen, there was a decided shift in opinion as the battles in Normandy progressed. Panzer Lehr Division was actually shifted to the American front, and there is no doubt that other divisions would have been shifted to oppose the Americans had they not been tied down by continued British pressure and the overall lack of reserves. We recognised all along that Montgomery was more methodical than most commanders, and we admired the quick deft stroke which cut the Cherbourg peninsula and the speedy regrouping of American forces following the fall of Cherbourg itself.

This shift in opinion was too late. Rommel may be partly to blame; his experiences fighting Montgomery in North Africa meant that Army Group B would naturally place emphasis on the British Army as a known quantity. The Americans' initial lacklustre performance in Tunisia had also helped to cloud German perceptions of their fighting abilities.

In early July Panzer Lehr had transferred out of Panzergruppe West's area of responsibility to 7th Army's and joined General Dietrich von Choltitz's LXXXIV Corps west of St Lô. On its left flank were the 17th SS Panzergrenadier Division and the 2nd SS Panzer Division respectively, covering the area east of Périers. Beyond them were three infantry divisions. South of St Lô lay the weakened II Parachute Corps consisting of the 3rd Parachute Division and the 352nd Infantry Division, the latter having few of its complement of self-propelled guns and assault guns combat ready. Hausser's 7th Army numbered less than 35,000 men and about eighty armoured vehicles.

By late July, OB West, Army Group B and Panzergruppe West continued to assess a British breakthrough at Caen with a thrust toward Paris as the greatest threat. The Germans reorganised and the panzer divisions of Panzergruppe West were gathered in the Caen area as the key defensive sector. The Allies' airpower negated most German daytime movements and in turn prevented any large-scale counteroffensives. This effectively meant that the Panzergruppe's mission remained a defensive one designed to prevent a British breakthrough in the direction of Falaise and Paris.

Of the three Panzer Corps, I SS, II SS and XLVII, the latter two were to be relieved by the LXXIV Infantry Corps which was in Brittany. The plan was that Panzergruppe West would have two panzer corps, with the two panzer divisions acting as strategic reserves. Predictably things did not go according to plan. To try and free up the panzers, a total of five additional infantry divisions were attached to the Panzergruppe, but, frustratingly, the panzers were only ever able to achieve local offensive success.

After nearly two months of almost continuous combat the 21st and 12th SS Panzer Divisions had been seriously mauled. Although the 1st SS, 9th SS, 10th SS and 2nd Panzer Divisions had suffered losses they still retained about 75 per cent of their fighting power and the 116th remained fresh. Only the 21st, 1st SS, 10th SS and 12th SS remained committed, with the 2nd, 116th and 9th SS held in reserve, the 116th having only just completed its reorganisation. Similarly the 2nd and 9th SS had been pulled out to complete this process.

The fighting power of Panzergruppe West comprised about six panzer divisions and four infantry divisions, while three other infantry divisions (the 89th, 271st and 272nd) were in the process of being transferred over. The 271st and 272nd Infantry Divisions were supposed to relieve the 10th SS and the 21st Panzer, respectively, on the left wing of the LXXXVI Infantry Corps. Both these infantry formations, though, were held up by Allied air attack, especially crossing the Seine, and only their leading elements had reached the front by 24 July. The process was not completed until the end of the month. In addition, on the 28th the 331st Infantry Division was ordered to join Panzer-gruppe West and by 11 August a *kampfgruppe* was operating in the L'Aigle-Gracé area about 12–30 miles (20–50kms) east of Argentan.

On their western flank the Germans were now roughly outnumbered in tanks by a ratio of ten-to-one. General Omar N Bradley's US 1st Army, at the start of Operation Cobra, mustered 1,269 M4 Shermans and 694 M5A1 light tanks, supported by 324 M10 and M18 tank destroyers. Eventually launched on the 25th, Cobra signalled the beginning of the end for 7th Army and Panzergruppe West. General Bradley threw six divisions, numbering about 70,000 men, over 660 tanks, 3,000 aircraft and forty-three battalions of artillery, at the Germans.

The Americans had good intelligence on LXXXIV Corps' and II Parachute Corps' main components, though over estimated their reserves. In fact LXXXIV Corps' reserve consisted of one infantry division supported by a single battalion of armour; II Parachute Corps had none and Hausser's only reserve was part of an infantry division behind LXXXIV Corps. In contrast, Hausser's intelligence on the American order of battle was faulty and underestimated the Americans' strength, in particular Major General J Lawton Collins' VII Corps.

On the Germans eastern flank, the Canadians launched a simultaneous attack to assist the American momentum by slowing the redeployment of I and II SS Panzer Corps. Conducted from 24–27 July, Operation Spring was designed to capture the strategic Bourguébus and Verrières Ridges south of Caen and open up the Falaise road. The 1st SS, 9th SS, 12th SS and 21st Panzer Divisions easily killed the Canadian offensive, but LVIII Panzer Corps had to be despatched from Toulouse so that 2nd and 116th Panzer of XLVII Panzer Corps could shift from the British sector to help counter Cobra.

To the west things began to unravel very quickly. The very day that Spring came to a stop, German troops, lacking reserves, began to withdraw in the face of the American onslaught. In the meantime the British maintained the unrelenting pressure round Caen by drawing in German forces and capturing Mont Pinçon with Operation Bluecoat, which ran from 30 July to 7 August.

The arrival of 116th Panzer Division on the 30th slowed the American advance eastward, but did nothing to arrest their progress south. Similarly 2nd Panzer was unable to stop the Americans crossing the Vire. Within a week and a half the Americans had broken through and, having overrun Coutances and Avranches, were sweeping west into Brittany and east toward Vire and Mortain. Elements of Panzer Lehr, 2nd Panzer, 2nd SS and 17th SS were swept away. Hausser lost 20,000 men captured and LXXXIV Corps and II Parachute Corps were effectively destroyed.

Hausser was reduced to plugging holes by 1 August, with whatever units were available. Facing the American forces were the 2nd, 2nd SS, 17th SS and 116th, along with the remains of Panzer Lehr. All that remained of the local infantry divisions were the 243rd and 353rd. West of Caen, 21st Panzer had been moved south of Caumont, the junction between the British 2nd Army and the US 1st Army. The 1st SS, 9th SS, 10th SS and 12th SS Panzer Divisions, along with the 271st, 272nd, 277th and 346th Infantry Divisions, were deployed south of Caen, fending off the British and Canadians.

Mortain: the panzers strike back

Panzergruppe West was renamed 5th Panzer Army on 5 August, with responsibility for 7th Army's right flank. Inauspiciously, in its first incarnation 5th Panzer Army fought in North Africa as a part of Army Group Afrika, surrendering on 9 May 1943 in Tunisia. In early August, Eberbach was visited by Lieutenant Generals Walter Warlimont and Buhle from OKW acting as Hitler's eyes and ears. They were far from pleased with Eberbach's prognosis; he advocated an orderly withdrawal covered by the exhausted panzer divisions. This was not what Warlimont wanted to hear and he questioned Eberbach on the proposed counterattack toward Avranches.

Eberbach considered this a hopeless cause; their forces were too weak; Allied air power too strong; any success would be short-lived as it would be impossible to fend off the Americans once they caught their breath. In addition, supplying the four panzer divisions earmarked for the attack would have to be conducted at night. Warlimont accused Eberbach of being a pessimist, but if anyone appreciated the reality of the situation it was Eberbach. The attack on Avranches would ultimately sound the death knell of 5th Panzer Army.

For this operation, conducted between 6 and 11 August, 2nd, 116th, 1st SS and 2nd SS (including a *kampfgruppe* from 17th SS Panzergrenadier Divisions) Panzer Divisions were committed. Although the Germans captured Mortain, RAF Typhoons pounced on some 300 armoured vehicles, destroying eight, and other squadrons followed up to take their share of the kills. On 8 August at 2115, 7th Army received orders from von Kluge to postpone the attack, following a British breakthrough south of Caen which had shaken 5th Panzer Army.

Hitler demanded the counterattack in the American sector be renewed and instructed Eberbach to assume command of the newly-activated Panzergruppe Eberbach on 10 August, while Sepp Dietrich took command of 5th Panzer Army. Eberbach saw this for what it was, a demotion, perhaps prompted by the failed assassination attempt on Hitler. The message was clear: replaced by an SS officer and subordinated to an SS officer. Despite these musical chairs with the senior German commanders in Normandy, time was rapidly running out. The Allied pressure on both the American and British sectors was such that, despite the panzers best efforts, the dam was about to burst in a very spectacular fashion.

Eberbach recalls:

> On 8 or 9 August, Field Marshal von Kluge gave me, over the phone, the order to give 5th Panzer Army over to General of the SS Sepp Dietrich. The attack on Avranches, according to an order from Hitler, would be repeated. With an emergency Staff, I have to take over the command of the Panzer Divisions provided for this attack, and will be subordinated to C-in-C of 7th Army, SS-Gen. Hausser.
>
> I again immediately say that I consider the attack hopeless, and again that my assignments to this post would therefore be very unpleasant to me. It did not help; the order stood. I had to go to 7th Army on the same day.
>
> Seventh Army was obviously not very pleased with my turning up there. The insertion of my Staff between the Army Staff and the Corp Staff was unnecessary, and meant, in the prevailing situation, a very unpleasant lengthening of the command channel.

Captain Harry C Butcher, USNR, Naval Aide to General Dwight D Eisenhower, Allied Supreme Commander, recalled that the renewal of the Germans' Avranches/Mortain attack was anticipated with glee, observing on 11 August:

> We have a good chance of catching the Germans in a giant trap if Patton's forces manage to get around to Argentan, the British-Canadians close in from the north to Falaise, and the remaining gap of some 15 or 16 miles (24–25km) is sealed off. At the moment the Germans are expected again to counterattack near Mortain, where they had amassed five and a half of their seven Panzer Divisions, the remaining one and a half still being opposite the British-Canadians. Some 475 to 500 German tanks were thought to be against us in the Mortain area. The weather was to continue good and Bradley [Lieutenant General commanding the US 12th Army Group comprising Lieutenant General Courtney H Hodges' US 1st and Lieutenant General George S Patton's US 3rd Armies] and his staff were optimistic as to the result. Hoped to 'suck in' more Germans.

There was, though, some concern that the panzers might find one of the weak spots in Patton's extended US 3rd Army. The following day Butcher noted: 'I mentioned to Ike last night that the Germans had about 500 tanks against us in the Mortain area, and he said, "We've got 3,500; what are we scared of?"'

In reality, for the renewed attack Eberbach could only gather 124 tanks, seventy-seven Panzer Mark IVs and forty-seven Panthers, roughly the same inadequate numbers that had been launched in the initial attack. His efforts, though, were stillborn once the Americans were south of Argentan. All thoughts of counterattack were abandoned in favour of trying to extricate as many units as possible from the American, British, Canadian and Polish pincer movement now coming to fruition.

Eberbach blamed the failure of the German attack on Avranches squarely on the German High Command. Referring to the transfer of Panzergruppe West's armour to 7th Army for the operation, he commented:

> These forces might have sufficed to stop the American advance if they had been transferred to 7th Army in time. This was never the case. The failure was caused by the fact that the Panzer Divisions of Panzergruppe West (5th Panzer Army), committed at the front, were not relieved by infantry divisions in due time. The Armed Forces High Command is to blame for this. It did not authorise C-in-C West to act freely, and delayed the transfer of the divisions.

After Avranches, Panzergruppe West became responsible for the supply of 7th Army, which controlled the 12th SS Panzer and 17th SS Panzergrenadier Divisions, a role it was singularly ill-suited to do.

The British, Canadian and Polish armour attacked along the Caen–Falaise Road on 7–13 August in Operation Totalise, an effort to capture Falaise. This then developed into Operation Tractable, designed to close the neck of the Falaise salient containing 5th Panzer Army, Panzergruppe Eberbach and 7th Army.

The German position in Normandy became completely untenable on 15 August when 94,000 Allied troops landed in the South of France in Operation Dragoon. Winston Churchill had wanted the operation launched into Brittany, which would have piled the pressure on the Germans in Northern France, but there was a lack of satisfactory ports as the Germans resolutely clung onto them. Churchill even threatened to resign but Eisenhower and the American Chiefs of Staff would not be moved.

In strategic terms Dragoon was largely nugatory, as it had not been conducted in parallel with Overlord due to shortages of amphibious transport. Moreover, if Overlord succeeded, Army Group G would be forced to withdraw from southern France to avoid being cut off. Additionally the Germans had very few panzers remaining in Southern France. All of Army Group G's panzer divisions, 2nd SS, 9th and 17th SS Panzergrenadier along with elements of the

271st, 272nd, 276th and 708th Infantry Divisions had already been drawn north to the fighting in Normandy. Only 11th Panzer remained in the south, which was refitting after being mauled on the Eastern Front.

By the end of the month, Free French Forces had liberated Toulon and Marseilles, driving Blaskowitz's dazed Army Group G northeastward. It was only a matter of days before Germans were facing final defeat in Normandy in the Falaise pocket. The fate of the panzer divisions was to vary greatly – but the ultimate outcome after all the bloodletting was to have very serious consequences for the Allies.

Chapter 3

Throw them back into the Sea – 21st Panzer Division

The preliminary stages of Operation Overlord commenced late on 5 June 1944 with the steady drone of hundreds of Allied aircraft making their way across the English Channel towards the French coast. The first formations consisted of over 1,000 aircraft of Bomber Command, directed at the ten strongest German coastal batteries along the Normandy coastline. Their task had to be completed by 2300 hours D-1, in order to clear the area ready for the incoming airborne troops. In their way stood the 21st Panzer Division. Gefreiter Werner Kortenhaus, Panzer Regiment 22, 21st Panzer recalled:

> *Our panzers were very well prepared; that was one thing we did not have to worry about. We had spent months and months previously getting them ready. We knew our panzers, we had full command of them.... we assumed we would be able to push back a sea landing. Indeed, we took it for granted. You know, people are amazed by this but we were young panzer men burning at the thought we were perhaps going to be involved in some action. Of course, we had no idea what that would mean. No idea at all.*

Generalleutnant Edgar Feuchtinger, commander of 21st Panzer, designated one of the reserve units, did not start moving northwards until 1600 hours on the 6th. His counterattack towards Bieville failed and his troops were driven eastwards. By the end of the day Feuchtinger had lost twenty panzers and the British were only just halted at Lebisey, a mere two miles (1.2km) north of Caen. From then on the division's performance was to be decidedly lacklustre, its greatest contribution to the defence of Normandy was helping to halt Operation Goodwood.

Combat experience

Created from the 5th Light Division, the 21st Panzer Division came into being in August 1941, commanded by General Karl Böttcher. Erwin Rommel's Panzergruppe Afrika was formed in North Africa in July 1941 and included the newly re-designated 21st Panzer, where it fought under a series of commanders.

After the decisive Battle of El Alamein the division was down to just four panzers and, in covering the retreat into Tunisia, was only able to operate as a series of *kampfgruppen*; its last major action was against the Americans at Kasserine Pass. The remains of the division under Heinrich-Hermann von Hulsen surrendered on 13 May 1943, along with the rest of the German and Italian forces in North Africa.

Rising from the ashes, the division was reformed in Normandy in July 1943 under Generalleutnant Edgar Feuchtinger, largely from scratch, and remained in France on occupation duty. Between January 1944 and May 1944 General-major Oswin Grolig and Generalleutnant Franz Westhoven commanded the division respectively, until Feuchtinger resumed responsibility again on 8 May.

Considering 21st Panzer's key role in the early stages of the Battle for Normandy, Feuchtinger seems to have been a decidedly uninspiring individual. He began his military career in the artillery, so was not strictly a panzer leader, but by early 1943 was in charge of Schnellen Brigade 931, which formed the cadre for the new 21st Panzer. The former was an occupation unit, bulked out with transferees to bring it up to divisional strength. One unit specially formed for the new division was Flak Abteilung 305, equipped with 8.8cm and 2cm flak guns. However, by far the best tank-killers were the dedicated 8.8cm Pak 43 anti-tank guns of Panzerjäger Battalion 200.

Oberst Hans von Luck, commander of Panzergrenadier Regiment 125, had a fairly dim view of the capabilities of his divisional commander, particularly his lack of recent combat experience or knowledge of armoured warfare. Paris seemed to hold a greater attraction for Feuchtinger than the responsibilities of his division.

Fortunately for Feuchtinger, the officer in charge of the division's Panzer Regiment 22 was a very able man. The forty-five year-old Oberst Hermann von Oppeln-Bronikowski was a veteran of the First World War and the invasions of Poland, France and Russia. On the Eastern Front he had served with 4th Panzer Division's Panzer Regiment 5, assuming command from Oberst Heinrich Eberbach (later commander 5th Panzer Army and 7th Army in Normandy) in January 1942. He subsequently commanded Panzer Regiments 204 and 11 and, wounded at Kursk, eventually found himself in France

In the run up to D-day the 21st Panzer Division was far from idle. With its limited, and in some cases antiquated, resources it made every preparation it could for the anticipated Allied attack. Nineteen year old Gefreiter Werner Kortenhaus recalled:

> In April 1944 we were still stationed in Brittany but were then moved
> to the area of Caen at the end of the month. I believe that this was at

the order of Rommel himself. In the weeks that followed we actually occupied ourselves less with military training, but more with manual work because we had to dig holes in which to bury our tanks, so that only the gun barrel was above the earth. It was very strenuous physical work for young people, and when we had finished that, there were still the lorries and munition stores to dig in. And added to all this was also the fact that the large flat plain where we were was expected to be a site for enemy air landings, so we stuck lots of trees – chopped down trees – vertically into the earth. We called these 'Rommel's asparagus,' because it was Rommel who had ordered them.

Petrol and ammunition shortages, though, greatly hampered training; while each panzer had its full complement of 100 shells, for live firing the crews were only allowed to expend one or two rounds. Like all soldiers food became a preoccupation with the men constantly grumbling about the rations, or rather the lack of them, and their quality. Understandably, the local French farmers did not go out of their way to supply the division and in the name of good discipline Feuchtinger's officers did all they could to prevent theft and looting. It was made clear that anyone caught stealing would be imprisoned.

Despite all the hard work and lack of supplies, 21st Panzer's morale remained high. In the back of the *panzertruppen*'s minds they knew that strategically, following Stalingrad and El Alamein, things were not going well; the task in front of them was another matter and they were confident about that.

The 21st Panzer Division's organisation was largely unique in Normandy; unlike the other panzer divisions (with the exception of 10th SS) it had no Panther tank battalion. Instead it had an assault gun battalion and an anti-tank battalion with towed 8.8cm guns. In addition, each of its infantry regiments had one battalion equipped with armoured half-track personnel carriers. At the beginning of June 1944 the 21st had a total of 104 Panzer IVs, including six with the short barrel 7.5cm gun. In manpower terms it was almost at full strength, nearing some 17,000 men.

The II Abteilung of Panzer Regiment 22 was also equipped with a variety of captured French tanks, while Panzer Artillery Regiment 155 and Sturm-geschütz Abteilung 200 were armed with self-propelled and assault guns, also converted from French tanks. The latter, under Major Alfred Becker, were not in reality Sturmgeschütz as they had open fighting compartments and could not really function as assault guns. Based on the French Hotchkiss H-39 chassis, armed with a 7.5cm or 10.5cm gun plus additional armour, these vehicles were perilously overloaded. They were unable to engage Allied tanks on anything like equal terms and when the time came could do little more than conduct a fighting withdrawal.

The chain of command for 21st Panzer was a horrible muddle that made little sense. While Feuchtinger was responsible to Schweppenburg's Panzergruppe West, he was immediately subordinate to the 716th Infantry Division under Generalleutenant Wilhelm Richter. The latter wanted anticipated Allied airborne landings swiftly mopped up and had a free hand with Feuchtinger's infantry and guns, but he could not commit Oppeln-Bronikowski's tanks, which were considered part of Rommel's reserves, and at the crucial moment the latter was on his way back from Germany. To further complicate matters Richter's division was subordinate to General Erich Marcks' LXXXIV Corps.

Invasion: they're coming!

At 0020 hours, D-Day, 6 June, the quietness of the night was shattered as the gliders of the British 6th Airborne Division landed by the Caen canal bridge at Bénouville and the Orne River bridge near Ranville. The paratroopers leapt from their gliders and after a short sharp exchange with the startled German guards, both bridges were successfully secured. Other units also succeeded in destroying the Merville battery and seized the four bridges over the River Dives and its tributaries. This secured the left flank of the British invasion.

At the same time Gefreiter Kortenhaus and four of his comrades were patrolling north of Falaise. Little did they appreciate the significance of the birthplace of William the Conqueror or realise that the British 6th Airborne was in the process of securing the important crossings over the Orne and Caen Canal. Although they were used to aircraft droning by high above, the noise was much lower and Kortenhaus assumed that fifth columnists were being dropped in the darkness. They found no parachutists and the sound of aircraft engines did not abate so they returned to their unit, which they found awake and alert.

Kortenhaus felt a sense of apprehension but also had more mundane things to worry about:

> As we got close to the village where our tanks were dug in, the moonlight was coming through the clouds, and we could see that the crews were at their tanks. This was unusual because most of them would normally be asleep. 'What's going on?' I asked. It occurred to me that it might be some sort of night exercise. They said, 'No, it's an alarm.' This was about 00.45. As the others prepared the tank, I remembered that my laundry was still with the French woman who did our

washing. I woke her and said, 'I need my clothes straight away.' She said, 'But they're still wet.' I said, 'I must have them anyway,' and paid for them, and ran to my tank.

After months of waiting, Kotenhaus finally found himself going to war with wet laundry. His division was ready in remarkably quick time, but now the dithering of the German high command took a hand in ensuring that the British and Canadians did not find an unpleasant surprise waiting for them just behind the beaches.

From General Feuchtinger to the lowest *panzertruppen*, a sense of frustration ultimately permeated the division. Kortenhaus and his comrades were baffled beyond belief; after all their anti-invasion training they just sat there kicking their heels:

> I would say that we were ready to march at 2am at the latest. As well as the earlier alarm, news of an airborne landing at Caen had meanwhile come through on the telephone, and we were ready to go. The engines of the tanks were running, but we didn't receive any marching orders. We thought, 'If we have to march, let's do it now while it's dark and the enemy planes can't see us.' We waited for orders, and we waited. Just stood there, inactive by our tanks. We couldn't understand why we weren't getting any orders at all.

In the meantime, all General Richter could do was order Panzergrenadier Regiment 192's II Abteilung into action against the British in Bénouville at 0200. Oberleutnant Hans Höller, commanding a section of 7.5cm self-propelled guns in the 8th Schwere Kompanie of II Abteilung drove east from Cairon and fought his way into Bénouville, held by the 7th Parachute Battalion. Under the cover of darkness they later withdrew to Lebisey.

Glider Pilot Alexander Morrison, 6th Airborne Division, who landed east of the Orne in the Ranville area recalls:

> In our briefing, we had been told that the German 21st Panzer Division was located further east of our position and that the anticipated armour counterattack would first come from them. Accordingly when at 4am we could distinctly hear the sound of tracked vehicles, we realised that we were now 'for it' because a 45-ton Tiger tank presents a formidable proposition! But miracles happened and this time we were saved by the Navy. Warned of the danger, an Army spotter plane was airborne at first light and located the squadrons of German tanks assembling for the attack. Fortunately, the pilot was in direct

communication with the Navy who promptly alerted HMS *Warspite* which was standing offshore. After a couple of sighters, she let loose with tremendous shelling and heavily blasted the whole area.

It was a fantastic experience to witness the terrible firepower of this battleship and to hear the huge shells roaring overhead like express trains to land with devastating effect right on the German assembly. The carnage must have been appalling and the severely damaged tanks shortly abandoned their attack and retired on Caen.

Feuchtinger was in Paris and eventually his performance would cost him dearly. Hastening back to his command he recalled:

> I waited impatiently all night for some instructions. But not a single order from a higher formation was received by me. Realizing that my armoured division was closest to the scene of operations, I finally decided at 6.30 in the morning that I had to take some action. I ordered my tanks to attack 6th Airborne Division which had entrenched itself in a bridgehead over the Orne. To me this constituted the most immediate threat to the German position.
>
> Hardly had I made this decision when at 7 o'clock I received my first intimation that a higher command did still exist. I was told by Army Group B that I was now under the command of the 7th Army. But received no further orders as to my role. At 9 o'clock I was informed that I would receive any future orders from LXXXIV Infantry Corps [General Marcks], and finally at 10 o'clock I was given my first operational instructions. I was ordered to stop the move of my tanks against the Allied airborne troops, and to turn west and aid forces protecting Caen.

The upshot was that the British 6th Airborne was spared a nasty mauling and the bridges it had secured remained in Allied hands. In the meantime Feuchtinger, Kortenhaus and their comrades miraculously were not strafed or bombed as the 21st trundled toward Caen. The city itself was not so lucky. As Kortenhaus related, they were on borrowed time:

> The long road from Falaise to Caen rises to a hill where one can suddenly get a view over Caen, and as we drove over this hill we got a shock because the city of Caen was burning. I had never seen the city before, never been there at all, and all I could see was a huge black cloud over Caen as though oil had been burnt. At that point, I realized for the first time that I was at war. As we got closer to Caen

our tanks had difficulty getting through the city because the streets were covered with rubble. So we lost a lot of time while some tanks went west around the city and others went east.

Despite all the chaos, the British landings remained vulnerable as Feuchtinger manoeuvred into position to attack. Between the British beach codenamed Sword and the Canadians' Juno beachhead to the west, the Germans held a four-mile (6km) wide strip that ran all the way to the coast. British Royal Marine Commandos had been unable to force their way through at St Aubin and Lion-sur-Mer to link the two. Feuchtinger's artillery was on the ridge above the village of Périers, south of Hermanville and Lion, protecting the salient and providing a potential springboard for a German counterattack against either the British or Canadians.

Major General T G Rennie's British 3rd Infantry Division, having landed on Sword, was driving on Caen from the north and Major General R F L Keller's Canadian 3rd Infantry Division, which had landed on Juno, approached from the northwest. Luckily for the 21st Panzer, Rennie's division showed a complete lack of flare; having captured Hermanville, it dug in instead of trying to outflank the Germans at Périers. It did not reach 6th Airborne at the Bénouville Bridge until the end of the day and only got to within three miles (5km) of Caen.

In the northern outskirts the 21st Panzer found itself struggling through a tide of frightened French refugees. Hauptmann Herr's twenty-five panzers of I Kompanie reached the area between Lebisey and Biéville at about 1500. Hauptmann Wilhelm von Gottberg with the II and III Kompanies reached Périers ridge at about 1600 while the I Abteilung, Panzergrenadier Regiment 192, headed for the coast. Feuchtinger found the odds not to his liking:

> Once over the Orne river, I drove north towards the coast. By this time the enemy, consisting of three British and three Canadian Infantry Divisions, had made astonishing progress and had already occupied a strip of high ground about six miles (10km) from the sea. From here, the excellent anti-tank gunfire of the Allies knocked out eleven of my tanks before I had barely started. However, one battle-group did manage to bypass these guns and actually reached the coast at Lion-sur-Mer, at about seven in the evening.

Into action

Feuchtinger had started the day with 124 tanks. However, while manoeuvring from the southwest of Caen northwards to attack the invaders, he lost thirty-four to Allied air attack and mechanical problems. By 1600 the British had reached Biéville, but beyond the village in Lebisey wood, just two and a half miles (4km) from Caen, they bumped into forty panzers under von Oppeln-Bronikowski.

Before the attack, Oppeln-Bronikowski was briefed by General Marcks, commander of LXXXIV Corps, who placed him under no illusions about the seriousness of his mission. 'Oppeln, the future of Germany may very well rest on your shoulders,' he said, adding, 'If you don't push the British back to the sea, we've lost the war'.

Feuchtinger and Marcks watched the tanks go in. The 21st finally counter-attacked in two places; thirty-five panzers under Gottberg struck at the Périers ridge four miles (6km) from the coast, while von Oppeln-Bronikowski with another twenty-five tanks tried the ridge at Biéville.

Tanks of the British Staffordshire Yeomanry south of Biéville reported German panzers rolling northward at 1600. They were well prepared, supported by 17-pounder anti-tank guns of the 20th Anti-Tank Regiment, Royal Artillery, and 6-pounder anti-tank guns of the Shropshire Light Infantry. The four lead panzers were 'brewed up' and the rest swung away for the cover of some nearby woods. The British gave chase and the panzers swung east towards the Périers ridge.

They bumped into another squadron of the Staffordshire's tanks hulled down on Point 61 and in the following firefight the 21st Panzer lost another dozen tanks. Bronikowski lost six tanks and Gottberg ten. They had little choice but to dig in. While Feuchtinger claimed he only had seventy tanks left by the end of the day, the British only counted twenty abandoned panzers, with RAF Typhoon fighter-bombers claiming another six on the outskirts of Caen. Only six panzers and a handful of infantry made it as far as Lion-sur-Mer.

In the meantime Kortenhaus and his company had been detached to secure the Orne against the activities of 6th Airborne Division. By 2000 hours Feutchinger's divided command was ready to push down the open salient, but at that point a massive Allied airborne reinforcement arrived and the panzers wavered. East of the Orne these airborne reinforcements bumped into seventeen tanks of IV Kompanie, which formed part of Kampfgruppe von Luck. Luckily darkness was falling and in the confusion the panzers advanced on their own panzergrenadiers and the attack was called off.

During the fighting on the 6th, Panzer Artillery Regiment 155 lost two batteries, leaving just seven batteries to cover a 15 mile (25km) front. This meant that the assault gun battalion and the infantry had to give up their batteries and self-propelled guns, respectively, to the artillery.

Feuchtinger then tried to coordinate his efforts with the 12th SS Panzer Division, recalling:

> About midnight, Kurt Meyer [commander 12th SS Panzergrenadier Regiment 25] arrived at my headquarters. He was to take over my left and we were to carry out a combined operation next morning. I explained the situation to Meyer and warned him about the strength of the enemy. Meyer studied the map, turned to me with a confident air and said, 'Little fish! We'll throw them back into the sea in the morning'.

By daybreak, though, the British and Canadians had closed the gap and 21st Panzer had lost it golden opportunity to rupture the bridgehead. In reality, any attack would probably have been hemmed in and decimated by naval gunfire and Allied fighter-bombers.

While Feuchtinger and Oppeln-Bronikowski may have wrung their hands in despair over the lack of firm direction and lost time, they had thwarted the British securing Caen on day one of the invasion. Although the 6th Airborne had valiantly secured the Allies' left flank, the British 3rd Division had failed to take Caen, a major D-Day objective, thanks to the presence of 21st Panzer. Similarly the Canadians failed to capture Carpiquet airfield three miles (5km) west of Caen.

The city itself was pivotal to the British break-out and all the time it remained in German hands it was an obstruction to General Montgomery's plans. The fate of France and indeed Panzergruppe West now rested with the outcome of the battle for Caen and 21st Panzer's ability to hold onto it.

Kortenhaus was shocked at the rapid rate with which the division lost its tanks:

> My company was under the control of Kampfgruppe von Luck. We made two attacks, one on 7 June and one on the 9th, and had a lot of losses – of our seventeen tanks, only one survived. The rest were destroyed. That had a big effect on us, and we sat around afterwards very crushed in spirits. It was now clear to us that we weren't going to do it, we weren't going to push the Allies back. The Allied attacks were too strong, particularly because of their air superiority. There was hardly any chance of avoiding a bad ending. But when an order came to attack we still did it – it must have been the same on the Allied side – because if a commander says, 'Attack!' or 'Tanks advance!' no one could say, 'I am not doing it.'

Trooper Peter Davies, 1st East Riding Yeomanry, found himself up against the 21st Panzer on 7 June:

> We had a nasty time at a tiny hamlet of a dozen places called Galmanche [northwest of Caen]. We were mortared all day by German infantry, and shelled by artillery, and we had to hold it without infantry. We fought there for five hours. It was said afterwards that we were lucky we weren't annihilated, that B Squadron had taken the brunt of the battle. We lost a lot of commanders dead or wounded. I think it was eleven out of nineteen in one day....
>
> The Germans had the greater firepower. We were outgunned on a number of occasions. Their tanks were better than ours, their guns were better than ours – I don't think their crews were better than ours. I have to say that, but I believe it was true. We were faster, we could manoeuvre better – we could survive better....
>
> It was mostly the 21st Panzer Division in front of us. We had fewer tanks than they had, but to kid them we had a lot more we used to stick the barrel through the hedge, stay there for ten minutes, quarter of an hour on watch, pull back and run down the hedge and stick it through somewhere else and kid the Germans there were tanks all along the hedge. Whereas there might have been only two or three.

Panzer Grenadier Regiment 125's combat team was involved in tough fighting with the British paratroops on 7 June. Feuchtinger could sense that the odds were stacked against his men:

> Already at this early date the enemy's superior weight in men and materiel became obvious. He was constantly being reinforced by sea and air, while the division did not have any reserves worth the name to call on, and those units that were arriving the High Command had to commit northwest of Caen.

He found the 7th very frustrating, adding:

> The whole day long it was difficult to cover the left wing of the division, as the 3rd Canadian Division was trying to envelop it, the 12th SS Division not having arrived yet.
>
> I SS Panzer Corps, to which the division had been subordinated since 2200 on 6 June, had ordered the 21st Panzer Division and the 12th SS Panzer Division to continue their attacks on 7 June with the objective of throwing the enemy into the sea. This attack was

never launched, as only one regiment of the 12th SS succeeded in establishing connections with the 21st Panzer Division on 7 June, and that only at 1600 hours.

Allied air attacks were responsible for this delay, only one panzer battalion and one panzergrenadier regiment from the 12th SS managed to reach 21st Panzer's left wing north of Épron.

On the 8th the division fended off another British attempt on Caen, destroying eighteen British Churchill Armoured Vehicle Royal Engineer (AVRE) tanks in the process. Allied firepower, though, accounted for twenty-five per cent of the panzers and fifty per cent of the infantry committed during this bitter fighting. British naval gunfire also impeded the movement of supplies, particularly ammunition. Soon the local dumps were drained, forcing vulnerable motor vehicles to forage further afield, exposing them to air attack. The complete lack of support by the Luftwaffe did not go unnoticed either.

Montgomery was planning a two-pronged attack. The first involved Major General D C Bullen-Smith's 51st (Highland) Division and the 4th Armoured Brigade striking toward Cagny from the airborne bridgehead east of the Orne. Werner Kortenhaus and his fellow *panzertruppen* of Kampfgruppe von Luck spoiled the Highlanders' plans with a pre-emptive attack on 9 June, though with some losses:

> We rolled through the gap one after the other, the Panzergrenadiers storming on behind us, weapons at the ready, trying to shelter behind their tanks as they deployed into broad front formation on the other side of the attack which was to steamroller us into Ranville. The firing began when we were only 30 yards from the hedge, and the first of the grenadiers dropped groaning to the ground. Panzer 432 was hit, and lost a track. Thirty seconds later Panzer 400 was hit and our company commander, Oberleutnant Hoffmann was staring in horror at the bloody mess which had been his leg, while Panzer 401 exploded, blowing open the hatches and literally flinging the crew out.

General Fritz Kraemer, Chief of Staff I SS Panzer Corps, recalled on the 9th the rising toll inflicted on the division:

> An enemy air attack on the Panzer Regiment of the 21st Panzer Division put it out of action for almost one and a half days and a critical situation developed in this sector. Direct damage from the bombing attack was slight, but at least 50 per cent of the sixty tanks were rendered inoperative, in most cases by mechanical damage arising from the tanks being buried in mud.

Montgomery's other attack was to push Major General G W Erskine's 7th Armoured Division toward Villers-Bocage. If they and the 51st broke through, the 1st Airborne Division was to be dropped into the gap, trapping the German defenders. Things did not go according to plan when 7th Armoured ran into elements of Schwere Panzer Abteilung 503 and the Panzer Lehr Division.

By 11 June, 21st Panzer had lost about forty per cent of its manpower killed, wounded or missing, it had also lost fifty per cent of its tanks and thirty per cent of its guns. In total it could field about thirty or forty Panzer IVs and Vs. By mid-month the division had suffered 1,864 casualties, by 11 July this had risen to 3,411 and by the end of July stood at 4,703. Crucially, replacements for this entire period amounted to only 2,479 men, some of which are believed to have come from the 16th Luftwaffe Field Division. During the second week of June, the 21st Panzer was transferred to 15th Army's LXXXVI Corps; Kampfgruppe von Luck had already been under this Corps' control since the 6th.

The 21st Panzer was thrown into the attack again, making some headway. Kortenhaus remembered a particularly bizarre moment during the fighting:

> I can paint you a strange picture which stays with me still. On 28 June we mounted an attack west of Caen and succeeded in getting through the British line. The battle lasted a very long time, from ten in the morning until five in the afternoon, but around midday there was a lull in the battle. Suddenly the battlefield was filled with dance music. Some infantrymen had gone and played with an English radio set, and dance music had come on, filling the air. It was a little unusual.

Stopping Goodwood

The 21st Panzer Division stayed in the line until 5 July when the 16th Luftwaffe Field Division finally relieved it. Within just over a week it was back resisting Goodwood launched on 18 July. The British offensive, employing the 7th, 11th and Guards Armoured Divisions, was intended to seize the high ground south of Caen and stop the panzers switching west before the Americans could launch Operation Cobra.

In the path of the British lay a series of stone-built villages amidst hedge-lined fields and orchards. General Eberbach and Field Marshal Rommel exploited these to the maximum. General von Obstfelder's LXXXVI Corps consisted of three infantry divisions supported by the 21st and 1st SS Panzer Divisions, while the 12th SS at Lisieux constituted I SS Panzer Corps reserve. In addition, Tigers of the 503 and 101 SS heavy tank battalions were also available.

The British assessed the German defences to be to a depth of three miles (5km). Rommel and Eberbach had in fact built five defensive zones covering 10 miles (16km). The first consisted of the infantry, then sixty tanks from 21st Panzer and thirty-nine Tigers; next a chain of fortified villages and then the artillery on a gun line including the Garcelles-Secqueville woods and the Bourguebus ridge, supported by Panzergrenadiers and Panther tanks from the 1st SS. The final zone comprised two *kampfgruppen* from the 12th SS.

The German defences were not as formidable as they appeared, in fact the best defensive weapons in the Main Line of Resistance (MLR) were just seventeen Pak 43s, the dedicated tank-killer version of the 8.8cm flak gun, belonging to Becker's Panzerjäger Abteilung 200. Just eight 8.8cm flak guns from the division's Flak Abteilung 305 supplemented these. Divisional artillery was a hotchpotch of captured French and Russian guns deployed on the reverse slopes of the Bourguébus ridge.

Werner Kortenhaus recalled Goodwood's preliminary bombardment: 'It was a bomb carpet, ploughing up the ground. Among the thunder of the explosions we could hear the wounded scream and the insane howling of men who had been driven mad'.

Panzer IVs of Panzer Regiment 22, along with Tiger tanks from Schwere Panzer Abteilung 503, were caught in the Allied saturation bombing near Château de Manneville, 16 miles (10km) east of Caen. The effects were devastating with tanks simply tossed upside down like they were toys. From a force of about fifty panzers over half were lost, many others suffered mechanical problems. At least three Tigers were caught.

Hans von Luck arrived from leave in Paris just in time to help rally the situation; ironically it had been Feuchtinger and Dietrich who had persuaded him to celebrate his birthday and visit his girlfriend. He returned just after 0900 to his *kampfgruppe* drawn from the battered 21st Panzer and the 16th Luftwaffe Field Division. Driving from his Frénouville HQ toward le Mesnil-Frémentel he saw that Cagny, off to his right, had been destroyed, but could not reach his men.

The bombardment had severed all communications and von Luck could not raise any of his units, so he rumbled off down the Vimont–Caen road in his Panzer IV:

> I approached the village of Cagny which lay exactly in the middle of my sector and was not occupied by us. The eastern part as far as the church was undamaged; the western part had been flattened. When I came to the western edge of the village, I saw to my dismay about twenty-five to thirty British tanks, which had already passed

southward over the main road to Caen … where my number I Abteilung ought to be, or had been, in combat positions. The whole area was dotted with British tanks, which were slowly rolling south against no opposition.

Discovering a dazed Luftwaffe captain with four 8.8cm flak guns by Cagny church, von Luck drew his pistol and forced him to redeploy them in a nearby apple orchard, where they claimed sixteen British tanks. General Wolfgang Pickert's III Flak Corps had been placed under Panzergruppe West's control upon the latter's activation on 10 June; however, this did not mean that all of Pickert's batteries were immediately released for frontline duty with the Panzergruppe. Although the 8.8cm flak gun also made an effective anti-tank weapon, it was normally against standing orders for flak artillery to be used in the ground fighting. In fact, as late as the end of August Field Marshal Wilhelm Keitel, Chief of Staff OKW, repeated this directive.

The 16th Luftwaffe Field Division was incapable of withstanding the bombardment and enemy tanks, and in reality was little more than a sacrificial lamb. The 21st's Panzergrenadier Regiment 192 was in danger of being overrun and I Abteilung Panzergrenadier Regiment 125 was cut off at le Mesnil-Frémentel; to the east, though, II Abteilung was holding on at Emiéville and Guillerville. Irritatingly the divisional reconnaissance and pioneer battalions were tied up at Bourguébus screening the anti-tank battalion.

The village of le Mesnil-Frémentel lay right in the middle of the British line of attack in this area. Major Becker's five batteries from his assault gun battalion were deployed at Démouville, Giberville, Grentheville and the farms of le Mesnil-Frémentel and le Prieuré, supported by von Luck's Panzergrenadiers.

On the eastern half of the battlefield they represented the Germans' only mobile tactical reserve. These forces attempted to hold up the British advance, but those guns at Cuverville and Démouville were lost in the opening bombardment and the battery at Giberville withdrew northwest of Bras and, along with those at Grentheville, shelled British tanks to the east and west. The two batteries at the farms, lacking infantry protection, were also soon forced back by the relentless tide of tanks.

The assault gun battalion engaged the British 29th Brigade's lead regiment, the Fife and Forfar Yeomanry, destroying more than twenty Shermans before conducting a fighting withdrawal towards the 1st SS 'stop line' on Bourguébus ridge. By the end of the day most of Becker's so-called assault guns were wrecks.

Just after 0930, determined to hold Cagny and the vital Bourguébus ridge, the Germans threw the 21st Panzer and Abteilung 503 at the Guards and

11th Armoured Divisions with orders to regain the Caen–Troarn road. The Panthers of the 1st SS also rolled down from Bourguébus ridge, driving back the British. In the process of trying to drive them back to Caen–Troarn, the two panzer divisions lost 109 tanks, while by the end of the first day the British had suffered 1,500 casualties and 200 tanks destroyed for the gain of just six miles (10km) beyond the Orne. However, the north–south line from Frénouville to Emiéville held and, with the commitment of the 1st SS, Goodwood came to a grinding halt over the next few days. The remnants of the 16th Luftwaffe Field Division were attached to 21st Panzer on 19 July.

The sector east of Troarn held by 21st Panzer was taken over by the 272nd Infantry Division in late July. The division was then transferred to the LXXIV Corps and the II Abteilung Panzer Regiment 22 was sent to Mailly-le-Camp and was still there in mid-August.

Final days

The division's final days in Normandy were spent fighting alongside the 1st SS and 12th SS trying to prop open the northern shoulder of the Falaise pocket. In particular with the remaining elements of the 89th Infantry Division it struggled to hold back Major General R K Ross' 53rd (Welsh) Division west of Falaise, before fleeing east. During August the division lost 3,000 men, giving a total loss of 8,000 for the entire campaign.

Chapter 4

Formidably Equipped –
Panzer Lehr Panzer Division

Following the D-Day landings in the early hours of 6 June, it was not until 1400 that the German armoured reserve, Panzer Lehr and 12th SS Panzer Divisions, were released for combat operations. It would take up to three days to bring them into action. The Allied air forces did all they could to impede the panzers' progress to the front and Panzer Lehr did not escape their unwanted attentions. Most of the Luftwaffe was tied up resisting the Allies' strategic bombing campaign over Germany or on the Eastern Front.

Panzer Lehr's commander, General Fritz Bayerlein, soon found that the constant air attacks and High Command's insistence on radio silence created a state of chaos within his strung-out units. Panzer Lehr's principal role would be desperately, but futilely, trying to fend off the American breakout, by which time it had suffered losses of 6,000 men. Almost swept away by the American offensive, Panzer Lehr remarkably avoided being trapped in the Falaise pocket.

Combat experience

Panzer Lehr had been formed at Potsdam in November 1943, from demonstration units of the various Panzer schools, and placed under the leadership of Generalleutnant Fritz Bayerlein. The division was then transferred to France in February 1944 and on to Hungary in April of that year, where it absorbed Infanterie-Lehr-Regiment 901. It then returned to France for garrison duties.

Bayerlein was Bavarian, hailing from Würzburg, and like so many of his comrades he had served in the trenches during the First World War. During the invasions of Poland and France he had served as General Heinz Guderian's First General Staff Officer. In North Africa he served under Erwin Rommel and that other leading panzer exponent, Wilhelm von Thoma. He was lucky to escape the German defeat in Tunisia, being sent back to Italy just before the Axis surrender on 12 May 1943. He then commanded the 3rd Panzer Division in Russia.

In Bayerlein's capable hands, Panzer Lehr was one of the most formidably equipped panzer divisions in Normandy and was also one of the few divisions at almost full strength. By the beginning of June, Bayerlein's command amounted to 14,699 officers and men. Including those forces of the attached Panzer Kompanie 316 (Funklenk – radio controlled), Panzer Lehr amassed ninety-nine Panzer IVs, eighty-nine Panthers, thirty-one Jagdpanzer IVs, ten Sturmegschütz IIIs and eight Tigers (three Tiger Is and five Tiger IIs), giving an impressive total of 237 panzers and assault guns. Initially, Panzer Lehr was stationed in the Chartes–Le Mans–Orléans area.

Fate partly favoured the Allies when it was decided to ship the Panthers of the I Abteilung Panzer Regiment 6, which was on loan from the 3rd Panzer Division, to the Eastern Front. The day before D-Day, the first train bearing this unit reached Magdeburg in Germany, whilst the last was loitering in Paris. Once the Allied landings were underway the battalion was ordered to retrace its steps.

Again fortunately for the Allies, the half dozen Tiger IIs of Panzer Kompanie 316 (Funklenk) were defective prototypes that were due back in Germany. Because they could not be moved by rail they were left at Chateaudun and eventually blown up. Panzer Kompanie 316 (Funklenk) was attached to Panzer Lehr in Normandy for tactical purposes with about ten tanks, though by early July all but two were undergoing repair. It operated closely with the division's Panzer Lehr Regiment, starting with an operational strength of nine StuG assault guns and three Tiger Is.

The divisional Panzer Artillery Regiment 130 also included Hummel and Wespe self-propelled guns, adding to its armoured fighting vehicle contingent. In addition, all the panzergrenadier units were equipped with armoured half-tracks and an array of heavy support weapons.

Bayerlein recalled the almost immediate aerial assault on his division:

> We moved as ordered [at 1700], and immediately came under air attack. I lost twenty to thirty vehicles by nightfall. It's hard to remember exactly the figures for each day, but I do remember very well being strafed personally near Alençon.
>
> We kept on during the night with but three hours' delay for rest and refuelling. At daylight, General Dollmann [commander 7th Army] gave me a direct order to proceed and there was nothing else to do. The first air attack came about 0530 that morning, near Falaise. By noon it was terrible: my men were calling the main road from Vire to Beny-Bocage a fighter-bomber race-course – *Jabo Rennstrecke*.
>
> I was driving in front of the middle column with two staff cars and two headquarters signal vans along the Alençon–Argentan–Falaise road. We had only got to Beaumont-sur-Sarthe when the first

fighter-bomber attack forced us to take cover. For once we were lucky. But the columns were getting farther apart all the time. Since Army had ordered radio silence we had to maintain contact by dispatch riders. As if radio silence could have stopped the fighter-bombers and reconnaissance planes from spotting us! All it did was prevent the division staff from forming a picture of the state of the advance – if it was moving smoothly or whether there were hold ups and losses, and how far the spearheads had got. I was forever sending officers or else seeking out my units myself.

We were moving along all five routes of advance. Naturally our move had been spotted by enemy reconnaissance. And before long the bombers were hovering above the roads, smashing cross-roads, villages and towns along our line of advance, and pouncing on the long columns of vehicles.

Hauptmann Helmut Ritgen also experienced first hand the division's difficulties trying to reach the enemy:

Marching at night turned out to be reasonably safe and Panzer Lehr made their way to the Flers-Vire area on previously reconnoitred routes.

My battalion was attacked by aircraft during a supply halt near Alençon. Bomb and gun bursts set tanks and POL [Petrol, Oil and Lubricant] trucks on fire, soldiers were killed and wounded. Similar incidents happened to all the columns. Some mushroom clouds of smoke were guiding the fighter-bombers to their targets. In spite of increased vehicle distance and dispersion to small groups, marching in daylight under repeated air attack was a risky venture, costing time and losses.

The pilots of the Allied fighter-bombers attempted to wreak havoc on the division, though there is some dispute as to the exact numbers; losses of over 200 armoured fighting and wheeled vehicles were reported. While the columns of Panzer Lehr struggled toward their objectives under rolling air interdiction, General Bayerlein was severely cut up when his car was attacked; his aide and his driver were both killed. He himself got away, slightly wounded but violently shaken.

Like Bayerlein, his ordnance officer, Hauptmann Alexander Hartdegen, was demoralised by the constant air attacks, recalling:

Unless a man has been through these fighter-bomber attacks he cannot know what the invasion meant. You lie there, helpless, in a

roadside ditch, in a furrow on a field, or under a hedge, pressed to
the ground, your face in the dirt – and then it comes towards you,
roaring. There it is. Diving at you. Now you hear the whine of the
bullets. Now you are for it.

Our staff car was a gutted heap of metal on the road; it was
smouldering and smoking. Corporal Kartheus lay dead in a ditch.
As if by a miracle General Bayerlein got away with a few cuts and
shrapnel wounds. As for me, I was saved by the culvert.

Just as crucial were the delays. The Panzer IVs of Panzer Regiment 130 did not
reach the woods to the north of Alençon until early on 7 June. The result was
that the Panzergrenadier Regiments 901 and 902 and Panzerjäger Abteilung
130 were committed in a piecemeal fashion over the next three days. The
Panthers did not arrive until the 10th.

Major Peter Selerie, Sherwood Rangers Yeomanry, came into contact with
the Panzer Lehr on 7 June:

We now pressed on to capture the St Léger feature southeast of
Bayeux. It was here that we caught our first glimpse of German tanks
since the end of the war in Africa. There were about three or four
of them and they withdrew southwards before we could engage
them. Subsequently we learned that the enemy had thrown together
a series of veteran training cadres to form the crack Panzer Lehr
Division. In addition the 12th SS (*Hitlerjugend*) Division was moving
up on our front. Our old desert adversaries – the 21st Panzer
Division – were also reported near Caen. . . .

It became increasingly obvious that our 75mm guns would not
penetrate the frontal armour of the German Mark VI (Tiger) or the
Mark V (Panther) tanks. It was exceedingly difficult to get on their
flank and fire on the side armour.

Into action

Coming up from Lisieux on the 7th, Bayerlein remembered what a bizarre
spectacle his division must have seemed:

Every vehicle was covered with tree branches and moved along hedges
and the edges of woods. Road junctions were bombed, and a bridge
knocked out at Condé. This did not stop my tanks, but it hampered
other vehicles. By the end of the day I had lost forty tank trucks
carrying fuel, and ninety others. Five of my tanks were knocked out
and eighty-four half-tracks, prime-movers and self-propelled guns. . . .

These were serious losses for a division not yet in action. I was just east of Tilly on 7 June and ready to attack. My attack took Ellon [on the 9th], and I could have gone straight to the sea down the corridor between the American and British forces, splitting them apart. I was ordered to hold Ellon because units on my right flank had been delayed. I was a day behind my schedule, because of air harassment.

At Lingèvres Panzer Lehr was thrown into the fray as Leutnant Ernst recalled:

We reached Lingèvres [on 11 June] and straightaway joined in the counterattack. In the narrow streets the noise of the tracks and engines of our tanks was deafening. Our tracks screeched as we turned just in front of the church, where we came across the hulk of a British signals tank that had been knocked out. Along a stony track, we headed for a small wood about 300 metres away.

'Battle stations! Close hatches!' came the order from Hauptmann Ritgen. Inside 'Zitrone' there was tension in the air... Ahead of 'Zitrone' three other tanks were moving in single file up the narrow track.'

Turning westward, Ernst and the others skirted a small wood. Suddenly they found themselves in the midst of a fire-fight with British tanks. He remembered the fierce action:

Suddenly, the gun-layers heard the tank commanders shout: 'Take aim, enemy tank at 11 o'clock – fire!

I shouted to my gun-layer: '*Feuer!*' and our round grazed the top of the Cromwell's cupola and flew past it. .... The enemy disappeared behind the hedge; then we came under fire from the other side. 'To the left!' I shouted, and the PzKpfw IV heaved round with a jolt. The shape of the enemy tank grew larger in the gun sight. The recoil jarred the tank backwards as the round flew towards the thicket. It sounded like a direct hit. Smoke rose up in the sky. Nothing further moved. Evidently they must have been as surprised as we were, and got out of the tank on impact and thus escaped being killed.

Carrying their wounded, Ernst and the other tanks of Panzer Lehr withdrew from Lingèvres.

Although only three days into the Allied invasion, Werner Kortenhaus was already full of doom and gloom:

Hitler should have ended the war on 9 June at the latest because, after all, he had said that if we weren't successful in pushing back the

Allied landing, we would have lost the war. We had three fronts –
Poland, Italy and the West. It would have been impossible to win.

After some difficulty, the bulk of Panzer Lehr came into the line to the left of
the 12th SS on 9 June, having driven 90 miles (144km) from Chartres. By this
stage the frequent air attacks were causing unwelcome shortages with those
troops now engaged in the fighting. The division needed 8,000 rounds of 8.8cm
and 60,000 rounds of 2cm ammunition, much of it probably expended shooting
at aircraft, but while the quartermaster was sympathetic, petrol shortages meant
nothing was reaching him. Even more alarming for Panzer Lehr's *panzertruppen*, there was no tank ammunition to be had.

They first went into action opposite the Canadians, but then side-stepped to
attack up the road towards Bayeux. The battle of Le Mesnil-Patry resulted in
them halting just three miles (5km) from the city on 11 June. Panzer Lehr then
went onto the defensive around Tilly-sur-Seulles and, as the rest of its units
arrived, British XXX Corps' advance was blocked. By the 11th the division had
lost about twenty-five per cent of its manpower, twenty per cent of its tanks
and ten per cent of its guns. In total about sixty Mark IV and V tanks remained
serviceable.

This forced the British to shift their efforts west of Caen to the flank of
Panzer Lehr and the high ground beyond Villers-Bocage. The idea of a right
hook was Major-General G W Erskine's, commander of the 7th Armoured
Division, and was first discussed at XXX Corps HQ on 10 June. It was hoped
the move would break up the resistance in front of Major General D A H
Graham's 50th (Northumbrian) Division; it was also hoped to encircle the
now-troublesome Panzer Lehr.

When 50th Division drove against Panzer Lehr, 7th Armoured Division
swung to the west, driving three quarters of a circle into the American sector,
then south through the gap in the German line and eastwards behind Lehr at
Villers-Bocage. There, on 13 June, they ran into Tiger tanks of Schwere SS-
Panzer Abteilung 101. The British were stopped dead in their tracks.

Oberstleutnant Kurt Kauffman, Operations Officer Panzer Lehr, assembled
three field guns, two 8.8cm and some rear echelon troops, which he led in a
successful attack against Villers-Bocage, while panzergrenadiers of the 2nd
Panzer Division began pushing up from the south. By 1600 hours the German
attacks had been beaten off, with Bayerlein reporting the loss of six precious
Tigers and several PzKpfw IVs. On 14 June Panzer Lehr was transferred to
General von Funck's XLVII Panzer Corps control.

That day the British XXX Corps launched a series of attacks using 50th
Division against Tilly and Panzer Lehr's Panzergrenadier Regiment 901, in the

hope of forcing Lehr back to enable 7th Armoured Division to continue its own ill-fated offensive. 50th Division's failure to get forward, the arrival of 2nd Panzer (which fanned out northwest of Caumont, north of Livry and northeast of Villers-Bocage), plus the two-day delay in the British build-up, meant the 7th Armoured was in danger of being crushed.

The division formed a defensive box of about 1,000 by 700 yards, which was attacked on three sides by German armoured forces on 14 June. Colin Thomson of the 11th Hussars recalled:

> The 3rd and 5th Royal Horse Artillery were firing over open sights into the woods 300 yards away.... The result was unbelievable carnage. This battle lasted until 10.30pm when Jerry decided to retire and presumably regroup.

Lieutenant General G C Bucknall, Commander of XXX Corps, failed to ask 2nd Army for direct infantry support for 7th Armoured's beleaguered tanks. In consequence, when Bucknall was visiting 7th Armoured's Tactical HQ he had both his escort tanks knocked out by lurking Tigers, and on returning to his own HQ concluded Erskine's communications were in danger of being severed.

By 18–19 June, however, Panzer Lehr had lost about 100 of its 240 tanks in the bitter fighting in the Villers-Bocage area. Bayerlein claimed this had weakened his division to such an extent that it was no longer capable of launching an armoured thrust towards the sea. Between 26 June and 5 July the 276th Infantry Division, previously deployed in southwestern France, relieved Panzer Lehr, moving into position on its right flank. By this stage the division had lost almost 3,000 killed, wounded and missing. Panzer Kompanie 316 (Funklenk) still had seven operational StuG on 1 July and was pulled out of the front later in July to join the newly-formed Panzer Abteilung 302 (Funklenk).

Cobra strikes

Panzer Lehr was placed in reserve and sent just nineteen replacement panzers. However, the rest was brief and within five days it was committed against the Americans in General Dietrich von Choltitz's LXXXIV Corps sector. On 11 July, Panzer Lehr counterattacked the Americans at Le Désert and made some ground. The attack, launched in the early hours, caused the American 30th Infantry Division problems, though the initial success of the panzers was due to a gap between the American 39th and 47th Infantry Divisions southwest of Le Désert. The Americans rushed in reinforcements, but to the west a column of ten panzers reached south of la Scellerie before losing three Panthers and being driven off.

By 1600 it was clear that Panzer Lehr had failed to break the American lines. American ground forces claimed about fifty panzers and the air force claimed another twenty-two, fighter-bombers reportedly destroying thirteen out of fourteen panzers near le Hommet-de-Arthenay. In reality, Panzer Lehr lost just twenty-two tanks to all causes during 1–15 July. Nevertheless, by 2100 on the 11th the Americans had reoccupied their old positions and the net result of Panzer Lehr's attack was simply to delay the American 9th Infantry Division by a day. By this stage the division had lost 3,140 casualties.

While Panzergruppe West was given the lion's share of the resources to fend off the British, General Hausser's 7th Army facing the Americans was starved of troops. It only had 30–35,000 men divided into two corps, though the Americans estimated its strength as 17,000, with 375 tanks and assault guns. When General Montgomery launched Goodwood on 18 July it convinced Field Marshal von Kluge that the main threat remained in the British sector.

Panzer Lehr now formed the main striking force of von Choltitz's LXXXIV Corps, which was guarding the front from St Lô westward to the coast. Scathingly, Rundstedt's verdict of Choltitz was 'decent but stupid'. Choltitz was a veteran of the Eastern Front, having initially fought as a regimental commander at Sebastopol. Promoted to lieutenant general, he also served in Italy before moving to Normandy. His experience directing panzer forces was patchy.

Although an infantry general, in Russia he commanded 11th Panzer for two months in early 1943, followed by the XLVIII Panzer Corps, which included the 3rd and 11th Panzer Divisions, for about five months. The latter suffered heavy losses during the battle of Kursk and, notably, General der Panzertruppen Heinrich Eberbach replaced him. In Italy he had briefly commanded General Traugott Herr's LXXVI Panzer Corps, consisting of the 26th Panzer and 29th Panzergrenadier Divisions, from 1 March–15 April 1944. He assumed command of LXXXIV Corps in mid-June after his predecessor, Erich Marcks, was killed in action.

Choltitz's command also included the only other armoured formations on the American front, the 2nd SS Panzer Division and the 17th SS Panzergrenadier Division. Kluge advised Hausser to use two reserve infantry divisions to replace Panzer Lehr and 2nd SS, but Hausser was reluctant to do so. The II Parachute Corps, under General Eugen Meindl, had its 3rd Parachute Division and 352nd Infantry Division deployed east and south of St Lô, respectively.

Choltitz's infantry formations consisted of the 243rd, 275th and 353rd Infantry Divisions and the 91st Airlanding Division. Following the battles in the Cotentin Peninsula these units were completely depleted. The 275th, which had arrived in Normandy piecemeal as Kampfgruppe Heintz, was divided amongst Panzer Lehr, 2nd SS and LXXXIV Corps. The remains of the 91st were largely attached to the 2nd SS and 243rd.

Similarly, the 353rd was split amongst the 91st, 243rd and II Parachute Corps. The 243rd had just four weak infantry battalions, nine artillery batteries and eight anti-tank guns. Panzerjäger Abteilung 243 had just three Sturm-geschütz remaining from a complement of ten, plus fourteen Marder self-propelled guns. These formations along with Panzer Lehr would bear the brunt of Operation Cobra.

By 20 July, Panzer Lehr had been redeployed west of St Lô, still facing the Americans, though the exhausted reconnaissance *abteilung* and II Abteilung Panzergrenadier Regiment 902 were withdrawn to the Percy area for refit. Word of the failed assassination attempt on Hitler quickly reached Panzer Lehr as Hauptmann Ritgen recalled, with dismay at the possible outcome:

> My command post was in a farm house in a village and it was under attack. Normally we never wore steel helmets, but this time my adjutant told me to put mine on. It was much too small for me – it perched on top of my head. Well, we had no idea what was happening in Berlin.... Although I loathed Hitler, his death would have been a disaster at that time and have caused such confusion that the enemy would have been confirmed in his goal – the destruction of Germany.

Hitler's mistrust of his generals became even more marked, further hampering the direction of the Normandy campaign. Otto Henning of Panzer Lehr felt 'the worst thing for us was that we were no longer allowed to salute in a normal military fashion with our hand raised to our caps. We had to have our arms raised in the Hitler [Nazi Party] salute'.

Just prior to Operation Cobra, Panzer Lehr had eighty tanks, of which only fifteen Panzer IVs and sixteen Panthers were operational, and was rated suitable only for defensive missions. When the Americans launched Cobra it was the Panther tanks that were at the front. Luckily Bayerlein's Panzer IVs had been withdrawn to form a reserve and in fact only a few Panthers and tank destroyers were lost to the preliminary bombing.

The division was also reinforced with elements of the 5th Parachute Division, in the form of Fallschirmjäger Regiment 14 that had recently moved up from Brittany. Its arrival was a mixed blessing; the unit was understrength and under-equipped and did not bring any supporting artillery or flak guns with it. Panzer Lehr also had under its command a battalion of infantry from the 275th Infantry Division, which were the remains of Kampfgruppe Heintz, along with Kampfgruppe Brosow from the 2nd SS.

During the night of 23/24, von Choltitz reported to Hausser's 7th Army that there was evidence of American armour concentrating north of the St Lô–Périers road; 'nonsense', replied 7th Army, 'The Allies will hit in the Caen sector'. In the prelude to Cobra on 24 and 25 July, Panzer Lehr's positions were heavily bombed. Bayerlein got a warning phone call at his command post at the chateau at Canisy at about 1100. It was a battalion commander from his Panzergrenadier Regiment 901, stationed along the St Lô–Périers road: 'American infantry [across the road] are abandoning their positions. They are withdrawing everywhere'. In fact they were pulling back out of the way of the imminent bombardment that would herald Cobra.

Cobra's opening aerial attack fell squarely on Panzer Lehr and Bayerlein chronicled the destruction of his division:

> Units holding the front were almost completely wiped out, despite, in many cases, the best possible equipment of tanks, anti-tank guns and self-propelled guns. Back and forth the bomb carpets were laid, artillery positions were wiped out, tanks overturned and buried, infantry positions flattened and all roads and tracks destroyed. By midday the entire area resembled a moon landscape, with the bomb craters touching rim to rim, and there was no longer any hope of getting out any of our weapons. All signal communications had been cut and no command was possible. The shock effect on the troops was indescribable. Several men went mad and rushed dementedly round in the open until they were cut down by splinters. Simultaneously with the storm from the air, innumerable guns of the American artillery poured drumfire into our field positions.

Initially, von Kluge at La Roche-Guyon assumed Panzergruppe West had been bombed and phoned General Eberbach for a situation report. When the latter informed him Caen was quiet the penny dropped, it was Bayerlein who was on the receiving end of things. Calling Hausser, von Kluge was still unsure what all the air activity actually meant. Panzer Lehr weathered the first attack on the 24th losing just 350 men and ten vehicles.

The following day the bombing cost the division 1,000 men and numerous vehicles caught near the St Lô–Périers road; in particular, a number of Panther tanks were lost. Ironically, the Americans inflicted more casualties on their own men when the bombers dropped their payloads short. Many of Panzer Lehr's casualties, though, are assessed to have been missing or captured rather than dead. The Allied bombers also cut Choltitz's communications with Bayerlein, so he sent a runner but received no reply.

Nonetheless, the preceding fighting had proved a heavy drain on Panzer Lehr's manpower and during June and July they lost almost 6,000 men; replacements numbered less than 2,500. Lacking infantry, it meant Panzer Lehr had to increasingly rely on its tanks and artillery, but this became increasingly difficult in the face of ammunition and fuel shortages. Bayerlein's men were in no condition to withstand the American onslaught about to be unleashed on them.

By the end of the 25th Bayerlein stoically recalled:

> I don't believe hell could be as bad as what we experienced. Luckily, the regimental reserves in the main defence line were still in good shape and were committed at once. They had done most of the day's fighting for the division and to their credit slowed the 9th Infantry Division's advance considerably.

On the 26th, four Panzer IVs and an assault gun attempted to hold the road junction at St Gilles against elements of the US 2nd Armored Division. In response an Allied air strike claimed two tanks and the American armoured column took out the rest. The Americans penetrated seven miles (11km) with the loss of just three tanks. Panzer Artillery Regiment 130 lost its guns north-west of Marigny, which lay between Coutances and St Lô, to the US 3rd Armored Division. Just two days after the American attack opened, Bayerlein had to abandon almost thirty panzers at the repair facility at Cerisy-le-Selle.

Fighting withdrawal

Choltitz's LXXXIV Corps, in danger of being enveloped, attempted to retreat toward Coutances with the US 2nd, 3rd and 4th Divisions pressing on its heels. With the American forces driving on Avranches, Panzer Lehr was subordinated to General Funck's XLVII Panzer Corps.

On the 27th Bayerlein set up a command post at Dangy, south of Marigny. All that remained of his division was a small *kampfgruppe* with some engineers and anti-aircraft guns deployed at Pont-Brocard. The rest of his men, number-ing some 2,300 with Panzergrenadier Regiment 901, twelve tanks and six self-propelled guns, had retreated south to Villedieu-les-Poeles south west of Percy. Suddenly, tanks of the US 2nd Armored Division swept round his command post, driving off those Panzer Lehr units still at Pont-Brocard.

By the afternoon, Bayerlein found his command reduced to seven officers and fourteen enlisted men, gathered in a farmhouse outside Percy. The arrival of American tanks at dusk, which began to shell the building, meant it was every man for himself. Bayerlein, narrowly missing being blown to smithereens, was the last to leave and in the gathering darkness found himself alone, heading toward Percy. He reached the town at midnight and, finding a radio, reported the loss of his division.

In the meantime, following the failure to hold Cobra, Kluge ordered the dismissal of von Choltitz and 7th Army's Chief of Staff, General Max Pemsel. The latter was replaced by Oberst Rudolf-Christoph Freiherr von Gersdorff, who was to later conduct himself with some valour in the Falaise pocket. Choltitz's poor handling of Panzer Lehr and LXXXIV Corps not only saw him lose his command, but also gain the poison chalice that was the post of military governor of Paris. Generalleutnant Otto Elfeldt commanding the 47th Infantry Division in the Calais–Boulogne area replaced von Choltitz as LXXXIV Corps commander.

By 1 August Bayerlein could muster just over 11,000 men with thirty-three panzers and Sturmgeschütz, although another forty-four were under repair, and just nine howitzers. The only good news was that the division could still field almost 400 armoured half-tracks. In light of the condition of Panzer Lehr, which urgently needed refitting, four days later Kampfgruppe von Hauser was put together with a company of Panzer IVs and a mixed artillery battalion and subordinated to Meindl's II Parachute Corps. Panzer Lehr now found itself under LVIII Panzer Corps.

General der Panzertruppen Walter Krüger and his LVIII Reserve Panzer Corps staff (von Schweppenburg's old command) stationed in Toulose, were ordered to Le Mans to help direct the fight against the Americans. Created in France in 1943, the Corps was transferred from Rambouillet to Mödling, Austria, before taking part in the occupation of Hungary in March 1944. The following month it returned to France, this time to Toulouse, coming under General Blaskowitz's Army Group G. From mid July 1941 to the beginning of January 1944 Krüger had been in command of the 1st Panzer Division.

His new command dropped its reserve designation on 6 July and departed on the 27th, joining Panzergruppe West two days later, though it was subsequently subordinated to 7th Army and Panzergruppe Eberbach. It formed the southern flank of the counterattack near Avranches with responsibility for elements of Panzer Lehr and the 17th SS. Amongst Krüger's corps assets in Normandy were thirty-eight wholly inadequate Panzer Is.

Krüger and his HQ thus avoided the liberation of Toulouse on 19 August, following the Allied landings in southern France. Only two days earlier, Blaskowitz had been ordered to abandon the city and start withdrawing north. General Ferdinand Neuling's LXII Corps at Draguignan, a few miles northwest of Le Muy were not so lucky and found themselves surrounded, his two infantry divisions lost in Marseilles and Toulon.

The rest of Bayerlein's forces were instructed to move to Alençon to refit between the 9th Panzer Division and 708th Infantry Division by 9 August. From these units another *kampfgruppe* was formed, including panzergrenadiers from 9th Panzer, and deployed between Joblains and Conlie. By 11 August, 7 Army's tactical headquarters was at St André, the subordinate II Parachute Corps comprising the 3rd Parachute Division supported by a *kampfgruppe* from Panzer Lehr was holding a line from Chênedollé to Vire.

Final days

By the 12th, Kampfgruppe von Hausser was retiring eastward toward Fontainbleau. The following day Bayerlein ordered the rest of the division to follow and it was soon east of Argentan, thereby missing the chaos of the developing Falaise pocket.

Panzer Lehr saw action again in the Nonant-le-Pin–St Lombard area, but on the 17th was relieved by the 344th Infantry Division and was able to continue on its way to Fontainbleau and safety. Only Kampfgruppe Kuhnow remained and on the night of 16/17 August it crossed the Orne at Mensil-Jean to join the battered 12th SS.

Chapter 5

Fanatical Nazi Teenagers –
12th SS Panzer Division *Hitlerjugend*

Along with the 21st Panzer Division, the 12th SS Hitlerjugend was the nearest armoured division to the Normandy beaches. On 7 June the division counterattacked the Canadian Army but, despite inflicting heavy losses, crucially failed to break-through to the beachhead. Seven days later a British naval barrage killed their divisional commander. Thirty-three year old SS-Standartenführer Kurt Meyer took command, becoming the youngest divisional commander on both sides.

By 9 July the battered division had suffered a staggering 12,000 casualties and was forced to withdraw south of Caen. The 12th SS had little rest, resisting Operations Goodwood, Totalise and Tractable. The survivors fought in some cases to the very last to keep the Falaise pocket open, allowing thousands of survivors to escape.

Combat experience

The idea to create a Hitler Youth or *Hitlerjugend* division was initially raised with Hitler by Gruppenführer Gottlob Berger in early 1943. His plan envisaged drafting all Hitler Youth members born in 1926 and assigning them to a combat formation. Hitler liked the proposal and ordered Berger to commence organizing a division and the official order was issued on 10 February 1943. Berger nominated himself to be the first divisional commander, but Himmler gave that duty to a former Hitler Youth member, Oberführer Fritz Witt, instead, as he had been commanding one of the 1st SS Panzer Division's panzergrenadier regiments.

Witt had won the Iron Cross and Knight's Cross in Poland and France respectively. In the Balkans his men from the 1st SS were instrumental in opening the Klidi Pass, the heart of Greece; during the fighting there, Witt's younger brother, Franz, had been killed. He then fought in Russia, seeing action at Rostov and Kharkov.

Hitler signed off on a number of additional decrees in April 1943 relating to the formation of the *Hitlerjugend* Panzergrenadier Division. On 1 May the first batch of 8,000 volunteers reported for six weeks training, although they only received four. At the beginning of July the graduating class were released for service, while a second batch of 8,000 were inducted for training. By 1 September 1943, 16,000 trained recruits were listed on the rosters of the newly-formed *Hitlerjugend* division and were assembled at an SS training facility located at Beverloo, near Leopoldsbourge, Belgium.

In March 1944, C-in-C West von Rundstedt and I SS Panzer Corps' commander, SS-Obergruppenführer Josef 'Sepp' Dietrich, visited the division at Beverloo. During this highly-publicized and stage managed event the two generals were introduced to the division's staff and officers including: SS-Sturmbannführer Arnold Jürgensen, commander of I Abteilung SS-Panzer Regiment 12; SS-Sturmbannführer Karl-Heinz Prinz, commander of II Abteilung SS-Panzer Regiment 12; SS-Sturmbannführer Karl Bartling, commander of III Abteilung SS-Panzer Artillery Regiment 12; SS-Sturmbannführer Hubert Meyer, Ia (General Staff Officer, Operations) and SS-Hauptsturmführer Fritz Buchsein, IIa (General Staff Officer, Personnel). Also present were SS-Standartenführer Kurt Meyer, commander of SS-Panzergrenadier Regiment 25, and SS-Obersturmbannführer Wilhelm Mohnke, commander of SS-Panzergrenadier Regiment 26, whose units conducted exercises for Runstedt's benefit.

On 20 April 1944 Witt was promoted to the rank of SS-Brigadeführer and on 27 May celebrated his 36th birthday. Well-wishers and officers from all over the division attended the celebration at the divisional headquarters in Tilières-Sur-Avre castle, Belgium. Witt commanded the 12th SS from 24 June 1943 to 14 June 1944.

On paper, the 12th SS was an extremely powerful armoured formation with a reported strength of 20,540. On 1 June, however, some 2,438 of these troops were probably with the division's replacement battalion stationed in Arnhem in the Netherlands. Elements of this unit were directed to Normandy, but did not arrive in time to take part in the fighting.

In addition, the Panzerjäger and Nebelwerfer, or rocket launcher, battalions were not combat ready on D-Day. SS-Panzerjäger Abteilung 12 only had a company's worth of Jagdpanzer IV tank destroyers; in total it only received twenty-one Jagdpanzers and the battalion was unable to join the division until 19 July. Similarly, the Nebelwerfer battalion lacked its prime movers, rendering it immobile.

It has been estimated that the 12th SS arrived in Normandy with about 17,000 men. SS-Panzer Regiment 12, under SS-Obersturmbannführer Max Wünche, had an authorised strength of 101 Panzer IVs and seventy-nine Panthers; its actual strength was close to this with ninety-one combat-ready Panzer IVs and another seven in the workshop, along with sixty-six Panthers and two undergoing maintenance at the beginning of June. A further thirteen Panthers were despatched to the division on 7 June.

SS-Artillery Regiment 12 included the usual complement of six Hummel and twelve Wespe self-propelled guns along with the standard towed artillery batteries. Of SS-Panzergrenadier Regiment 25 and 26, only SS-Panzergrenadier Regiment 26's III Abteilung was fully equipped with armoured personnel carriers, although altogether the division had 333 of these vehicles.

Early on 6 June, 12th SS was put on alert, but SS-Panzer Regiment 12 did not receive its orders until just before midday at 1130. Its I Abteilung assembled in Le Neubourg and then made its way through Thibouville and Bernay to Orbec.

Allied fighter-bombers soon forced the panzers to seek shelter amongst the nearby trees. Panthers of III Kompanie withdrew to Chateau De Launcy near Orbec and that evening combat elements drove through St Pierre-sur-Dives, past Falaise, over the Orne near Thury-Harcourt and concealed themselves in a defile at Maizet.

Into action

On D-Day Hitler dithered, hoping that his infantry would hold the invasion. After midday he passed control of the 12th SS over to General Dollman's 7th Army. Kurt Meyer, commander of SS-Panzergrenadier Regiment 25, came under air attack on 6 June as he graphically relates:

> A chain of Spitfires attacks the last section of the 15th Kompanie. Missiles and cannon reap a devilish harvest. The section is passing through a narrow pass; it is impossible to get away. An elderly French woman is coming towards us screaming, 'Murder, Murder!' An infantryman lies in the street. A stream of blood comes out of his throat – his artery has been shot through. He dies in our arms. The munition of an amphibious vehicle explodes into the air – high tongues of flame shoot up. The vehicle explodes into pieces.

Over the next two days the Hitler Youth of the 12th SS threw themselves with gusto at the British and Canadians. The latter were thrown back for two miles (3km), but their line did not break. The Allies then tried to drive the Germans from Caen, but the only place that the 12th SS gave ground was at Cambes on 9 June. The Allies would learn to fear these Nazi teenagers.

The SS-Aufklärungs Abteilung, or reconnaissance battalion, under SS-Sturmbannführer and Ritterkreuzträger Gerd Bremer, was among the first units to reach the front on the 7th. Upon arrival it manoeuvred through eight miles (13km) of no-man's land to the division's far left flank to establish a security line. The battalion beat off numerous heavy attacks during 7–11 June, during which Bremer's command vehicle was knocked out and he was wounded by shrapnel. Twice wounded, he nevertheless remained with his *abteilung* until the situation was secure.

The Allies penultimate attack came on 11 June when the British 50th (Northumbrian) Division struck, employing an infantry battalion and eighty-four tanks. This was repulsed with seven Sherman tanks destroyed and the British suffered over 250 casualties. At the battalion command post in Cristot, one of the Shermans was salvaged by Hauptsturmführer von Reitzenstein and Untersturmführer Wieneke and placed over the command post bunker as protection against shrapnel.

On the night of 6/7 June, Fritz Witt reached the HQ of the decimated 716th Infantry Division. It had taken him eight hours to get to them; a good four of which had been spent grovelling in roadside ditches avoiding air attack. The 716th, raised in 1941, had been under 15th Army until June 1942 when it was sent to the Caen area to join Dollmann's 7th Army. Totally inexperienced, it was one of the weakest divisions in Normandy, numbering just 7,771 men in early May 1944. The division had only twenty-one anti-tanks guns, half of which were self-propelled, and forty artillery pieces of Czech and French origin. Initially the division had found itself stretched from Carentan to the Orne estuary until the 352nd Infantry Division arrived and was deployed east of Carentan.

Shortly after, SS-Standartenführer Kurt Meyer arrived and galvanised the situation, proposing a counterattack on the left flank of 21st Panzer. His SS-Panzergrenadier Regiment 25, part of Kampfgruppe Meyer/Wünsche went into action against the Canadians north of Caen on 7 June, supported by fifty Panzer IVs of II Abteilung SS-Panzer Regiment 12 commanded by Sturm-bannführer Prinz. The Canadian 3rd Division was driving on the strategic Carpiquet airfield west of Caen when its 9th Brigade ran into an accidental ambush and was driven from Authie and Buron northwest of the city.

The counterattack was timed for 1600, but four Panzer IVs of V Kompanie under Untersturmführer Porsh ran into Sherman tanks along the Franqueville–Authie road. Three of the panzers were knocked out and it became impossible to wait. Wünsche gave the order and V and VI Kompanies advanced left of the Ardennes Abbey, with VI claiming ten enemy tanks for the loss of five Panzer IVs.

SS-Sturmmann Hans Fenn was almost killed in this battle:

> Ours the fifth panzer, took a direct hit between the side of the hull
> and the turret ... The shell ripped a leg off my commander, Ober-

scharführer Esser. As I heard later, he managed to get out of the turret. The incendiary shell immediately set fire to all parts of the panzer. I lost consciousness. . . . Somehow, I managed, without being fully conscious, to crawl over the hatch of the loader. I could only remember clearly the moment when I dropped headfirst out of the hatch to the ground. With bad, third-degree burns, I walked back toward our advancing grenadiers. They looked at me as if I were a ghost.

The attack was broken up by Canadian artillery, naval gunfire and air strikes followed by a counterattack by the Sherbrooke Fusiliers. That evening the *kampfgruppe* of panzergrenadiers and panzers held defensive positions stretching from the railroad line between Caen and Luc-sur-Mer to Rue Nationale 13 from Caen to Bayeux. Although the Canadians had pushed through the Carpiquet airfield, the 12th SS had stopped them in their tracks, destroying a total of twenty-seven tanks for the loss of fourteen Panzer IVs. Over the next few days the Canadian 3rd Infantry Division, striking from the Caen–Bayeux railway near Bretteville, fought the 12th SS.

On the 8th, Panzergruppe West's commander, General Schweppenburg, arrived at Meyer's HQ at Ardenne Abbey outside Caen and unnerved him slightly by saying: 'My dear Herr Meyer, the war can only be won by political means.' However, on that day the 12th SS, 21st Panzer and Panzer Lehr were thrown into the attack.

The 12th SS found Carpiquet airfield deserted by the Luftwaffe and unoccupied by the Canadians. They now turned on the Canadian 7th Brigade, also part of the Canadian 3rd Division, driving it from Bretteville l'Orgueilleuse and Putot-en-Bessin, though the Canadians in turn recaptured Putot, claiming six Panthers.

Around 2200, SS-Panzergrenadier Regiment 25, supported by Panthers, struck toward Bretteville from three directions. The attack from the south resulted in the platoon commander's tank being immobilised in the town and surrounded. The attack from the southwest was ordered to rescue him, but the lead tank was knocked out and the rest driven off. In the attack from the west, three Panthers were hit simultaneously by concealed Canadian anti-tank guns; two managed to withdraw, but the other burned like a torch, though its crew managed to escape. The following morning the attack was broken off.

During the withdrawal Wünsche was wounded, as SS-Untersturmführer Chemnitz records:

> The Panzers were returning from the attack. Since the road ran on top of an embankment, the Panzers had to be directed in order to

get onto it. Initially, the commander of the Panzer Regiment, Max Wünsche, did this himself until I took over from him. One of the Panzers had turned around on the road. I stood in front of it directing the driver. Wünsche stood behind me to the right. The orderly officer of SS-Panzer Regiment 12, Untersturmführer Nehrlich, stood behind me to the left. At that moment, the Panther took a shell hit from a Canadian tank to the front armour. Wünsche was wounded in the head by a fragment. I took a shower of small fragments from my head to the knees. Nehrlich was so critically wounded by a fragment that, although he was immediately put into the sidecar of a motorcycle to be driven to the dressing station, he bled to death during the drive.

On the 9th, Panthers of III Kompanie, SS-Panzer Regiment 12, under SS-Obersturmführer Rudolf von Ribbentrop, having missed the attack on Bretteville, moved on Norrey with the Caen–Cherbourg railway embankment protecting their right flank. With Wünsche temporarily out of action, Kurt Meyer probably directed this attack. Ribbentrop had been wounded, so Hauptmann Lüdman led his twelve Panthers. However, once beyond the cover of the railway bank well-concealed anti-tank guns knocked out seven tanks and the advance was halted. Crew losses were also heavy, with eighteen of the thirty-five men involved killed.

The Kompanie moved to Fontenay-les-Pesnel to the west, but, with all its tanks suffering mechanical problems, withdrew to Harcourt. Two days later the division's tanks claimed thirty-seven Shermans for the loss of three panzers in the fighting south of Le Mesnil

The stark reality of war soon came home to Emil Werner, serving with Meyer's SS-Panzergrenadier Regiment 25:

> Until Cambes everything went well. So far as we were concerned, the village looked fine. But on the outskirts we came under infantry fire and then all hell broke loose. We stormed a church where snipers had taken up positions. Here I saw the first dead man from our kompanie; it was Grenadier Ruehl from the headquarters platoon. I turned his body over myself – he'd been shot through the head. He was the second member of our company to die. Dead comrades already; and we still hadn't seen any Englishmen. Then the situation became critical. My section commander was wounded in the arm and had to go to the rear. Grenadier Grosse from Hamburg leapt past me towards a clump of bushes with his sub-machine gun at the ready, screaming 'Hands up! Hands up!' Two Englishmen emerged with

their hands held high. As far as I know, Grosse got the Iron Cross, second-class, for this.

The British and Canadians were dismayed at the Hitler Youth's apparent fanaticism, little realising that they could expect little else from youngsters raised under the harsh dictates of National Socialism. Sergeant Leo Gariepy of the Canadian 3rd Division saw little reason for leniency toward these Nazi teenagers:

> The morale of the men was very low indeed. So many of their long-time comrades had stayed behind on the battlefield, the battle itself had been so savage, so furious, that every man felt that the 12th SS Panzer had a personal grudge against our tanks. Silently, grimly, we were looking at each other, knowing exactly what was in the other man's mind.... Mostly, everyone was rather vindictive, and silently swearing revenge.

Colonel H S Gillies, King's Own Scottish Borderers, 15th (Scottish) Division, could not forget the hot reception meted out by the 12th SS at Cambes:

> The attack entailed crossing a distance of about one thousand yards of open cornfield, which fell away from Cambes Wood. We had barely crossed the start line when the enemy reacted fiercely, with well-sited machine gun and intense mortar fire, which enfiladed the companies as they moved forward.... After a sharp battle at close quarters, the village was cleared at dusk, but we were then subjected to an intense barrage of gun and mortar fire, which caused many more casualties. At best, it was only possible in the pitch darkness to establish a tentative defence system and we expected the enemy to launch a counterattack at the first opportunity. They had now been identified as the notorious 12th SS (Hitler Youth) Panzer Division.

The battle for Hill 112 was a brutal affair. SS-Schütze Zimmer experienced the British attempts to dislodge them on 10 June:

> From 6.30 to 8.00am, again heavy machine-gun fire. Then Tommy attacks with great masses of infantry and many tanks. We fight as long as possible but we realise we are in a losing position. By the time the survivors try to pull back, we realise that we are surrounded.

On the 11th, the Canadian 6th Armoured Regiment lost thirty-seven of its seventy-six tanks in the fighting around Le Mensil-Patry. By now the 12th SS had lost about twenty-five per cent of its manpower, twenty per cent of its tanks and ten per cent of its guns. In total about sixty Panzer IV and V tanks remained serviceable. Fritz Witt was killed at Venoix on the morning of the 14th when his HQ was caught in an Allied naval bombardment and shrapnel stuck him in the face. Following his death, Kurt 'Panzer' Meyer, took command of the division.

By 15 June it was decided to withdraw the depleted 716th Infantry Division to the south of France and Chevallerie's 1st Army. In the event this proved difficult as units were with the 346th, 352nd and 711th Infantry Divisions and 21st Panzer. Having suffered 6,261 casualties its withdrawal was not completed until late July and then it ended up with Wiese's 19th Army on the French Riviera.

Containing Epsom

It seemed that the British Operation Epsom, designed to punch west of Caen on 25 June, could not fail; directly in its path lay the 12th SS holding the line from Fontenay-le-Pesnel through St Marvieu and Cheux, eastwards to Carpiquet airfield. Rommel moved the 2nd Schwere Panzer Kompanie (Heavy Tank Company) with Tiger tanks behind SS-Panzergrenadier Regiment 26. The British XXX Corps was to jump off first, followed by VIII Corps the following day. The latter had 60,000 men, 600 tanks, 300 guns and the support of another 400 guns from the flanking XXX Corps, plus naval and air support. It fell to SS-Panzer Regiment 12 and SS-Panzergrenadier Regiment 25 to resist VIII Corps, while just to the west of Caen SS-Panzergrenadier Regiment 25 was facing the Canadian 3rd Division

The plan was for the British VIII Corps to break through between XLVII Panzer Corps and I SS-Panzer Corps, force a bridgehead over the Odon River and take the strategic height of Hill 112. For the British it was a race against time as the II SS Panzer Corps and 2nd SS were heading for the sector; even if the attack pierced the in-depth defences of the 12th SS, the intervention of German armoured reinforcements could kill Epsom.

On 25 June, XXX Corps conducted Operation Dauntless, a subsidiary attack to secure VIII Corps' western flank before the main offensive carried out by the 49th (West Riding) Infantry Division, supported by the 8th Armoured Brigade. The 49th also conducted Operation Martlet, intended to capture Fontenay-le-Pesnel

Second Lieutenant Stuart Hills, Nottinghamshire Sherwood Rangers Yeomanry, 8th Armoured Brigade, was then a fresh faced twenty-one year-old who had only been with them since January, having arrived straight from the Officer Cadet Training Unit at Sandhurst. The Sherwood Rangers were assigned to support the 147th Brigade's attack on Fontenay. Recalling his role in Operation Epsom, Hills remembered a stiff reception from the 12th SS:

> The fighting in Fontenay was fierce and confused, with enemy tanks of 12th SS Panzer dug in defensively east of the town, and we did not have enough infantry to take the village. At about four o'clock in the afternoon the attack had clearly run out of steam, infantry losses had been heavy and we withdrew to the heights of Point 102 above Fontenay to replenish our stocks of ammunition, refuel and have something to eat.

The attack, though, was renewed, Fontenay captured and the road to Caen cut. A Squadron moved forward to attack Rauray. As Stuart Hills relates it was in for a nasty surprise:

> As they cleared Fontenay, they were suddenly confronted by an enormous tank coming round the bend in front. It was hard to know who was more surprised, but John [Semken, the Squadron Leader] shrieked, 'Fire, it's a Hun,' and they loosed off about ten rounds into the smoke. As this cleared away, it was observed that the crew were baling out as small flames came from inside the tank. It was a Tiger of 12th SS Panzer, the first Tiger to be captured in Normandy, and made an impressive sight at close quarters as both its size and the thickness of its armour became apparent.

Hot splinters from the driver's visor had caused the crew to abandon their tank, not the shells from the Rangers' Shermans. Some of Semken's tanks included the Sherman Firefly armed with the powerful 17-pounder anti-tank gun and by the end of the day they had accounted for thirteen Panzer IVs, a Tiger and a Panther tank.

Between Tessel Wood and Rauray, ten Tiger tanks were dug in and the SS-Panzer Regiment 26 repulsed the British attack through Le Manoir from Tessel towards Rauray and established positions near Le Haut du Bosc, facing toward Cheux. Assembling across the line Fontenay–Tessel–Bretteville to attack toward Juvigny, the heavy tank company's actions left SS-Panzergrenadier Regiment 26, which lay directly in the path of the British attack, unsupported. The latter was thrown into a counterattack at 0500 on the 26th

Hubert Meyer, Operations Staff Officer, 12th SS, expecting an armoured attack, tried to get the order rescinded but I SS Panzer Corps would not comply. The results were predictable:

At 0700 on 26 June, this great British attack of about 500–600 tanks on a breadth of about three miles (5kms) rolled over the Pioneers and the Panzergrenadiers. Eventually it came to a halt only because our artillery fire separated the enemy infantry from their tanks. Several pockets of resistance did considerable damage. The battle head-quarters of the Pioneer Battalion 12 under Sturmführer Siegfried Müller had been made into a strongpoint which was to be held until well into the night; then the survivors managed to get to the west of Le Haut du Bosc, and were picked up by some of our panzers advancing in a counterattack. As late as 28 June, our operators picked up radio messages from British tanks attacking the remnants of 3 Pioneer Kompanie which still held several strongpoints in the old frontline between St Mauvieu and Fontenay. We tried to convince I SS Panzer Corps that a well-planned counterattack by tank units from the southwest might restore the original front, or at least, relieve the surrounded units, but fresh forces were not available.

The 15th (Scottish) Division, with 11th Armoured Division and 31st Tank Brigade, also broke through the 12th SS defences. Likewise, the 43rd (Wessex) Division, supported by the 4th Armoured Brigade, reached Mouen. On the 27th, the 15th (Scottish) Division captured a bridge over the Odon and 11th Armoured Division moved to take Hill 112.

On the 28th a hastily-formed *kampfgruppe* from 12th SS supported by 21st Panzer's 4th Kompanie, Panzer Regiment 22, which had been redirected from the British airborne bridgehead, attacked along the railway embankment toward Mouen. The young panzergrenadiers broke through and drove the British back.

With the British pouring out of the Odon bridgehead, the Luftwaffe Motorised Flak Unit I/53 armed with 8.8cm dual-use guns, which had been protecting the 12th SS workshops, was moved forward. Its job was to relieve a battalion of 12th SS on Hill 112. What they found was half a company of exhausted teenagers who had fought hard to fend off encroaching British tanks the previous day.

The Luftwaffe's flak guns were soon engaging British armour coming through the village of Esquay to the southwest. The following day, British tanks and air attacks drove them from the hill. The British 20th Armoured Brigade withdrew from Hill 112 on the night of 29/30 June, not because of the dogged resistance by 12th SS but the arrival of II Panzer Corps with the 9th and 10th SS Panzer Divisions, which came into the line between XLVII Panzer Corps and I SS Panzer Corps.

The Germans had succeeded in containing Epsom but at a cost of over 2,600 casualties sustained by the 12th SS. Epsom cost the British VIII Corps 4,020 casualties; the 11th Armoured Division alone lost 100 tanks and suffered 1,000 killed, wounded and missing during 26–29 June.

By early July the SS holding Carpiquet airfield were expecting an attack by the Canadian 8th Infantry Brigade. The garrison consisted of just 150 Hitler Youth teenagers drawn from SS-Panzergrenadier Regiment 25; about 100 were on the airfield and the rest in the village of Carpiquet itself, supported by a few tanks and an 8.8cm gun. The attack was launched at 0500 on 4 July and the Canadians cleared Carpiquet village and then ran into the panzers and the gun. The Germans counterattacked the following day.

On 6 July panzergrenadiers of the 12th SS deployed to the northern suburbs of Caen. Within two days they and a regiment from the 16th Luftwaffe Field Division were ejected by Montgomery's frontal assault on the city known as Operation Charnwood, which commenced on the 7th. Initially Caen was heavily bombed and then, on the 8th, German defences were smothered by an artillery barrage. Major General R F L Keller's Canadian 3rd Division attacked on the German left, L O Lyne's inexperienced 59th (Staffordshires) in the centre and L G Whistler's 3rd Infantry on the right.

The Canadians sought to exploit their gains at Carpiquet, striking Caen from the west. To the east, the 3rd Infantry were to secure Lebisey and Herouville, their original D-Day objectives. The bombing, while impeding the progress of the attackers, did not completely neutralise the defenders and 7.5cm and 8.8cm anti-tank guns met the tanks. At La Bijude the 12th SS were well entrenched and it took two attempts before it was firmly in 59th Division's hands. They were then brought to a halt before Malan.

The British 3rd Division reached Lebisey and Herouville within an hour and brushed aside the 16th Luftwaffe Field Division, only to find Caen an impassable sea of craters and rubble. In the meantime, the 1st SS tried to mass their armour for a counterattack, but air strikes and naval gun fire drove back their thirty-five panzers, which suffered some losses.

At the village of Buron, northwest of Caen, elements of III Abteilung, SS-Panzergrenadier Regiment 25 were surrounded and on the verge of being overrun by Canadian tanks. Kurt Meyer and General Eberbach, Panzergruppe West's commander, were at the Ardenne monastery. Meyer recalled the dramatically unfolding events:

> All available tanks were sent towards Buron. The attack failed to get through. From the [Ardenne] monastery church tower I watched the tank fight as it surged back and forth. Both sides suffered heavy

losses. Then, suddenly, enemy tanks appeared from Authie [to the north], heading straight for Ardenne.

The tank *kompanie* of von Ribbentrop with its fifteen Panthers deployed against this mass of enemy tanks and they shot up the enemy armour, halting its advance. The last enemy tank was destroyed only 100 metres west of Ardenne but von Ribbentrop had saved the command post. His initial instructions had been to relieve the panzergrenadiers and clear the Canadians from Buron, however he was distracted by the Canadian armour to the left of the village and had to send a platoon of Panthers to deal with them. Reaching Buron, von Ribbentrop's Panthers knocked out several Canadian tanks.

Loathe to enter the village without infantry support, von Ribbentrop quickly found the tables turning as he noted:

Just then a well-camouflaged Canadian anti-tank gun must have opened fire, because two or three tanks to my right went up in flames one after another. There was nothing left to do but pull back to our starting position and support the hard-pressed infantry from there.

The company's remaining tanks spent the rest of the day under heavy artillery fire around the monastery. Several engagements with enemy armour took place, which prevented the enemy from advancing any further and enabled the monastery to be held until it had to be abandoned soon afterwards.

SS-Unterscharführer Freiberg, serving with Ribbentrop, found himself in one of the three Panthers knocked out:

We crossed the open field to the wall around the village of Buron at high speed. As we moved past an opening in the wall, there were suddenly two explosions. Sepp Trattnick's tank and another tank burst into flames. We immediately opened fire with both machine-guns on the opening of the wall. I saw some movement there and then a flash from the muzzle of an anti-tank gun. The round struck our gun mantlet and the solid projectile ended up in the fighting compartment. Our sight was smashed, and the gunner was wounded in the face. I received several fragments in my left arm.

The crew in the turret bailed out at once, and because of the heavy machinegun fire, took cover behind the Panther. My radio operator and driver had not bailed out, and were still calmly sitting in the tank, whose engine was still running.

> I therefore jumped back up onto the tank and grasped the throat
> microphone, which was dangling over the side of the turret. I called
> to my driver: 'Back up!'

His tank withdrew to Ardenne monastery, south of Authie, only to be attacked by Allied fighter-bombers. During the fighting in the Buron area 1st SS lost thirteen panzers to a Canadian 17-pounder anti-tank gun battery. Having secured Buron the Canadians took Ginchy, Authie and St Louet as the SS abandoned Carpiquet. During the heavy fighting on 8 July III Kompanie's Panthers destroyed twenty-seven tanks, eight Bren gun carriers and four anti-tank guns.

The British, suffering heavy losses, took Malan on the 9th, and the loss of the defensive chain of villages north of Caen now meant that the city itself was open to attack. At this point Kurt Meyer took the decision to withdraw south of Caen and back over the Orne to spare his men further slaughter. To the west of the city he also withdrew from Carpiquet airfield. South of the river his men entrenched themselves in the industrial suburbs of Colombelles and Faubourg de Vaucelles.

Although the 12th SS could not retain Caen they had, along with Panzer Lehr, denied it to the Allies for just over a month. By the 9th, the 12th SS had lost fifty-one Panzer IVs and thirty-two Panthers. Three days later the division received a welcome respite from the bloodletting when it was relieved by the 272nd Infantry Division and sent to Potigny, 20 miles (32km) north of Falaise, to recuperate.

Thus, at the time of Operation Goodwood on the 18th, the 12th SS was resting in reserve, except for a strong *kampfgruppe* under Max Wünsche, which Hitler ordered to the coast at the Orne estuary to counter a spurious invasion threat. With the onset of Goodwood the division was called back into the line and remained in the Caen area, fighting along the Caen–Falaise road.

Several *kampfgruppen* were formed including Wünsche, Olboeter, Krause and Waldmüller. On 6 August they tried to seal the Orne bridgehead after Major General O Lyne's 59th (Staffordshire) Division had crossed, but to no avail. The II Abteilung of Panzer Regiment 12 was in support of Kampfgruppe Krause near Grimbosq on the Orne, just over nine miles (14km) from Caen.

Battle for Falaise

On 1 August the inexperienced Canadian 4th and Polish 1st Armoured Divisions arrived in Normandy. Following the launch of Operation Totalise to take Falaise just six days later, these two divisions were tasked to breach the Germans' second defence line between St Sylvian and Bretteville, but they were to run into successive defensive lines held by the 12th SS and the 85th, 89th and 272nd Infantry Divisions forming Dietrich's I SS Panzer Corps. These defences included sixty hulled-down panzers, self-propelled guns and ninety 8.8cm anti-tank guns.

The initial attack for Totalise by the Canadian 2nd and British 51st (Highland) Divisions opened at 23.30 on 7 August, following a bombardment involving 1,000 heavy bombers. The 89th and 272nd Infantry Divisions all but collapsed, but, with stout support from Meyer's 12th SS, the 85th Division blocked the Allies' way. By dawn the Canadians had managed to advance just three miles (5km) before they ground to a halt. The Polish 1st Armoured on the left flank, east of Hautmesnil, and the Canadian 4th Armoured on the right, just north of Bretteville-sur-Laize, were thrown into the attack the following day to try to break the deadlock.

Kurt Meyer drove cross-country to Cintheaux to rally Kampfgruppe Waldmüller in an attempt to halt the British and Canadian Totalise offensive on 8 August. The significance of Falaise dawned on him:

> Suddenly, I realise that the fate of the city of Falaise and the safety of both armies depend on my decision. I am standing upright in the VW as we drive in the direction of Caen. More and more shocked soldiers come toward me and flee to the south. In vain, I attempt to halt the front, which is in motion. The terrible bomb attacks have broken the nerves of the units of the 89th Infantry Division.... I jump out of the car and stand alone on the road armed with a carbine.... The boys probably consider me crazy, but then recognise me, turn around, wave their comrades over and organize the defence of the height of Cintheaux. The town has to be held at all costs to gain time for the two *kampfgruppen*.

Kurt Meyer was to give both armoured divisions a bloody nose; Panthers of the 12th SS and Tigers of Abteilung 101 held the Canadians at Bretteville and Cintheaux; the Poles were countered at St Sylvain, losing thirty tanks while trying to barge the 12th SS out of the way. On the 9th, Max Wünche's Panthers, I Abetilung SS-Panzergrenadier Regiment 25 and troops from the 85th Infantry Division, the latter having only recently arrived in Normandy, counterattacked the Canadians on Point 140. In the bitter tank-to-tank battles the Canadians were driven off with the loss of forty-seven tanks; miraculously, SS-Panzer Regiment 12 lost none.

The following day, the 12th SS were involved in trying to stem the Canadian attack on Point 195. With Kampfgruppe Krause's flank at risk from the Poles to the northeast, who were trying to force the River Laison near Condé-sur-Ifs, a dozen panzers had to be diverted to counter this new threat.

By the end of 10 August Meyer had just fifteen Panzer IVs, five Panthers and fifteen Tigers facing 700 enemy tanks. However, in the area defended by the 12th SS alone, over 100 had been destroyed in the fierce close combat. By now the American breakout from Avranches was well underway and, with the US 1st and 3rd Armies charging westward, Totalise became Operation Tractable, intended to close the neck of the developing Falaise salient. The 12th SS now became instrumental in preventing this happening.

The Canadians attacked on 14 August and despite getting to within three miles (5km) of Falaise the neck was still 15 miles (24km) wide. To the south General Wade H Haislip's US XV Corps, instead of driving northward to Argentan and beyond to link up with the Canadians, was directed to Dreux and the Seine with the view of making a much wider envelopment.

Captured intelligence tipped the Germans off that Tractable would fall to the east of the Caen–Falaise highway, this gave the 12th SS the opportunity to make some hurried preparations. Meyer regrouped his exhausted division on the high ground in front of Falaise and the River Dives. The remains of the 89th and 271st Infantry Divisions redeployed to the hills to the northwest and the 89th along the River Laison. They would contest every inch of the way to Falaise.

Meyer and Wünsche knew that the key strategic ground northwest of Falaise lay around Point 159. The Canadians drove from Soignolles to Potigny and Sassy, while at Perrières and Jort the last few panzers were quickly put out of action. On the 15th, Point 159 was heavily bombarded and then assaulted by Allied tanks; they were stopped cold. SS-Sturmbannführer Karl-Heinz Prinz was killed, while to the right of the hill RAF Typhoons set about the panzers. The pressure was such that only a few panzers were able to cling to the reverse slopes and in the afternoon were forced to abandon their positions.

Final days

Although the Canadians reached Falaise on 16 August, the 12th SS held out in the town until the 18th, four days after Tractable commenced. By now the Battle for Normandy was all but over. Between 6 June and 22 August, Hitler's fanatical and resolutely fearless teenage Nazis lost around 8,000 killed in action, wounded and missing. This seemed a deathblow from which no unit could hope to recover.

Nonetheless, most of the division's combat arms and rear services were not encircled at Falaise, resulting in moderately low casualties during the latter half of August. Also, many of the missing who were not captured made their way back to the unit. For this reason, despite the disaster of Falaise, from 15–22 August the 12th SS lost less than 1,000 men, consisting of forty-five killed, 248 wounded and 655 missing. It would soon rise from the ashes of Normandy, ready to fight again.

Chapter 6

The Iron Fist –
17th SS Panzergrenadier Division
Götz von Berlichingen

Thrown into combat on 10 June 1944 near Carentan, the reconnaissance battalion of the 17th SS Panzergrenadier Division fought the American paratroops of the US 101st Airborne. Dubbed the Battle of Bloody Gulch, the paratroops were only saved by the arrival of the US 2nd Armored Division. The 17th SS then suffered during the American Operation Cobra and during the subsequent futile German counterattack at Mortain. The division escaped the Falaise pocket and was eventually withdrawn to Metz. It was the only panzergrenadier unit to fight in Normandy.

Combat experience

The grand sounding 17th SS Panzergrenadier Division *Götz von Berlichingen* was authorised by Hitler on 3 October 1943, though it did not start coming together until 15 November in France, within General Chevallerie's 1st Army area of responsibility. Created from replacement units and conscripts under SS-Gruppenführer Werner Ostendorff, the formation found itself relying on Romanian conscripts and French vehicles and assault guns. Under the circumstances it needed a man of some character to meld the fledgling division.

Werner Ostendorff's background was as a qualified Luftwaffe pilot and he had served in Russia on a technical exchange. In the mid-1930s he joined the SS and served in Poland during the invasion. In 1942 Ostendorff became Chief of Staff with Paul Hausser's SS General Kommando (later II SS Panzer Corps), seeing action at Kharkov and Kursk, during which time he gained a reputation as a highly-respected staff officer. The division was to have ten different commanders before the end of the war, with Ostendorff and SS-Standartenführer Otto Binge serving with *Götz von Berlichingen* twice.

The Division's title came from Götz von Berlichingen (1480–1562), a knight who lost a hand in battle near Landshut in 1504, during the Bavarian War of

Succession. His hand was replaced with an iron fist and this was adopted as the symbol of the 17th SS. Hitler's right-hand man, Reichsfuhrer-SS Heinrich Himmler, travelled from Berlin on 10 April 1944 to attend the division's formal activation, with Panzergruppe West's commander, Schweppenburg, and I SS Panzer Corps' commander, 'Sepp' Dietrich, at Thouars, northwest of Poiters. Divisional cuff titles were also bestowed on the unit.

The only other German divisions in the region were the 158th Infantry Division way to the west, deployed between Nantes and Fontenay-le-Comte, and the 708th Infantry Division to the southwest near Royan, guarding the bay of Biscay against possible Allied invasion. Elements of the latter division were also to end up fighting the Americans in Normandy. Even further south lay the 11th Panzer Division, the only armoured unit not to be drawn north to Normandy.

By the time of D-Day, the 17th SS was not fully combat ready and although some 17,321 men strong it lacked forty per cent of its officers and non-commissioned officers (NCOs). The division also lacked transport and by mid-May had just 257 trucks and towing vehicles. SS-Panzerjäger Abteilung 17 had received none of its Jagdpanzer IVs and the III Abteilung had just nine self-propelled guns.

By early June the situation was little better, with its armoured forces con-sisting of just forty-two StuG III assault guns equipping SS-Panzer Abteilung 17 and twelve Marder self-propelled guns with SS-Panzerjäger Abteilung 17. Three Panzer IV command vehicles did not arrive until 12 August. SS-Panzer Abteilung 17, though, was in capable hands; Sturmbannführer Ludwig Kepplinger was a Waffen-SS veteran who had fought in Russia with the 5th SS Panzer Division *Wiking*.

Two days after the Allies landed, the independent Sturmgeschütz Abteilung 902 with thirty-one assault guns, stationed at Tours on the Loire, to the north-east of Thouars, was placed under Ostendorff's control. These were a welcome supplement to the division's meagre armoured forces. En route, however, the battalion was side-tracked, for while the 17th SS was attached to General der Fallschirmtruppen Eugen Meindl's II Parachute Corps, Abteilung 902 ended up with von Choltitz's LXXXIV Corps. By 24 June it was with the 91st Airlanding Division and, escaping encirclement, it eventually ended up with Wiese's 19th Army in southern France.

On 6 June, the 17th SS divisional HQ was still at Thouars and it would take a week for Ostendorf to get the division to the front. The very day after D-Day, the division received orders to depart its marshalling area and head for Normandy. Under the designation of Operation Mimose (or Mimosa) the 17th SS Panzergrenadier Division redeployed from the area of General Chevallerie's

1st Army, south of the Loire, to the sector of General Dollmann's 7th Army, facing Lieutenant General Omar N Bradley's US 1st Army at the base of the Cotentin Peninsula.

The complete lack of transport meant that the division could only be moved piecemeal, and the most readily-available unit was SS-Panzeraufklärungs Abteilung 17, the reconnaissance battalion. A *kampfgruppe* had to be scraped together from three battalions. Nonetheless the division moved off in good spirits, happy at last that the uncertainty was over and that it would be seeing action. The Allies though were determined that this unit would not have an easy time of it.

Only four of the division's six infantry battalions moved on 7 June, the other two battalions had to rely on bicycles. Similarly, a flak battery and the artillery units began to move on the evening of the 7th, while the assault guns and self-propelled guns were loaded onto trains. Allied fighter-bombers quickly pounced on the freight cars, claiming one StuG III for the loss of two aircraft. Three days later they had been unloaded between Montreuil and la Feche and were rumbling toward Mayenne.

Some units, including SS-Flak Abteilung 17 and SS-Pioneer Bataillon 17, had to be left behind to protect the crossings over the Loire at Saumur, located between Angers and Tours. The flak battalion did not deploy to Normandy until the end of June and then I Battery and its 8.8cm guns were left to guard the bridges for the want of prime movers or tow trucks. Similarly the pioneer battalion, some 726 men, did not reach Normandy until mid-July.

A divisional Staff officer recalled how moving in daylight would soon draw the unwanted attentions of the Allied fighter-bombers:

> Our motorized columns were coiling along the road towards the invasion beaches. Then something happened that left us in a daze. Spurts of fire flicked along the column and splashes of dust staccatoed the road. Everyone was piling out of the vehicles and scuttling for the neighbouring fields. Several vehicles were already in flames. This attack ceased as suddenly as it had crashed upon us fifteen minutes before.
>
> An hour later the fighter-bombers were back inflicting even more damage, wrecking the division's anti-tank guns and even more vehicles. Werner Ostendorff's men gave up the advance and abandoned the road trying to camouflage their vehicles and equipment in the nearby farms and farmland. From now on the 17th SS would travel toward the battle at night, the cost of doing otherwise was simply too great.

Into action

By 8 June SS-Panzeraufklärungs Abteilung 17, although under fighter-bomber attack, reached Balleroy, halfway between St Lô and Bayeux. Two days later it went into action for the first time when it was committed to the 352nd Infantry Division's sector north of St Lô; the latter had suffered 1,200 casualties on D-Day. At the same time SS-Panzergrenadier Regiment 37 arrived at La Chapelle southeast of the city.

While the reconnaissance battalion was sent to help the 352nd Infantry near Caen, Ostendorff went forward to make contact with the 6th Fallschirmjäger Regiment defending Carentan, which had been advised by 7th Army, via LXXXIV Corps, that the SS were on the way. The German paratroopers were so short of ammunition that they requested an air drop by the Luftwaffe, but late in the afternoon of the 11th they abandoned Carentan to the Americans, just as the 17th SS were preparing to relieve them.

The US 101st Airborne Division captured Carentan on 12 June and the 17th SS adopted defensive positions to the south. The first real test of strength came on the 13th when the panzergrenadiers, supported by the StuG IIIs, set about the 101st Airborne southwest of the town.

The bulk of the 17th SS began to arrive in their assembly areas prior to a counterattack to recapture Bayeux on 11 June and was subordinated to II Parachute Corps. After D-Day, General Meindl's II Parachute Corps with the 3rd Parachute Division were deployed from Brittany to counter the Americans in the St Lô area.

Formed from the XIII Flieger Corps, Meindl's command came into being in February 1944 and deployed in reserve near Paris under C-in-C West. In May it was placed under Dollmann's 7th Army. Unusually for a command and control staff, Meindl's Corps had its own dedicated armoured unit in the shape of Fallschirm-Sturmgeschütz-Brigade 12 with eleven combat-ready assault guns. Numerous units, including the 17th SS, would pass through II Parachute Corps' hands.

Ostendorf and his operations officer, Obersturmbannführer Konrad, set up their command post at St-Sébastien-de-Raids southwest of Carentan to direct the attack. At 0700 on the 13th Sturmgeschütz of SS-Panzer Abteilung 17 got to within 500 yards of Carentan before being stopped by elements of the US 2nd Armored and 101st Airborne Divisions. Similarly SS-Panzergrenadier Regiment 37 made no progress and by midday it was clear the attack on Carentan had failed. By the 15th the division had suffered 456 casualties in its struggle with the Americans.

In the meantime, 7th Army's reserve, Panzer Abteilung 100, attached to the 91st Airlanding Division, faired poorly at Baupte, meaning that the Americans were soon threatening the flank and rear of the 17th SS Panzergrenadier Division. The battalion was in fact a training unit equipped with obsolete French tanks, stationed west of Carentan and covering Baupte and Ste Mère-Eglise. Panicked by the American airborne landings that had claimed a number of officers and men within two weeks, the unit had ceased to exist.

Ostendorf and Konrad were furious at the commander of the 6th Fallschirm-jäger Regiment for withdrawing southeast from Baupte and arrested the man. Only the intervention of the II Parachute Corps secured his release.

General Max Pemsel, Chief of the General Staff, 7th Army, noted:

> The failure of the attack launched by the 17th SS Panzergrenadier Division in the direction of Carentan was due not so much to the lack of air support as to the inadequate training of the young division, which ran into the simultaneously launched counterattack. The 100th Panzer Training Battalion had only a few obsolete and hardly manoeuvrable French tanks. It was intended to deceive the enemy by the name of this unit.

By mid-June nearly all the division's units had arrived, although the flak and pioneer battalions were held back at Saumur to assist with the crossings over the Loire river, which were under regular air attack. In total, the 17th SS Panzer-grenadier Division fielded about 15,500 men. On the 16th SS-Brigadeführer Ostendorf was wounded and relieved by SS-Oberführer Eduard Diesenhoffer.

The division was bolstered with a number of units of dubious utility. The disgraced Fallschirmjäger Regiment 6 was tactically attached to the 17th SS on 20 June, which had previously been part of von Choltitz LXXXIV Corps based south of Carentan. Two battalions of Soviet deserters, Ostbataillon 439 and 635, also came under its direction along with the remnants of 7th Army's Sturm-Bataillon AOK and Pionier-Bataillon Angers. The division was also assigned Fallschirm Pioneer Bataillon 5 from the wholly inadequate 5th Parachute Division in mid July. The battalion was of little value as it lacked small arms; in late May it had just twenty-eight rifles.

The presence of the 17th SS in the Carentan area helped persuade the Americans that they should first clear the Cotentin Peninsula and capture Cherbourg before making further efforts to strike southward. In the face of the US 4th, 9th and 79th Divisions the German garrison did not surrender until 26 June.

At the end of June the division's six infantry battalions were still alright, but the reconnaissance battalion had been considerably weakened. By this stage the 17th SS had lost nearly 900 casualties. Similarly, the panzer regiment only had eighteen combat-ready assault guns, supported by thirty-two 7.5cm anti-tank guns, including the self-propelled weapons and four powerful 8.8cm Pak 43s. During early July the 5th and 7th Kompanies from SS-Panzer Regiment 2 were attached to the 17th SS along the Périers–Carentan road. However, by the middle of the month it had lost another eight Sturmgeschütz and Kampfgruppe Fick was formed using SS-Panzergrenadier Regiment 37 and SS-Pioneer Abteilung 17 under SS-Obersturmbannführer Jacob Fick.

Other units facing the Americans were suffering much higher rates of attrition. Deployed to the east of St Lô, the 3rd Parachute Division, consisting of three regiments with little heavy equipment of note apart from nine 7.5cm Pak 40 anti-tank guns and twelve 10.5cm field guns, had suffered 4,064 casualties by 12 July. Likewise, the 352nd Infantry had been through the grinder and lost 7,886 casualties. All of the infantry formations west of St Lô fighting alongside the 17th SS were in similar dire straits.

This meant that the principal forces that would have to withstand and deflect the American's break-out offensive, Operation Cobra, were the 17th SS Panzergrenadier Division and Panzer Lehr Panzer Division. West of the Vire, the sector facing the American XIX Corps, was part of the 20 mile (32km) front held by the 17th SS. Its right wing consisted of Kampgruppe Heintz, employing units from the battered 275th and 352nd Infantry Divisions.

Cobra strikes

Just before the Americans attacked with overwhelming force, employing four infantry and two armoured divisions, the 17th SS reported to LXXXIV Corps that it could field just two weak infantry battalions with another five combat ineffective, ten assault guns, ten heavy anti-tank guns and five light artillery batteries. Mobility was poor and its heavy artillery was assigned to Panzer Lehr.

When the American blow fell, Sergeant Helmut Günther of the 17th SS reconnaissance battalion was caught up in the chaos following Cobra. He heard the neighbouring paratroop unit under attack on 23/24 July. Although not in the path of the assault he and his men were ordered to withdraw as the front collapsed. Günther recalls:

> We were marching, marching back all the time. One morning we were ordered to keep a road open, but we found that the Americans had already blocked it. The roads were crowded with American vehicles, and all that we could do was take to the fields on foot. On the fourth day, by sheer coincidence we ran into some of our own unit's vehicles, and kept going by road. But we were losing stragglers all the time – some of us later had letters from them from America. Once when we were moving to take up position an army staff car

stopped besides us. I saluted. The officer in it asked me where we were going. 'Have you gone crazy?' he said. 'The Americans are there already.' Then he drove on. In a ditch in a wood we met ten exhausted paratroopers who asked us for water. I suggested that they come with us, but they were reluctant. We moved off, and a while later heard shooting. One paratrooper caught up with us, and told us that all the rest were dead. They had tried to surrender, but it was too difficult.

With the American armour hot on their heels, Günther soon discovered that there was not even time to eat:

We found a pig in a farm, killed it and cooked it. We took sheets from the farmhouse and laid them out on the table and prepared to eat. Suddenly a Luftwaffe man burst in shouting: 'The Americans are right behind me.' We grabbed the corners of the sheet with everything inside it, threw it in the back of a field car, and pulled out just as the first Sherman came in sight. Eventually we met up with out battalion headquarters, who were expecting the enemy at any moment. From then on, I could not distinguish the days. I had seen the first retreat from Moscow, which was terrible enough, but at least units were still intact. Here, we had become a cluster of individuals. We were not a battle-worthy company any longer. All we had going for us was that we knew each other very well.

The 17th SS, driven south, were partly caught in the Coutances pocket, the division then fought closely with the 2nd SS, forming a joint battlegroup to break out from the Roncey pocket to the southeast. At Roncey survivors joined a huge, stationary, three-abreast column of vehicles on 29 July. To the south lay the American 2nd Armored Division barring their way; suddenly American fighter-bombers swooped in and wrecked a 2 mile (3km) stretch of vehicles. The strafing and the bombing continued for six hours. Eleven vehicles from the 17th SS assault gun battalion, escaping westwards from St Denis-le-Gast, bumped into American artillery and tank destroyers near La Chapelle during the night. All the vehicles were lost along with ninety men killed and 200 captured.

Survivors of the 17th SS, 2nd SS and the 6th Parachute Regiment continued to flee south along with the 91st Airlanding Division. By the end of July the LXXXIV and II Parachute Corps and their divisions facing the Americans had been destroyed and 20,000 German troops captured. Although many of the 17th SS escaped, they left much of their equipment littering the Normandy countryside.

The division's condition was such that by August it was withdrawn for refitting, although elements served with the 2nd SS during the Mortain counter-attack and later with 10th SS. Kampfgruppe Fick was expanded to include all the remaining battle-worthy elements of the division, but on 6 August C-in-C West ordered the 17th SS to be subordinated to the 2nd SS.

In early August about 5,000 men of the 708th Infantry Division were finally sent north to help contain the Americans and support the 17th SS, though by this stage the Americans had already broken out. Lacking mobility and equipped with old French and Russian artillery, the division was being sent to its doom and would be of little value to the SS-Panzergrenadiers. In the event, the division ended up scattered over a 26 mile (40km) area, with much of its artillery remaining in 1st Army's area.

Final days

SS-Panzerjäger Abteilung 17 finally received some of its thirty-one Jagdpanzer IVs from Germany in early August. Only III Kompanie of the battalion with the self-propelled guns had originally moved to the front with the assault guns. Now equipped with the Jagdpanzers and twelve Flakpanzers, it headed north, reaching Chateau Gontier with instructions to move westwards between Laval and Rennes.

The battalion finally went into action against the Americans on the 5th in the Laval area, where there were also elements of the 708th Infantry Division. On 6/7 August, the SS-Panzer Abteilung 17 commander, SS-Sturmbannführer Kepplinger, was killed near Laval by the French resistance. The fighting did not last long and it retreated toward Sablé-sur-Sarthe, where there were other elements of the 708th, which lost 4,000 men, mainly as prisoners. American forces had already bypassed Laval and by 9 August elements of the US 5th Armoured Division was south of Le Mans. The battalion was forced to fight its way eastward, suffering heavy casualties as it went.

Kampfgruppe Fick, joined a week later by Kampfgruppen Braune and Günther, drawing on men from SS-Panzeraufklärungs Abteilung 17 and a Reichsarbeitsdienst (RAD – Reich Labour Service) flak battalion, headed for the Saar and Metz. It was felt that these separate units would be less vulnerable than if the division tried to withdraw as a coherent whole. Therefore, because large parts of the division had already been withdrawn, it avoided the Falaise pocket, escaping to fight another day.

Chapter 7

The Tigers are coming! – The 503, 101 SS and 102 SS Heavy Panzer Battalions

The most potent panzers in Normandy were the fifty-seven ton Tiger I and sixty-eight ton Tiger II; fortunately for the Allies they were few in number. The popular perception in many Allied tankers' minds though was that all panzers were dreaded Tigers, leading to an inferiority complex.

In mid-June 1944, Schwere Panzer Abteilung 503, equipped with Tiger Is and IIs under Hauptmann Rolf Fromme, was assigned to Panzergruppe West. This was good news as the battalion was considered the most experienced Tiger tank unit in the whole German Army. The 503 were formed to assist Rommel in North Africa, but, with the end in sight in Tunisia, were sent to Russia. It had fought on the Eastern Front in the winter of 1942–43, seeing action at the Battle of Kursk. The battalion, operating Tiger IIs, was then transferred to Panzergruppe West, fighting round Caen and helping to stem the tide of Operation Goodwood. Although depleted, the battalion escaped the Falaise pocket.

Two other SS heavy tank battalions equipped with Tiger Is also served in Normandy. Schwere SS-Panzer Abteilung 101 thwarted the British 7th Armoured Division at Villers-Bocage, though notably most of its tanks were lost in the Falaise pocket. Its sister unit, SS-Panzer Abteilung 102, went into action on 9 July at Point 112, supporting the 10th SS and 12th SS Panzer Divisions. By 20 August the battalion had claimed 227 Allied tanks, but again was lost in the chaos of Falaise.

Combat experience

Schwere (Heavy) Panzer Abetilung 503 came into being in May 1942, drawing on men from Panzer Regiments 5 and 6. There were insufficient Tiger tanks so it had to be brought up to strength with Panzer III Ausf Ns. Although destined to serve Erwin Rommel in North Africa, the cancellation of the Porsche-designed Tiger in favour of the Henschel model delayed the battalion's deployment. Instead, in December it found itself destined for the Eastern Front and Field Marshal von Manstein's Army Group South.

The Tigers of this battalion soon gained a truly fearsome reputation. Its full complement of tanks did not arrive until April 1943, but during the third battle of Kharkov the battalion helped destroy the main Soviet attacking force, Mobile Group Popov. Abteilung 503 then took part in Operation Citadel in July, designed to crush the Kursk salient, during which it lost only eight tanks. In return it single-handedly claimed an incredible total of 501 Russian tanks, 388 anti-tank guns, seventy-nine artillery pieces and eight aircraft.

Abteilung 503 then became part of a heavy *kampfgruppe* including armour from the 6th Panzer Division under Oberst Dr Franz Bake. While covering the withdrawal of 6th Panzer on 20 July 1943, Bake, with six Tigers, caught the Soviets by surprise and knocked out twenty-three T-34s. Three days later his battle group claimed another thirty-three Soviet tanks.

The 503 were reassigned to assist the 19th Panzer Division, but in January 1944 thirty-four Tigers of the battalion found themselves part of Heavy Panzer Regiment Bake. Bake's panzers endured seven Soviet counterattacks, claiming 286 Russian tanks and assault guns.

During 4–8 February 1944, eleven Tigers and fourteen Panthers attempted to breakthrough to the German troops trapped in the Cherkassy Pocket, north-east of Uman. A second attack from the Rubany-Most area was more success-ful, knocking out eighty Russian tanks and assault guns. The rate of attrition against the Soviets was such that by 13 February Bake only had four Panthers left. At this point command of Schwere Panzer Abteilung 503 was assumed by Hauptmann Fromme, who was then to lead the battalion in Normandy. By mid-February, Bake's Tigers had helped 35,000 German troops escape the Cherkassy Pocket. Having lost all the Tiger tanks of Abteilung 503, on 6 March 1944 Panzergruppe Bake was created with the newly-arrived Schwere Panzer Abteilung 509.

The exhausted *panzertruppen* of the 503 were withdrawn to Lemberg on the Polish border and then on to Ohrdruf, Thuringia, in the spring of 1944 for refitting, along with almost a hundred Red Army 'volunteers'. By the summer it still had no tanks, but between 11 and 17 June the battalion received a shipment of thirty-three new Tiger Is and twelve Tiger IIs; the latter monsters had only recently come into service and were used to equip I Kompanie.

SS-Sturmbannführer von Westerhagen assumed command of the Schwere SS-Panzer Abteilung 101 when it was formed in July 1943 around a cadre from the 1st SS Panzer Division *Leibstandarte SS Adolf Hitler*. It was placed under the direction of I SS Panzer Corps and the battalion was then attached to its founding unit and sent to Italy in August 1943. Two companies were sent to Russia, where they remained until April 1944.

The 101 was then assigned to the I SS Panzer Corps, consisting of the 1st SS and 12th SS Panzer Divisions. Schwere SS-Panzer Abteilung 102, formed in October 1943, was attached to II SS Panzer Corps. It was also sent to Normandy, where it fought the Allies under the leadership of SS-Sturmbann-führer Weiss.

Villers-Bocage

At the time of the invasion, Schwere SS-Panzer Abteilung 101 was stationed in the Beauvais area with Corps HQ at Septeuil west of Paris; the latter moved to Baron-sur-Odon between Villers-Bocage and Caen on 9 June. The battalion reached Normandy on the 12th and II Kompanie, minus four tanks left with the workshop company under Obersturmführer Stamm, found welcome cover from Allied air attack in a small wood northeast of Villers-Bocage. I Kompanie under SS-Hauptsturmführer Mobius was deployed to their right; it is unclear just how involved Mobius' tanks were in the coming battle. The battalion had a theoretical strength of forty-five Tigers, but in fact numbered thirty-seven; less than half these were available at Villers-Bocage and by 1 July only eleven were fully serviceable.

The failure of Operation Perch on 13 June 1944, of all the setbacks the Allies suffered during the Normandy campaign, has to rank as one of the worst. In the space of just five minutes a mere handful of the dreaded Tigers destroyed the brigade spearhead of the 7th Armoured Division, saved the Panzer Lehr Division from encirclement, prevented the German line from being rolled up and stopped the Allies from breaking out to the southwest of Caen. In short, this engagement could have speeded the conclusion of the Normandy campaign; instead bad planning and bad luck resulted in a major setback for the British Army.

Sited at the head of the Seulles valley, Villers-Bocage dominated the approaches to Mont Pinçon, ten miles (16km) to the south, the Odon valley and Caen in the east. The road network for the whole region stemmed from the village, making it of strategic importance to both sides; anyone controlling Villers-Bocage controlled the roads.

What the British did not know was that the 2nd Panzer Division had been alerted to move from Amiens to Normandy to establish blocking positions in this sector, and that elements of Abteilung 101, I SS Panzer Corps reserve, under SS-Obersturmführer Michael Wittmann, had occupied Point 213. The British were outclassed from the start. The Cromwell, which had replaced 7th Armoured Division's Sherman tanks when they left Italy, was too lightly armoured and armed. In stark contrast, the Tiger tank could expect to remain unharmed by the majority of Allied tanks except at point blank range. In addition, the late arrival of 7th Armoured Division's second armoured brigade, due to bad weather, meant the division lacked 150 tanks and supporting infantry when it went into action.

To make matters worse, Wittmann was an established tank ace. In July 1941, in the Balkans as an SS-Unterscharführer, he had been awarded the Iron Cross II Class while commanding an assault gun in the *Leibstandarte SS Adolf Hitler* Division, and in September had gained the Iron Cross I Class on the Eastern Front. By December 1942 he had became an SS-Untersturmführer and the following year was given command of a Tiger I in 13 Kompanie of the *Leibstandarte*'s SS-Panzer Regiment. When he reached SS-Obersturmführer, on 20 January 1944, his kills stood at 117 vehicles. In April he took command of 2 Kompanie in the Schwere SS-Panzer Abteilung 101.

On the 13th the Germans had planned to carry out maintenance, until the British armoured column was spotted outside Villers-Bocage. Wittmann decided to reconnoitre to the northwest to see if the rumour that the British 7th Armoured Division had pushed into the left flank of Panzer Lehr was in fact true. With four, possibly five, Tigers and one Panzer IV from Panzer Lehr, he fanned out and advanced on Villers-Bocage. Upon seeing the British armoured column moving east towards Point 213 Wittmann realised the vital road junction must be secured at once.

In the meantime, the British had halted on the hill past the junction with the Tilly road. At 0905 hours the lead elements had reached the base of Point 213. The main column of vehicles had stopped several hundred yards away on the hedge-lined highway, while most of the tanks, including four Cromwells and one Firefly, spread out to the north.

Wittmann's gunlayer, SS-Oberscharführer Balthasar Woll, who had served him in Russia, and whose own tank was now under repair, grumbled: 'They're acting as if they've won the war already.' To which Wittmann replied: 'We're going to prove them wrong.'

Two or three of the Tigers drove parallel to the British column, but Wittmann to the north decided to circle round and attack without waiting for the others. Heading from the east he rammed aside a Cromwell blocking his way and drove into the town's high street, Rue Clemenceau. In the town square, the British tank crews had dismounted and were alarmed by the sight of a lumbering Tiger tank. Any six-pounder anti-tank guns that had been deployed were useless as their shells just bounced off the panzer's armour. The latter knocked out four British tanks.

Wittmann descended the slope down towards the Seulles River valley, past some bombed-out houses. At the road junction he bumped into British tanks parked on the Caumont road. A Sherman Firefly had heard all the firing and was confronted by a scout car and its frantically-waving driver. It drove round a corner to find Wittmann's Tiger 200 yards away, firing down a side street. The Firefly quickly poured four 17-pounder rounds into the Tiger which began to burn, but its turret rotated and a shell brought half a building down on the British tank. When it emerged the Tiger had vanished.

The battered and bruised Tiger beat a hasty retreat back up the hill, running into a Cromwell. Wittmann and his crew sustained two more hits before the Cromwell was brewed up and two of its crew killed. Lying to the left of, and parallel to, the highway was a narrow track. Clanking up this, Wittmann's first victim was a half-track at the base of the waiting column; this was followed by an unsuspecting Honey light tank. Further up the road a 6-pounder crew hurriedly swung their gun round, but a well-placed German shell hit the Bren carrier loaded with ammunition in front of it.

Wittmann's rampaging Tiger then proceeded to brew up the rest of the trapped column, knocking out a row of Bren Carriers and half-tracks as armour piercing shells continued to bounce off his impervious armour. British soldiers scattered in all directions, many taking shelter in the ditch behind the column. A tank tried to block Wittmann's path on the track so he drove onto the road, crushing everything in his way. Wittmann withdrew to the woods to the south-east. In just five minutes he had reduced the British advance to a shambles, destroying twenty-five vehicles single handedly.

The 7th Armoured's divisional reconnaissance regiment, to the north, advanced to help, but was engaged by four other Tigers and suffered heavy losses. In the early afternoon a triumphant Wittmann, rearmed and refuelled, returned to join the rest of his forces: four Tigers, the Panzer IV and possibly three other tanks (either from Lehr or 1 Kompanie) with infantry support. With these he attacked the remnants of the British forces trapped around Point 213. On the edge of the hill at least two Cromwells and one Firefly were knocked out blocking the road, while not far away, in the woods on the crown of the hill, two more Cromwells were brewed-up.

The battle for Point 213 was a one-sided affair with the Germans now pressing around Villers-Bocage and British attempts to send reinforcements failed. Three Cromwells and a Firefly under Lieutenant Bill Cotton tried to make contact. They managed to cross the town, but were unable to get over the railway embankment and turned back to take up positions in the square.

The survivors from the British 7th Armoured Division's 22nd Armoured Brigade, spearheaded by the 4th County of London Yeomanry and A Company, 1st Battalion the Rifle Brigade, were quickly overrun. The Rifles lost four killed, five wounded and seventy-six missing; at least twenty Cromwell tanks, four Fireflys, three Honeys, three scout cars and a half-track were destroyed.

A Company lost eighty men, including three officers; about thirty infantry managed to escape. By late afternoon both units had ceased to exist, which left only B Squadron precariously holding onto Villers-Bocage.

Supported by units of the 2nd Panzer Division, Wittmann now turned his attention back on Villers-Bocage. This time the British were not going to be caught out. B Squadron, with four Cromwells and a Firefly, took up defensive positions around the main square with a Queen's Regiment 6-pounder guarding the main street from a side alley, where it was hoped they would catch the Tiger's side armour.

Wittmann, over-playing his hand, noisily entered Villers-Bocage again, this time in strength, with two Tigers (possibly including Mobius) and a PzKpfw IV. Rounding the bend into the high street, he drove straight into the prepared ambush, 'When the Tigers were about 1,000 yards away and were broadside to us I told 3 Troop and my gunner to fire', recalled Lieutenant Cotton. 'The Firefly did the damage, but the 75s helped and must have taken a track off one which started to circle out of control'.

Wittmann's tank was hit by the anti-tank gun, the following Tiger by Sergeant Bobby Bramall's Firefly. Corporal Horne's Cromwell missed and the Panzer IV had driven almost past the second Tiger when Horne drove out behind the German and blasted him. It seems a third Tiger entered town but was also caught by B Squadron a few dozen yards from the main street at the crossroads of Rue Jeanne Bacon and Rue Emile Samson.

Lieutenant Cotton notes that the engagement was not all one way: 'They shot back at us, knocked the Firefly out, as its commander was hit in the head. However, at the end of a very few minutes there were three "killed" Tigers'. The German crews escaped because too few British infantry remained. Later, Lieutenant Cotton, armed with an umbrella, alongside Sergeant Bramall, carrying blankets and petrol, walked in the pouring rain to the German tanks and set fire to them to prevent recovery.

This series of brutal engagements fought throughout the 13th rendered it impossible for the British to hold onto Villers-Bocage. Their forces were split in two, with one group at Villers-Bocage and another at Tracy-Bocage several miles west; also, the 7th Armoured was strung out along the road from Villers-Bocage to Livry.

Alarmingly, 7th Armoured's intelligence estimated that up to forty Tigers from 2nd Panzer were in the area, with which it was feared the Germans would cut the road between Villers-Bocage and Caumont, trapping B Squadron. This estimate was not accurate; 2nd Panzer had no Tigers and its panzers did not arrive from Paris until 18 June, nor did the 12th SS Panzer Division have any

Tiger tanks. It is doubtful that Abteilung 101 had any more than a handful in the Villers-Bocage area on 13 June.

Panzer Lehr, likewise, had no spare tanks. It was being held down frontally by Major General D A H Graham's 50th (Northumbrian) Division and Kampfgruppe Kauffman's ad hoc forces showed what Panzer Lehr had in the way of reserves. Panzer Kompanie 316 (Funklenk), attached to Panzer Lehr, had six Tigers, of which only half were serviceable, and nine StuG assault guns. Therefore, the 7th Armoured Division even at this stage was still a considerable threat to the German flank. The British, though, in fear of the Tigers, were ordered to pull back at nightfall and hold Tracy-Bocage, concentrating on Hill 174.

At about 1700 hours, while the Germans were regrouping, the British withdrew two miles (3km) to the west. B Squadron was ordered to time its withdrawal to coincide with a covering barrage. In total the brigade lost 225 men, twenty-seven tanks, fourteen half-tracks, fourteen Bren carriers and a number of anti-tank guns. Wittmann's prompt action in thwarting the British enabled Villers-Bocage to be retaken later in the day by the Panzer Lehr Kamfgruppe and units of 2nd Panzer; thus plugging the gap. A few days later he was promoted to SS-Hauptsturmführer.

Stopping Goodwood

Wittmann's successful defensive action forced Montgomery to launch two more costly enveloping attacks, with Operation Epsom to the west on 25 June and Goodwood to the east on 18 July. In between these he launched Operation Charnwood, a frontal assault, on 8 July, losing 3,500 casualties and eighty tanks.

In the meantime, Schwere Panzer Abteilung 503 became the tactical responsibility of 21st Panzer Division. The tanks were entrained and shipped to Dreux by 5 July. They reached von Choltitz's LXXXVI Corps area with about forty-five Tigers, though on 23 July the *abteilung* was shifted to the I SS Panzer Corps. In early July the *abteilung*'s HQ, at the Château de Canteloup near Argences, southeast of Caen, was visited by Oberst Hermann von Oppeln-Bronikowski, commander of 21st Panzer's Panzer Regiment 22. The 503 departed the Dreux forest for Caen, going into action on 11 July alongside 21st Panzer, with III Kompanie claiming twelve enemy tanks near Cuverville.

Seven days later, German defences east of Caen were carpet bombed prior to Goodwood. One Tiger was burnt out, another tossed upside down like a child's toy, trapping the crew, and a third was seriously damaged. The *abteilung*'s HQ in a nearby Chateau was also caught in the bombing, but Hauptmann Fromme escaped with his life. That day, eight Tigers went into action, but by evening III Kompanie had just one operational tank left.

Goodwood made good initial progress until it ran into the in-depth prepared positions of infantry and armour, including thirty-six Tiger tanks and elements of the 1st SS and 12th SS Panzer Divisions. The offensive cost 6,000 British casualties and 400 tanks and was called off after just two gruelling days.

Abteilung 503's III Kompanie was withdrawn from the line and received fourteen Tiger IIs during the first week of August at Mailly-le-Camp. The company left on the 11th but missed the battle for Falaise. I and II Kompanies were instrumental in helping halt the British breakthrough, which reached Cagny to the southeast of Caen. The British lost forty tanks, many of them falling to Abteilung 503's Tigers. The battalion continued to fight with 21st Panzer and by the end of the month was in the Bretteville-sur-Laize area.

Battle for Hill 112

Tigers of Panzer Abteilung 102, supported by panzergrenadiers from the 9th SS Panzer Division, attacked Canadian positions at Hill 112 on 10 July. The battalion first went into action at Maltot to the northeast of the hill, when four Tigers securing the flank knocked out three Shermans, a surviving tank fleeing in the direction of Eterville. Fourteen Tiger tanks then struck toward St Martin to the southeast of Hill 112 and were met by more Shermans, which poured fire into the lead panzer.

Platoon commander Will Fey recalled the attack:

> Three enemy tanks were already silenced; the others kept on firing without pause. Then we finally had the most eager one in our cross-hairs. The two farthest to our right had already been knocked out by us with five anti-tank shells, when light bombers showed up above the battleground. Like eagles, they fell out of the sky, dropped their loads of bombs, pulled up, and climbed away again. They came at us like a swarm of hostile hornets and covered us with a hail of medium bombs. At the same time, smoke shells landed among us and covered everything around with an impenetrable white fog within minutes. This was a new way of fighting to us, something we had not encountered on any battleground before. We withdrew to the starting positions where at least the infantry was able to keep the enemy close-assault teams away from us.

The attack was renewed the following day, but an artillery barrage greeted the advancing Tigers, though they managed to knock out a few Churchill tanks. A smoke screen again descended on the panzers and Fey's tank took several hits to the rear and the turret, before stumbling upon enemy trucks and personnel carriers. Two Churchills were quickly knocked out. By the evening the Tigers had secured Hill 112. It would be fought over until the end of the month when the Germans finally gave up its scorched earth. In the meantime it would change hands repeatedly.

During the night of the 11th, the British moved back onto the hill and the isolated Tigers withdrew to St Martin. Two days later they counterattacked, recapturing the wooded area of the cattle pen on the summit. The heavy and devastating Allied bombardment of the hill ensured that the supporting panzer-grenadiers could not remain, and on the 15th the Tigers once again found themselves alone amid the shattered landscape. The following morning the 10th SS came to their assistance.

When the Canadians occupied Maltot, some Tigers were sent to clear them out. These were met by a deluge of artillery fire but caught a column of four Churchill tanks on the road, knocking out the first and last vehicle, trapping them. The two middle tanks were caught desperately trying to escape down the embankment; the last one was hit twice in the rear. Enemy anti-tank guns and fighter-bombers then greeted the Tigers and despite getting beyond Maltot, Will Fey and his comrades were recalled to their original positions.

On 24 July the Tigers intercepted eight Churchills striking from Maltot toward St Martin; none escaped. The next day the battalion was bombed when a raid covered Hill 112 all the way back to St Martin. Fey and his comrades were relieved by the III Kompanie and they withdrew, only to be thrown into the fight again on the 26th, around Hill 67 and the northern exit of St Andre, to the west of Feuguerolles.

In the fighting that followed, the Tiger next to Fey's tank was hit, smoke pouring from its hatches as those uninjured crew sought to escape. He witnessed the awful carnage:

> The driver of the knocked-out Panzer wildly waved the bloody stump of his arm from which his hand was dangling, held by some pieces of skin and flesh, and sought cover with the other survivors to the side. The radio operator had been killed by a direct hit. Our other Panzers then advanced from their standby positions to the ridge of the hills. Across from us, there was no more movement. Everything remained quiet.
>
> It appeared that the Canadian attempt to break through, which began with such high hopes, had been stalled by the valour and determination of our grenadiers. Its brutal force spent, it faltered. Then came another air attack. On the whole the Tiger tanks were able

to weather these steel storms; the main damage seemed to be to the antenna, tracks, radiators and ventilators. The thing they most feared was naval gunfire as this delivered the heaviest shells.

Totalise juggernaut

The Tigers helped halt the Guards Armoured Division near Estry and stopped the 11th Armoured Division's push toward the Vire-Vassy Road. On 1 August, Abteilung 102 was ordered to withdraw south under the cover of darkness to assist the 9th SS Panzer Division, which was involved in heavy fighting with British and Canadian armoured forces. Arriving in Vire, they found the place reduced to rubble by air attacks.

They then moved north to assist German paratroops under attack along the railway embankment. The following day, elements of Abteilung 102, along with the weak reconnaissance *abteilung* from the 10th SS and a company of paratroops, were ordered to counterattack north of Vire.

In the initial engagement the Tigers knocked out five Cromwell tanks. They then bumped into concealed Shermans, but these were also swiftly dealt with. In total, twenty-two tanks, belonging to the British Guards Armoured Division, were knocked out without any loss. The following day the battalion continued to take a toll on the British tanks. At 2300 on 3 August they withdrew, claiming twenty-eight enemy tanks and fourteen trucks destroyed, two armoured scout cars and two motorbikes captured.

Northwest of Vassy on 7 August the Tigers halted a massed armoured column with devastating effect. Opening fire at just 400 metres they knocked out fourteen of the fifteen attacking Shermans along with numerous other vehicles.

The next day, ten tanks of Abteilung 101 supporting Kampfgruppe Waldmüller, consisting of thirty-nine Panzer IVs, a battalion of panzergrenadiers and the escort companies from the 12th SS, were thrown against Operation Totalise, the British and Canadian attempt to break through to Falaise. The juggernaut of the Polish 1st Armoured and Canadian 4th Armoured Divisions were poised to roll.

Wittmann's Tigers were gathered east of Cintheaux behind a hedge, ready to do Kurt Meyer's bidding. The latter recalled:

> Once more I shake Michael Wittmann's hand and refer to the extremely critical situation. Our good Michael laughs his boyish laughter and climbs into his Tiger. So far, 138 enemy tanks in the East and West have fallen victim to him. Will he be able to increase this number of successes or become a victim himself?

The massive Allied air raid in support of their offensive failed to hit a single panzer. The Tigers, with the grenadiers behind them, struck toward the wood southeast of Carcelles where the Allied tanks were assembled. It was at this point that Wittmann's luck ran out.

Hauptsturmführer Wolfgang Rabe MD, Abteilung 101's physician, reported:

> Wittmann was east of the road to Caen with four or five Tigers. I was off to the side. The panzers came under fire, reportedly from English 15cm guns. Some of the Tigers went up in flames. I tried to determine if anyone got out. When I did not see anybody, I thought they might have left the panzer through the lower hatch and I tried to get closer. This was impossible since I came under fire as soon as I left the ditch in an easterly direction. We waited another hour or two for anyone of the crews to show up. Towards evening I drove over to Brigadeführer Kraemer, Chief of the General Staff, I SS Panzer Corps, and reported on developments. He ordered me, since I was the senior officer of the Abteilung, to lead the remains of the Abteilung back, and attached me to the SS Panzer Regiment 12, Wünsche.

Other reports stated that Wittman succumbed to Shermans and a Typhoon rocket attack. At the time of his death he was not only credited with 138 AFVs, most of them tanks, but also 132 anti-tank guns, which he had chalked up in under two years. His greatest victory, though, has to be inflicting the debacle of Villers-Bocage on the British. Through a mixture of luck and courage Wittmann, largely single-handedly, halted a British armoured thrust that could have encircled Panzer Lehr or even rolled up the entire German corps front. If this had happened the German collapse in Normandy could have been much swifter and perhaps even more catastrophic. Generalmajor Fritz Kraemer summed up the action very succinctly:

> Early in the morning of 12 June the commander of five tanks (Tigers) which had been placed in readiness north of Villers-Bocage sighted an enemy motorized column, including tanks, on the march from Tilly toward Villers-Bocage. Without hesitation he [Wittmann] drove against this column and exterminated with his tanks about thirty enemy tanks and a like number of motor vehicles. Thus, by the personal courage of this officer, the enemy's intention to break through by way of Villers-Bocage was frustrated.

Battle for Falaise

By 9 August the last of Abteilung 102's Tiger tanks were withdrawing from the Vire area toward Falaise. Their *kampfgruppe* was attached to the remains of the 271st Infantry Division, which was holding a line from St Germain to the southern edge of Bernay to the northern edges of Fresnay, Espins and Coisilles, against the British 59th (Staffordshire) Division.

The following day enemy armoured cars probed the 271st's left flank, followed by forty tanks advancing on Espins and Le Monsul. German infantry dropped their weapons and fled when twelve tanks supported by the armoured cars broke through southwest of Le Monsul. The Tigers of the II Kompanie rallied the reluctant infantry and counterattacked, claiming four tanks and putting the rest to flight northward.

During 12 August Abteilung 102 continued to support the 271st Infantry Division and the I and II Kompanies attempted to trap the advancing British armour. The latter broke through east of Barberie and II Kompanie moved to secure the roads to Espins and Fresnay. Six tanks also occupied the height on the northern edge of Zingal, catching seven enemy tanks. The British then brought down a massive barrage which stunned Ernst Streng, commander of II Kompanie:

> The English shells hit the roofs, walls, windows, and streets like hailstones. The force and violence of the artillery fire, never experienced at such intensity before, raced through the town [Bois Halbout] like a hurricane. Wounded soldiers were trapped under the rubble of crumbling roofs and walls. Helpless injured overflowed the hallways and rooms of the main dressing station. Whoever was still breathing was buried under the falling walls.

Five Tigers at Tournebous had to make a fighting retreat to Bois Halbout or face being overwhelmed. The Tigers then withdrew southeast of Claire-Tizon to refuel and take on ammunition. Six tanks needed repairing and were handed over to the mechanics. The retreating Tigers were then caught at the junction of the western ring road just outside Falaise on 13 August by rocket-firing fighter-bombers. They sought sanctuary in a nearby wood without loss and were ordered to defend the Tournebous area. Soon the British were in amongst the three Tigers that formed the command post of II Kompanie and two were quickly knocked out.

The remaining panzers retreated and north of Soulangy, at Hill 184, they found German infantry fleeing twelve Sherman tanks. The Tigers knocked out three as the daylight began to fail and the infantry dug in. The following day, Will Fey and his crew, returning from the repair company, were ordered to hold the Caen–Falaise road between Soulangy and St Pierre. Although Soulangy had fallen, a few panzergrenadiers from the 12th SS screened Fey and his men.

At the approach of the Canadians, Fey drove forward to engage them but they disappeared in Soulangy. Moving to rescue some trapped panzergrenadiers, he spotted a line of ten Sherman tanks threatening the foxholes of the German infantry. At 400 metres the Tiger knocked out the first and last Sherman and then finished off the rest at leisure. Covering the retreat of about thirty men from 12th SS, the Tiger knocked out an approaching column of armoured personnel carriers. After all this success, Fey's tank now refused to start and, in danger of being outflanked, had to be towed back to St Pierre.

Final days

The Tiger tanks withdrew to the Falaise road junction and on the night of the 15th the local *Maquis* were foolish enough to tangle with the *abteilung*'s sentries. By the morning the Tigers were at Versainville, just north of Falaise, and they moved forward to engage the Canadians just as the village was flattened. Their machineguns mowed down the numerous exposed advancing Canadian infantry; as long as no one surrendered they kept firing and it was soon the turn of the supporting Shermans.

When the Tigers fell back, the Canadian infantry bravely but vainly tried to deal with them. After abandoning Versainville, the Canadians continued to press them closely as they retreated to Eraines. The end was now in sight as Will Fey stoically noted:

> On the horizon, we saw columns of tanks and vehicles rolling east in the evening sun, tank after tank, with no break. This meant that the encirclement, which had been obvious around Falaise for days, was to be completed. But it was not the first encirclement we had to break out of!

It was only a matter of time before the last of the lumbering Tiger tanks had to be abandoned.

Chapter 8

Operation Lüttich – 2nd Panzer Division

While the 21st and 12th SS Panzer Divisions fought almost immediately to contain the Allied bridgehead, it was a week before they received any other armoured reinforcements. Panzergrenadiers of the 2nd Panzer Division first went into action on 13 June, but its tanks did not join the fighting until 27 June. The 2nd Panzer Division was a well-equipped and powerful formation by the time of D-Day. It was involved in the desperate attempts to contain the American breakout before being caught in the chaos of the Falaise salient.

Combat experience

As its designation implies, 2nd Panzer was one of Hitler's very first armoured divisions. Raised in October 1935 at Wurzburg, it was deployed to Vienna three years later following the Anschluss with Austria, where it remained until the invasion of Poland. After its role in the Polish campaign under General Rudolf Veiel, 2nd Panzer was sent to the Eifel area in readiness for the attack on France. It also supplied Panzer Regiment 4 to help form 13th Panzer Division on 28 September 1940 and was once again sent to Poland, this time for occupation duty.

The 2nd Panzer then saw action under Veiel's leadership in the Balkans during the invasion of Greece and Yugoslavia. After a brief deployment to France the division was sent to the central sector of the Eastern Front, where it was involved in the fighting at Moscow, Smolensk, Orel and Kiev. It subsequently fought at Kursk and the Dneiper, suffering heavy losses, and was sent to France under General Franz Westhoven for much needed refitting in 1944.

The division made the most of its well-earned rest and by late May/early June 1944 Panzer Regiment 3 had ninety-eight Panzer IVs and seventy-nine Panthers, of which only eight tanks were in the workshop undergoing maintenance. Panzerjäger Abteilung 38 also had about twenty powerful Jagdpanzer IV tank destroyers. These had been designed as a replacement for the Sturmgeschütz III/IV assault gun and had only started being issued to the tank hunter detachments of the panzer divisions in March 1944. Although also issued to the Panzerjäger *abteilung* of the 9th, 12th SS, 116th and Panzer Lehr Panzer Divisions, it was quite a rare armoured fighting vehicle in Normandy, where only about sixty were deployed.

Panzer Schwere Infanteriegeschütz Abteilung 38 was equipped with the Grille 15cm self-propelled gun on a Czech tank chassis. In addition, 2nd Panzer's Artillery Regiment 74 had six Hummel and twelve Wespe self-propelled guns, mounted on Panzer IV and II chassis respectively, and the panzergrenadiers had 476 armoured personnel carriers or armoured half-tracks. Manpower stood at 16,762, but this probably included 1,085 men belonging to the subordinated Panzer Abteilung 301 (Funklenk), although only the IV Kompanie of the latter unit accompanied 2nd Panzer to Normandy. On 5 June the battalion was sent back to Russia, leaving behind the IV Kompanie, which was supposed to form a cadre for the Panzer Abteilung 302 (Funklenk) that was just forming. The Kompanie consisted of two Panzer IIIs, six Sturmgeschütz and thirty-six Ladungsträger B IV remote-controlled demolition vehicles, totalling at the most 250 men. Panzer Abteilung 301 returned from the Eastern Front to be equipped with thirty Tigers, which were to be used as control vehicles for the Ladungsträgers.

Into action
On D-Day, the division, under General der Panzertruppen Heinrich Freiherr von Lüttwitz, who had reassumed command on 27 May, was deployed in the Amiens area. It was three crucial days before the division was instructed to move toward Normandy. Lütwittz received word in the early hours on the 9th, as he recalls:

> Toward 0300 hours, 9 June, the division received orders to march through Paris, and on into the Argentan–Sees sector. It was ordered that the march movement was to become effective with darkness on 9 June, and it was to be carried out only under the protection of darkness. The reason for the movement route through Paris was because all other bridges between Paris and the river estuary had been bombed out. Besides in the heart of Paris were the only passages still intact.
>
> By 1400 2nd Panzer was ready to move, two groups were to take to the road while nearly all the division's tracked vehicles were to be transported by train to save on unnecessary wear and tear. On the road losses to enemy air attack were to be kept to a minimum by travelling in small groups or individually. The lead elements arrived in Paris after dusk and at first things went smoothly until midnight

when an air raid caused chaos after the French traffic police fled to the shelters.

Because the Allied air forces had destroyed all bridges over the Seine from Paris to the coast, 2nd Panzer was obliged to make a longer journey when it moved from Amiens to Normandy. Instead of travelling via Rouen it had to take the detour via Paris, increasing the distance by more than 100 miles (150km). Moving mainly by road and by using the cover of darkness and periods of poor weather, the division managed to cover about 265 miles (400km) in two days, an impressive performance.

On the morning of the 10th von Lüttwitz arrived at the Panzer Corps HQ at Gallion. He was informed that it was intended that his division, along with Panzer Lehr Panzer Division, 17th SS Panzergrenadier Division and the 3rd Fallschirmjäger Division were to recapture Bayeux. Three days later, at 1700, 2nd Panzer was ordered to move to the Aunay-sur-Odon area on the left wing of Panzergruppe West to co-ordinate its efforts with Panzer Lehr and the 3rd Fallschirmjäger Division. For the attack on the 13th the division committed two *kampfgruppen*, one in the Jurques area and the other in the northern sector of the Bois de Homme. Some ground was taken but the lack of tanks greatly hampered operations.

Although elements of 2nd Panzer had been blooded, it was another six days before all of the division arrived in-theatre. Frustratingly, the Panther *abteilung* with fifty-two operational tanks did not arrive until the 19th; twenty were damaged in transit. Similarly the Panzer IV *abteilung* arrived with 75 per cent of its tanks operational and only two thirds of the Hummels and Wespes were combat ready.

The left battle group of 2nd Panzer advanced on Caumont and by nightfall on the 13th they had driven the British off Hill 174, near Cahagnes, and almost cut the road between Caumont and Amaye-sur-Orne.

Oberfeldwebel Hans Erich Braun, a senior NCO with Panzerjäger Abteilung 38, was with III Kompanie, equipped with nine 7.5cm anti-tank guns pulled by half-tracks. In total the division had twenty-five Pak 40 7.5cm towed anti-tank guns, while Abteilung 38's I and II Kompanies were equipped with the Jagdpanzer IVs. Braun was involved in the fighting southeast of Caumont and on 14 June noted that the British artillery ceased firing at around 0530. He was also grateful that it was too early for the enemy fighter-bombers, but an enemy artillery spotter plane was already up and about. He felt that the division was horribly exposed and recalled:

> From Caumont, especially from one of the town's highest towers, the enemy could see everything, and fired at the slightest movement

in the forward area, usually with several batteries combined. However, the three 7.5cm anti-tank guns of my troop were so well dug in and camouflaged, in the orchards and by the field paths which ran to the north, that it was impossible for anyone who did not actually know that they were there to spot them from a distance of twenty paces.

Braun and his men were hardened Eastern Front veterans and emplacing and hiding their guns was second nature. They had a steady nerve and allowed enemy patrols, tanks or armoured cars to get so close that their surprise fire was inevitably overwhelming and devastating. They were not afraid of hand-to-hand fighting either, but found their British counterparts were shy of such close-quarter combat. Braun adds:

> Often, we were accused of fighting fanatically, but we had long since learned the lesson, that one thing alone counts in war: to fire first, by a fraction of a second, and kill; or otherwise, be killed oneself.

At 0603 the British shelling resumed for fifteen minutes and Braun was stunned by the weight of the bombardment:

> A hurricane of fire raged through the countryside, wrapping everything in grey smoke and dirt; only once before, in the great battle near Orel [in Russia], had we ever experienced anything like this. Then, suddenly it stopped.

Then came the British Typhoons, followed by more artillery fire. Despite this deluge, the right-hand battle group of 2nd Panzer attacked on 15 June and, although suffering heavy losses, took Launay and St Germain d'Ectot. Two days later the left battle group reached le Quesnay.

Erich Braun was with the left-hand *kampfgruppe* that attacked under a covering barrage from its Hummel and Wespe self-propelled artillery:

> In spite of the enemy's strength in artillery and in the air, our left Battle Group assembled on the morning of 17 June for yet another attack towards the north. In our kompanie we had five operational anti-tank guns left; their task was to follow close behind the attacking grenadiers, down roads or paths, or across the patch-work of fields. At the start, I was with two remaining guns of my troop, in support of Panzergrenadier Regiment 304. Overhead, as we assembled, shrilled and whispered the protective barrage from Artillery Regiment 74. Our grenadiers rose up from their trenches and went forward, firing their machine-pistols and machineguns from the hip as they advanced.

In this way, and with some close combat, they got into the outskirts of le Quesnay. We pushed our guns forward, muzzle first, straining and heaving, to keep up with them.

Braun and his guns, taking up position behind a stone wall, were soon engaging advancing British tanks:

> I gave the command: 'Fire!' Simultaneously, some of the grenadiers let fly with their panzerfausts (which only tore holes in the ground short of the tank), and my gunner pulled the trigger.
>
> Bright-red flame: a terrific detonation: a violent blast of air. The shell screeched away towards the Cromwell, hitting the sloping top of the turret, and shooting straight up into the smoke-obscured sky, hissing and spitting. Unfortunate. The British gun began to wing in our direction, as the turret revolved. My crew re-loaded with solid shot, and fired again before the enemy gun could bear. The shell went straight through the turret and thinking that the enemy gunner was probably out of action, my crew recommenced firing with the appropriate ammunition, this time into the lightly-armoured side. Immediately a deep blue flame, surrounded by a bright flash, leapt up from the tank; there was a terrific explosion; and the Cromwell literally burst apart.

To Braun's left the panzergrenadiers claimed another Cromwell using panzerfausts. Reaching le Quesnay it took them an hour, fighting house-to-house and cellar-by-cellar, to drive the British out, though they clung on in the northern part of the town and in the neighbouring orchards. Braun's guns were used to fire explosives at point-blank range to crumble the buildings.

Following an artillery bombardment of southern le Quesnay, 2nd Panzer was counterattacked by British tanks and infantry. For a moment disaster loomed, but as Braun recalls quick thinking and discipline saved the day:

> Then the first waves of retiring grenadiers began to pass us, and we could hear the roar of the enemy tanks above their artillery and mortar fire. The British had forced their way back into le Quesnay, and cut the line of retreat for the German half-tracks and lorries. It could have been a catastrophe, but energetic officers and NCOs stopped the panic and the British attack halted. At the end of the day, we were back precisely where we had started from.

Driven back, Lüttwitz's 2nd Panzer attacked again the following day, seizing le Quesnay once more and pushing through to Briquessard at considerable cost.

However, all the abandoned tanks and weapons which they had lost on the 17th were recaptured and found to be in good order; ultimately, though, what had 2nd Panzer gained? – a little ground for irreplaceable manpower. It was a war of attrition the division could ill-afford.

On 14 June in the Villers-Bocage area, an American artillery 'serenade' broke up an attack by 2nd Panzer, knocking out eleven panzers, though the tanks of the British 7th Armoured Division were still in serious danger of being cut off. The 2nd Panzer's divisional reconnaissance group, on entering Villers-Bocage, found an almost intact Sherman, its turret was removed and the vehicle pressed into service as a much-needed recovery vehicle.

For the rest of June the division fought in the Caumont area, although the Panthers were despatched to resist the British Epsom offensive. When the British broke through east of Tilly-sur-Seulles on the front held by Panzer Lehr on 25 and 26 June, the 12th SS, supported by the I Abteilung Panzer Regiment 3, counterattacked on the right. On the 28th the Panthers destroyed fifty-three British tanks and fifteen anti-tank guns. By 1 July they had claimed eighty-nine enemy tanks, thirteen Bren carriers and nineteen anti-tank guns for the loss of twenty panzers.

The division, like many other German units in Normandy, did not escape the attention of the Allied air forces, especially the bombers. Air Marshal Arthur Harris, in charge of RAF Bomber Command, wrote:

> On June 30th it was learned that the 2nd and 9th Panzers division were moving up through Villers-Bocage to make an attack that night; there was a network of roads here which it would be almost impossible for the enemy to by-pass and it was therefore the obvious place in which to bomb the Panzer Divisions and their equipment – the enemy had also established a supply point there. This time Bomber Command attacked in daylight and dropped 1,100 tons of bombs; the Panzer Divisions had to call off the planned attack.

Cobra strikes

By early July the division still had eighty-five Panzer IVs in the field with another eleven in the shop, and twenty-one operational Panthers and thirty-eight undergoing maintenance. In addition it still had its twenty Jagdpanzer IVs. On the 2nd, IV Kompanie Panzer Abteilung 301 (Funklenk) was given sanction to remain with 2nd Panzer and Panzer Kompanie 316 (Funklenk) was earmarked for Panzer Abteilung 302 (Funklenk). The latter, stationed near Vouziers, was not destined to see action in Normandy and instead was sent to Warsaw in mid-August.

On 15 July the British launched Operation Greenline, a subsidiary of Goodwood, tying down the 2nd, 9th SS and 10th SS Panzer Divisions west of Caen, along the Epsom Salient, and forcing the 1st SS to hold the Orne. Goodwood was launched east of Caen three days later.

Elements of the 326th Infantry Division, deployed in the Pas de Calais area with 15th Army, crossed the Seine and remained in the Caumont area. Lüttwitz and his men were pulled out of the line on 21 July after the 326th Infantry relieved them. Although the Panzerjäger Battalion of the 326th included Marder self-propelled guns and Sturmgeschütz IIIs, the Panzer IVs of the I Abteilung Panzer Regiment 3 remained in welcome support for a week.

By 28 July the Germans realised that Operation Cobra represented the Allies' main effort to break the deadlock in Normandy. The Germans could not get 9th Panzer to the disintegrating American front for at least ten days, so von Kluge summoned the 2nd and 116th Panzer Divisions from the British front. Belatedly, General Krüger's LVIII Panzer Corps began to move northwards from Toulouse to free up General der Panzertruppen Hans Funck's XLVII Panzer Corps, which shifted from the British sector taking 2nd and 116th Panzer to confront the Americans at Avranches.

By the end of the month 2nd Panzer was pushing westward to link up with Panzer Lehr and the 2nd SS. Field Marshal von Kluge attempted to prevent the Americans spilling over the Vire by sending 2nd Panzer to Tessy-sur-Vire southeast of St Lô. The lead elements of 2nd Panzer went into action near the town on the 28th when they counterattacked.

Further to the west a 2nd Panzer *kampfgruppe*, including twenty panzers, reached the cross roads at la Denisiére, on the road between St Lô and Villebaudon to the south. On the 30th they found themselves under attack not only from the north, but also on their southern flank near Denisiére as the Americans attempted to surround them. Although cut off, the *kampfgruppe* knocked out twenty-five American tanks before it was overwhelmed. Just seven panzers managed to fight their way east to Moyon.

Hitler instructed Operation Lüttich (Liège) to close the developing American breach and von Funck's XLVII Panzer Corps was given the job of overseeing the Avranches counterattack. This meant it needed it to disengage. To the southeast of St Lô, II Parachute Corps also began to withdraw and on the 31st the Americans entered Torigni-sur-Vire northeast of Tessy. In the meantime the Americans seized Troisgots, just 4.5 miles (7km) north of Tessy-sur-Vire, where 2nd Panzer and remnants of the 352nd Infantry Division resisted to the end. The town fell to elements of the US 2nd Armored Division on 2 August, just as XLVII Panzer Corps was withdrawing through Pont-Farcy to the south.

Mortain counterattack

The Avranches counterattack was to be launched by 2nd, 116th, Panzer Lehr, 1st SS, 2nd SS and 17th SS, supported by two infantry divisions. In total the panzers were down from 1,400 tanks to 800, of which just 120–185 were allotted to Operation Lüttich. According to German sources the attack force involved no more than seventy-five Panzer IVs, seventy Panthers and thirty-two StuGs. The Americans were tipped off by the highly secret ULTRA intelligence intercepts and prepared to repel the Germans.

On the night of 6/7 August the 2nd Panzer, with about 80 tanks, was the first to strike west, between the La Sée sector and the St-Barthélemy-Juvigny road. Specifically, the panzer forces consisted of sixty Panzer IVs and Panthers as well as fifteen Jagdpanzer IVs. Then, supported by a panzer battalion from the 1st SS, the division was to force the Juvigny–Avranches road with an attack via St-Bathélemy, with the rest of the 1st SS following up.

Reinforced by Panzergrenadier Regiment 304, the right attack group of 2nd Panzer moved on Le Mesnil-Adelée via Mesnil-Tôve against weak American forces. Unfortunately, the right flank of 2nd Panzer was exposed when the 116th called a halt to its contribution to the operation. The left *kampfgruppe*, with Panzergrenadier Regiment 2, took Bellefontaine, but the Americans were not so easily ejected from St-Barthélemy and it took two attacks before they captured the area along with a hundred American prisoners.

Then, in the face of Allied air power, a crucial factor throughout the entire campaign, the German counterattack died out. Tantalisingly for Hitler, the attack got to within nine miles (14km) of Avranches; had they reached the coast they could have cut off twelve American divisions way to the south.

Although they took Mortain, the 2nd SS were unable to dislodge American troops of the US 30th Division from Point 317. Some seventy panzers penetrated US VII Corps front, but fifty were lost and the attack was not renewed on the 11th as instructed by OKW. Following the Mortain attack, once the Americans had gathered their wits, American Lightning, Mustang and Thunderbolt fighter-bombers, as well as British Typhoons, set about Lüttwitz's division at Le Coudray, halfway to Avranches. The 1st SS and 2nd SS were also caught in this rain of fire. In one RAF Typhoon strike the 2nd Panzer Division reportedly lost sixty tanks and 200 vehicles. This was a deadly taste of things to come. In total eighty-one panzers were knocked out, fifty-four were damaged and twenty-six abandoned. Hundreds of armoured cars, trucks, Volkswagens and guns were also lost.

However, Allied fighter-bomber claims during the Mortain counterattack are greatly exaggerated and were often the result of double counting or simply misinterpretation of a target. Between 7 and 10 August the British 2nd Tactical

Commander-in-Chief West Generalfeldmarschall von Rundstedt confers with SS-Standartenführer Kurt Meyer, commander SS-Panzergrenadier Regiment 25. The 12th SS Panzer Division's commander, SS-Brigadeführer Fritz Witt, stands in the centre. After he killed on 14 June 1944 Meyer assumed command. *(via Author)*

Generalfeldmarschall Erwin Rommel, commander Army Group B, wanted the Panzers within striking distance of the coast, this lead to friction with Rundstedt and General von Schweppenburg, commander Panzergruppe West. *(via Author)*

A relaxed looking SS-Obergruppenführer Josef 'Sepp' Dietrich, commander I SS Panzer Corps, which formed part of Panzergruppe West. He succeeded General Heinrich Eberbach as commander Panzergruppe West/5th Panzer Army in early August 1944. *(Author's collection)*

SS-Obersturmführer Michael Wittmann, commander II Kompanie, Schwere SS-Panzer Abteilung 101. His prompt action at Villers-Bocage on 13 June 1944 saved the Panzer Lehr Division from encirclement, prevented the German line from being rolled up and stopped the Allies breaking out to the southwest of Caen. *(via Author)*

Generalleutenant Dietrich von Choltitz replac[e] General Marcks, killed on 12 June, as comman[d] LXXXIV Corps. Rundstedt's verdict of him w[a] 'decent but stupid.' Choltitz's poor handling [of] Panzer Lehr and his corps saw him lose his command and gain the poison chalice of milit[ary] governor of Paris. *(US Army Archives)*

General Walter Krüger, commander LVIII Panzer Corps meeting men of Panzer Lehr. His Corps formed the southern flank of the counterattack near Avranches with elements of Panzer Lehr and the 17th SS in early August 1944. *(ECP Armées)*

General Otto Elfeldt, von Choltitz's successor commander of LXXXIV Corps, was captured Hill 113 on 20 August 1944 by the Polish 1st Armoured division. He had the dubious hon[our] of being the most senior officer taken during [the] fighting to seal the Falaise pocket. *(USAA)*

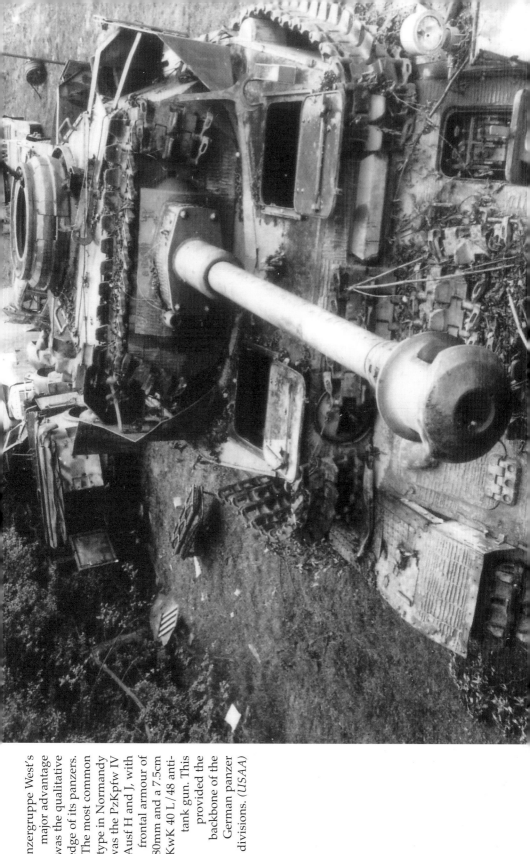

Panzergruppe West's major advantage was the qualitative edge of its panzers. The most common type in Normandy was the PzKpfw IV Ausf H and J, with frontal armour of 80mm and a 7.5cm KwK 40 L/48 anti-tank gun. This provided the backbone of the German panzer divisions. (USAA)

American Military Police escort US P-47 Thunderbolt pilots to examine their handiwork on 19 July 1[...]
The PzKpfw V or Panther represented the pinnacle of German tank production, mounting the powe[...]
7.5cm KwK 42 L/70 gun that could penetrate 120mm of armour at 1,094 yards. The main models
deployed in Normandy were the Ausf A and G. *(USAA)*

French villagers get a closer look at an abandoned Tiger. While the PzKpfw VI Tiger I was a formida[...]
weapon with 100mm frontal armour and 8.8cm KwK L/56 gun, only three battalions were deployed [...]
Normandy. *(USAA)*

Captured teenage SS-panzergrenadiers, the 9th SS, 10th SS and 12th SS deployed youngsters such as these. What they lacked in experience they made up for with fanaticism. *(USAA)*

Another common armoured fighting vehicle with the panzer divisions in Normandy was the Sturmgeschütz or StuG III assault gun armed with the 7.5cm StuK40 L/48. *(USAA)*

The main self-propelled anti-tank weapon was the Marder armed with a 7.5cm PaK 40/3. This particular example lies shattered after an encounter with the American Army. *(USAA)*

The principal self-propelled artillery in Normandy comprised the Wespe, seen here, based on the Panzer II armed with a 10.5cm gun and the Hummel self-propelled 15cm howitzer, mounted on the Panzer IV chassis. (USAA)

French civilians trudge past a knocked out Sdkfz 135 7.5cm Pak 40/1 auf Lorraine Schlepper, proba from Major Alfred Becker's Sturmgeschütz Abteilung 200, 21st Panzer. The Germans deployed a ra of hybrid self-propelled guns based on French tank and ammunition tractor chassis. (USAA)

Dead panzergrenadiers lay strewn by their camouflaged SdKfz 251 armoured personnel carrier, which were used to equip the panzergrenadier regiments. *(USAA)*

By far the best tank [ki]ller was the dedicated [8].8cm Pak 43, the anti-tank version of the 8.8cm Flak 36. These helped take a very heavy toll on British armour during the Goodwood offensive. *(Author's collection)*

Rows of 7.5cm Pak 40 anti-tank guns; the Germans had this weapon in abundance in Normandy. *(USAA)*

The most common Allied tank in Normandy was the American M4 Sherman. Mechanically reliable
was handicapped by thin armour, a gun lacking sufficient punch and a tendency to burn. *(USAA)*

The French *Maquis* played a key role harassing German troop movements and gathering intelligenc
Most notably the 2nd SS fought running battles with them as it moved north to Normandy.
(Author's collection)

The Americans developed tank destroyers based on the Sherman that could penetrate at least 80mm of armour at 1,000 yards, notably the M10 Wolverine armed with a 3-inch gun, though these were not available in sufficient quantities. *(USAA)*

The prelude to D-Day saw the Allied bomber fleets attacking ailways and the bridges over the Seine to prevent reinforcements oving up and to hamper escape. *(USAA)*

While the German armed forces were largely able to ride out Allied air attacks, they greatly underestimated naval gunfire. This hampered the panzers' efforts to counterattack in the Caen area following D-Day. *(USAA)*

Although Canadian armour pushed through to Carpiquet airfield on 8 June 1944 the 12th SS stopped them in their tracks, destroying a total of twenty-seven tanks for the loss of fourteen panzers. (USAA)

The American architects of the southern flank of the Falaise salient: Generals Bradley, Gerow, Eisenhower and Collins. Bradley's decision to halt the US XV Corps at Argentan partly ensured Falaise was a flawed victory. (USAA)

Sturmgeschütz of SS-Panzer Abteilung 17, 17th SS Panzergrenadier Division, got to within 500 yards of Carentan before being stopped by elements of the US 2nd Armored and 101st Airborne Divisions on 13 June 1944. (USAA)

man armour caught in the Roncey pocket – these abandoned Marder self-propelled guns belong to 17th SS Panzergrenadier Division or the 2nd SS Panzer Division. *(USAA)*

erican armour pours into Avranches five days after the launch of Operation Cobra, this opened the for the swing west into Brittany and east toward the Seine. *(USAA)*

Following the Mort[ain] counter-attack XLVI[?] Panzer Corps was n[o] match for the US X[V] Corps' French 2nd Armoured Division, seen massing here, [with] the US 5th Armored Division. *(USAA)*

By 10 August strong American forces including the US 5th Armored Division, seen here, had successfully pivoted from Le Mans northwards, striking toward Alençon, which fell two days later. *(Author's collection)*

Officers and men of the 2nd Panzer Division surrender t[o] the Canadian Army [on] 19 August in St Lambert-sur-Dives. During the bitter two[-] day battle for the village the Germans suffered 300 dead, 5[00] wounded and 2,100 captured. *(USAA)*

roops stream into Argentan on 20 August. Its capture helped seal the fate of those German forces inside the Falaise pocket. *(USAA)*

shattered remains of an army – the end of the road for many Germans in the Falaise pocket.
ing this final battle the Wehrmacht lost approximately 10,000 killed and 50,000 captured, though
claimed 40,000 escaped. *(USAA)*

Eisenhower during his tour of the Falaise pocket examines an overturned Tiger II. He recalled: 'Forty-eight hours after the closing of the gap I was conducted through it on foot, to encounter scenes that could be described only by Dante'. (USAA)

thers and Panzer IVs, now little more than junk gathered in a scrap yard, following Panzergruppe
t's defeat in Normandy. (USAA)

ish troops pour over pontoon and Bailey bridges thrown across the Seine. The Americans first
sed at Mantes-Gassicourt on 19 August, though the German Rouen bridgehead lasted another ten
s and about 240,000 Germans and 135 panzers escaped. (via author)

When von Choltitz capitulated Paris on 25 August there were still 2,000 Germans in the city and fighting continued in the suburbs. *(Author's collection)*

Astoundingly, despite the losses suffered in Normandy, just four months later all the reconstituted panzer divisions were involved in Hitler's major counterstroke. His Ardennes gamble did not pay off as these bodies from SS-Panzergrenadier Regiment 25, 12th SS, testify – this time there would be no miraculous recovery. *(USAA)*

Air Force claimed a total of 140 panzers, whilst the US 9th Air Force bagged another 112. The problem with this is immediately evident: it was more than the Germans actually deployed for Operation Lüttich.

The Allies' operational research teams who scoured the battlefield afterwards only found forty-six panzers and self-propelled guns and only nine of those had clearly been knocked out by air attack. Similarly, another thirty-two combat vehicles had been lost, but only twelve of these had been hit from the air.

By 9 August, Krüger's newly-committed LVIII Panzer Corps had taken over command of the 2nd and 10th SS Panzer Divisions. A penetration on its right wing was eliminated when 2nd Panzer counterattacked west of Le Neufbourg, the division then repelled enemy attacks in the area of Mesnil-Tôve. All this activity had to be carried out in the face of heavy artillery fire and constant fighter-bomber attack.

The 2nd Panzer Division then found itself counterattacked frontally and on its flanks by the American 4th Infantry division. When Le Mesnil-Tôve was recaptured, the 2nd Panzer *kampfgruppe* was cut off around Le Mesnil-Adelée. With its main body annihilated, the division was forced onto the defensive. It was, though, able to repulse successfully all attacks directed against its frontline on 10 August.

Final days

By this date Panzergrenadier Regiment 2 could still muster 820 combat effectives; Panzergrenadier Regiment 304 some 760 men; Panzeraufklarüngs Abetilung 2 some 360 and the Panzer Pioneer Battalion 38 just 280. Lüttwitz found that his division could field about 4,000 troops, twenty-five to thirty still-functioning panzers, 800–900 vehicles and forty guns.

For the attack on Alençon, XLVII Panzer Corps was to assemble the 1st SS, 2nd SS, 2nd and 116th Panzer Divisions in the Forêt d'Ecouves to strike the US 5th Armored and French 2nd Armoured and push on to Mayenne and further southwest. General Eberbach, demoted to command Panzergruppe Eberbach for a renewed effort against the Americans, by the afternoon of 13 August had gathered the remains of 2nd Panzer, 116th Panzer and the 1st SS; but with just seventy panzers they were no match for the US XV Corps' 5th Armored Division and the French 2nd Armoured Division.

The attack had to be abandoned after the enemy thrust through Alençon and reached south of Argentan, and Panzergruppe Eberbach was forced onto the defensive. The 2nd Panzer had not even reached the assembly area when it was given orders to gather east of Carrouges. Losing communication with the 9th Panzer Division, 2nd Panzer, under air attack, moved in two columns, reaching Domfort-Flers on the 13th. Only the reconnaissance battalion reached south of

Carrouges and 300 men from the division were captured. Losing contact with General Eberbach, 2nd Panzer was placed under XLVII Panzer Corps.

The 2nd Panzer and 1st SS were encircled at Falaise, along with elements of the 10th SS. On 17 August the division was ordered to withdraw from the pocket via St Lambert-sur-Dives. The following day, the remaining tanks of Panzer Regiment 3 and men of Panzergrenadier Regiment 2 reached the town in good order. During the fierce fighting in an around St Lambert, some officers and men of the division were forced to surrender to the Canadians. By the end of the month 2nd Panzer had lost up to 7,000 men in Normandy; its role in the war, though, was far from over.

Chapter 9

Tough Resistance –
1st SS Panzer Division *Leibstandarte*
Adolf Hitler

Although the 1st SS Panzer Division was recuperating from the fighting on the Eastern Front in Belgium, it did not enter the fray in Normandy until mid-July. The British, intending to pivot at Rauray and swing over the River Odon, driving southeast in an attempt to isolate Caen, attacked on 25 June. The British VIII Corps managed to secure a bridge near Baron and by 30 June had forced a bridgehead two and a half miles (4km) wide and one mile deep (1.6km). Subsequently, tough resistance was encountered from battle-hardened elements of the 1st SS, 2nd SS and 10th SS Panzer Divisions. Then in early August the 1st SS were switched to the American sector and although escaping the chaos of the German collapse lost all its' panzers.

Combat experience

The 1st SS dated back to 1925, with the creation of the *Schutz Staffel* (SS), Hitler's protection squad, building on the Nazi's short-lived Sturmabteilung (SA) *Stabswache* (Headquarters Guard). In March 1933 Joseph 'Sepp' Dietrich established the *SS-Stabswache Berlin*, consisting of 120 men, and these along with the *SS-Verfügungstruppe* were the forerunners of the Waffen-SS. Initially the unit was based at Berlin's Alexander Barracks but was later moved to Berlin-Lichterfelde.

SS-Stabswache Berlin was re-designated *SS-Sonderkommando Zossen* and, along with the newly-raised *SS-Sonderkommando Jüterbog*, was merged in September 1933 and designated *SS-Leibstandarte* (Bodyguard) *Adolf Hitler* (LAH). The following year it was re-designated *Leibstandarte SS Adolf Hitler* (LSSAH) and grew to regimental strength.

LSSAH took part in the Anschluss with Austria as a part of XVI Corps under General Heinz Guderian and later in the annexation of Czechoslovakia. During the invasion of Poland it served with Army Group South under the leadership of SS-Oberstgruppenführer Sepp Dietrich. It later took part in the invasion of France and the Low Countries, where it was mainly held in reserve, though it was used against the retreating British troops at Dunkirk. LSSAH was attached to XIV Corps during the second and final phase of the invasion of France.

The LSSAH was then upgraded to brigade strength in August 1940 for the planned invasion of Britain (*Unternehmen Seelöwe* or Operation Sealion). When this was called off, LSSAH was transferred to Romania for the attack in the Balkans. It fought its way through Yugoslavia and Greece, chasing the Allied troops to Kalamata, from where they took flight by sea to Crete. Kurt Meyer, commanding *Liebstandarte*'s reconnaissance battalion, captured 11,000 men after attacking the Klussura Pass and the brigade took the surrender of at least sixteen divisions before the Greeks surrendered.

In June 1941 LSSAH expanded to a full motorised infantry division and took part in the invasion of the Soviet Union, Operation Barbarossa, as part of Army Group South and was involved in the fighting at Kiev and Rostov. The division was sent to France for refit in 1942 and upgraded to a panzergrenadier division. Sent back to the Eastern front in 1943 under SS-Brigadeführer Theodor Wisch, it fought at Kharkov and Kursk. After the failure at Kursk, LSSAH was sent to Italy on anti-partisan duty, but it soon was deployed back to the Eastern Front as a panzer division.

In January 1944 the division was involved in the rescue of those troops trapped in the Cherkassy pocket. The tanks of SS-Panzer Regiment 1 cut through four Russian divisions and thanks to its efforts some 32,000 men escaped, but the depleted 1st SS was left with just three panzers and four assault guns. By mid-March the division had less than 1,250 men. LSSAH was one of the divisions encircled near Kamenets-Podolsk and, though rescued by the 9th SS Panzer Division *Frundsberg* and 10th SS Panzer Division *Hohenstaufen*, it suffered heavy losses. The division was then sent to Belgium for rest and refitting in 15th Army's area of responsibility.

On 18 April 1944 the remainder of 1st SS under Wisch was sent by train to northwest France and established its headquarters at Turnhout in Belgium, where it became part of the I SS Panzer Corps. The problems of manpower and equipment were soon addressed. Over 2,000 men from the 12th SS were transferred to the division and in early May Hitler ordered it should get new equipment, much of it straight from the factory floor.

A month later the 1st SS was far from combat ready. The week before D-Day the division stood at 19,618 strong, though many of the new recruits were untrained and 1,081 men, mainly drivers and vital technicians, were still in Germany. Wisch was still awaiting replacement Panzer Mk IVs and Vs and these did not arrive until the weeks following D-Day. Motor transport was lacking, the division only had 1,691 of 3,887 authorised trucks and over a third of those were in maintenance. None of the panzergrenadiers' armoured half-tracks were operational.

The division's SS-Panzer Regiment 1 was commanded by veteran SS-Obersturmbannführer Jochen Peiper, who had made a name for himself in the campaigns fought in Poland, where he had commanded 10 Kompanie of the LSSAH, and in France and Russia. He then commanded III Abteilung of the newly-motorised division's SS-Panzergrenadier Regiment 2.

Peiper fought with distinction during the recapture of Kharkov and at Kursk. In November 1943 he succeeded SS-Obersturmbannführer Schönberger as commander of SS-Panzer Regiment 1. He was later to achieve notoriety for the Malmedy massacre perpetrated by the 1st SS during the German Ardennes offensive in the winter of 1944.

SS-Panzer Regiment 1 mustered forty-two Panzer IVs in its I Abteilung under SS-Sturmbannführer Kling, thirty-eight Panthers in II Abteilung commanded by SS-Hauptsturmführer Pötschke and forty-four StuG IIIs in SS-Sturmbannführer Heimann's SS-Sturmgeschütz Abteilung 1. A further eight Panzer IVs and a StuG were in the workshop. In total the 1st SS was to field 103 Panzer IVs, seventy-two Panthers and forty-five StuG IIIs during the fighting in Normandy. Divisional artillery also included five Hummel and eight Wespe self-propelled guns mounted on Panzer IV and II chassis respectively.

Nazi indecision ensured that the 1st SS were kept away from Normandy for two crucial weeks. Although not combat ready, just two days after the Allied invasion it had been decided to send what units it could to help. Fortunately for the Allies, the Germans changed their minds and the division was not embarked onto its freight trains until 17 June.

Stationed at Enghen, Belgium, on 9 June, expecting an attack across the Pas de Calais, the 1st SS was ordered to move east of Bruges as a safeguard. Five days later the Panther *abteilung* arrived east of Rouen and eight days later other units were unloaded west of Paris, but elements of the division totalling 5,800 men remained in Belgium.

Into action
Equally frustratingly for Rommel, Schweppenburg and the others, only the SS-Panzergrenadier Regiment 1 could be committed belatedly to help resist the British Epsom Operation along National Highway 175. A *kampfgruppe* under SS-Obersturmbannführer Albert Frey from SS-Panzergrenadier Regiment 1 went into action on the 28th. Although the panzergrenadiers arrived in the Caen area it would be another week before other elements arrived. In the meantime

the 12th SS were left to fend off the Epsom offensive, aimed at securing Caen, largely unassisted.

SS-Panzer Regiment 1 had not been brought together by 1 July and the bulk of the division was not in the line before the 9th. By early July, Kling had thirty Panzer IVs, Pötschke twenty-five Panthers and Heimann thirty-one StuGs. The division initially gathered south of Caen between Thury-Harcourt and Bretteville-sur-Laize, then to the north of Potigny between Caen and Falaise and also Bretteville-sur-Laize and Caen. Wisch reported to Sepp Dietrich's I Panzer Corps, which included the battered 12th SS.

From 7 July, for three days, elements of 1st SS fought with the 12th SS to the southwest of Caen to halt Operation Charnwood, the British frontal assault on the northern outskirts. They found themselves up against Major General R F L Keller's Canadian 3rd Division, which struck toward the Odon. The British attack opened with 460 bombers carpet-bombing the city and a regiment from the 16th Luftwaffe Field Division suffered seventy-five per cent casualties. Within two days the Germans had been driven from all of Caen north of the Orne. On 10 July the British tried to barge the Germans out of the way to the west with Operation Jupiter.

Following Charnwood, General von Obstfelder's LXXXVI Corps, which included 21st Panzer, assumed I SS Panzer Corp's responsibility for the whole sector east of Caen. The 1st SS then assumed responsibility for the sector taking over from the exhausted 12th SS. Between 12–17 July the division's HQ was just to the northwest of Bretteville at Fresnay-le-Puceux. On the 15th the British launched Operation Greenline, pinning 2nd Panzer, 9th SS and 10th SS west of Caen and obliging 1 SS to return to the fight to hold the Orne.

In mid-July the 272nd Infantry Division gradually relieved the 1st SS. The former, part of Army Group G's 19th Army, had been ordered to move from the Mediterranean coast on 2 July. After being sent by train to the Le Mans area, the 272nd began to move into defensive positions on the night of 13/14th. By 15 July the Germans had suffered 97,000 casualties, an attrition rate of 2,500 to 3,000 per day. Replacements numbered just 10,000, of whom only 6,000 had reached the front. Tank losses totalled 225, with just seventeen replacements.

Stopping Goodwood

By the 18th, the 1st SS was in reserve at Falaise, way to the south of Caen, when the British launched Operation Goodwood. Just prior to this, the 1st SS between Eterville and Mondeville were directed eastward towards Cagny. Subsequently the 1st SS and 12th SS were redeployed to the south and east of

Caen on a line from Bras-Bourguébus-Frénouville-Emiéville, while 21st Panzer lay between Emiéville and Troarn along with the Tiger tanks of Abteilung 503.

British intelligence underestimated the German defences, which were almost 10 miles (16km) deep, supported by 230 panzers, although other armoured fighting vehicles brought the total for this force to nearly 400. The initial defences, comprising of the 16th Luftwaffe Field Division and 21st Panzer's inadequate assault gun battalion, were unlikely to hold up the British tanks for any length of time, especially once they had been pulverised by the Allied bomber fleets. A lot rested on the panzergrenadiers of Kampfgruppe von Luck, drawn from 21st Panzer.

To the south, the German gun line on the Bourguébus Ridge included seventy-eight 8.8cm guns, 194 field guns, twelve heavy flak guns and 272 Nebelwerfer rocket launchers. In reality, much of this equipment was spread throughout the entire German defensive zones. Most of the 8.8cm anti-aircraft guns belonged to General Pickert's III Flak Corps, which was under strict orders from Panzergruppe West to defend the Caen–Falaise road from air attack. Most of his guns were therefore to the south and east of Bourguébus, with air defence a priority.

The anti-aircraft 8.8cm Flak 36, while it could be used in an anti-tank role, was not much better than the 7.5cm anti-tank gun, which German units had plenty of. In addition, its inability to achieve a first-time kill at long range, and its high silhouette, meant that it was very vulnerable in ground combat. The III Flak Corps had three *flakkampfgruppen* intended to help the ground forces resist enemy tanks; they arrived just in time for Goodwood but were to prove largely useless. They claimed about twenty tank kills for the loss of thirty-five 8.8cm guns and another seventy light Flak guns. This meant that responsibility for holding the ridge rested squarely with the 1st SS and elements of the 21st.

Goodwood opened at 0745 on the 18th and the 1st SS rushed north to join 21st Panzer to halt the British attack on their left flank. About forty-six panzers of I Abteilung, SS-Panzer Regiment 1, were thrown into action against the British in the area of Bourguébus at 1620. Taking up positions on the Bourguébus Ridge, the division inflicted heavy casualties on the British 7th and 11th Armoured Divisions, who received a very nasty surprise with the appearance of the 1st SS.

The British armour had 3,000 yards of open ground to cover before they reached the ridge marked by the villages of Bras, Hubert Folie and Bourguébus itself, all of which were German strongpoints. They got to within a few hundred yards before the Germans opened fire, knocking out four tanks in quick succession, followed by at least another seven to their right. The 3rd Royal Tank Regiment, with 11 Armoured, swiftly lost thirty-four of its fifty-two tanks.

Exhausted by the fighting, the panzers of 1st SS wanted to break off combat on the Bourguébus Ridge, but their request was denied due to the activity of Allied fighter-bombers, presumably on the grounds that if they stayed in close proximity to the British they were at less risk of air attack. Although German losses were high, they achieved the desired effect and the 11th Armoured Division lost 106 of its tanks. West of Cagny, the Guards Armoured Division was also held up, having lost sixty tanks.

On the eastern side of the British corridor General von Obstfelder's LXXXVI corps was able to deploy a number of anti-tank battalions, including elements of Artillerie-Pak Abteilung 1039 and 1053, which between them could muster twenty-seven 8.8cm Pak 43 and sixteen 7.5cm Pak 40. The British lost a total of 200 tanks on that first day of Goodwood. Just as it was getting dark, Panthers and two captured Shermans from the 1st SS counterattacked after the 2nd Northants Yeomanry tried once more to force the ridge.

Now that the Bourguébus Ridge was such a bloody killing ground, when the panzergrenadiers from 1st SS moved up on the night of 18/19 July they must have been fearful that the Allied bombers would repeat the previous day's attack. The British brought up artillery on the 19th to cover the advancing tanks. The Northants Yeomanry, however, veered towards Ifs, to the west of Bras, and were driven back toward Caen. At Bras the 1st SS defenders were not so lucky and were ejected at 1900 with the loss of a dozen self-propelled guns and many dead. By 1740 the entire III Abteilung, SS-Panzergrenadier Regiment 1 had been destroyed in and around Bras. Although I SS Panzer Corps had been prevented from moving west to fight the Americans it had been at great cost.

Heavy rain and the actions of the 1st SS and 21st Panzer Divisions brought Goodwood to a halt on 20 July. The Churchill, Cromwell, Honey and Sherman tanks of the three British armoured divisions suffered extremely heavy casualties in men and equipment. In just two days the British 2nd Army had lost 413 tanks – some thirty-six per cent of its total tank strength.

The 1st SS, 12th SS and 21st Panzer had effectively hemmed in Goodwood. By this point, the 1st SS had gathered seventy Panzer IVs and Panthers west of Bourguébus at Verrières on the far side of the Caen–Falaise road. Also, a *kampfgruppe* from 2nd Panzer and the 272nd Infantry Division were also on the ridge, while the 116th Panzer was in the process of moving up behind the 12th SS. When word of the assassination attempt on Hitler on the 20th filtered through to the SS there was a sense of outrage. SS-Hauptsturmführer Hans Bernhard of the 1st SS summed up their feelings:

> We felt it was treason and a great crime. We knew these people had to
> be enemies of the Reich. Legally this was high treason, which helped

our enemies and not us. The generals were too short sighted. They were willing to lose the war in order to get rid of Hitler. Traitors normally get shot in most countries of the world.

Bernhard was also amused by the visits from neighbouring army generals keen to prove their loyalty and the Nazi party salute was enforced on all. Also on the 20th, the 1st SS launched their counterattack from Verrières against Major General C Foulkes' Canadian 2nd Division, which had been foolish enough to renew the attack on the Bourguébus Ridge under the guise of Operation Atlantic.

The 1st SS remained engaged between the N158 Caen–Falaise and N13 Caen–Lisieux roads and on 25 July took part in the counterattack at Tilly-la-Campagne. The division held the Caen–Falaise highway until the end of the month, by which time it had suffered 1,500 casualties, but, through a combination of new deliveries made in the face of Allied air attack and the maintenance staff pulling out all the stops, 1st SS could field sixty-one Panzer IVs, forty Panthers and twenty-three StuGs. In fact by now all of Peiper's SS-Panzer Regiment 1 had arrived in Normandy, although some artillery, rocket launcher, flak and reconnaissance units remained behind in Belgium.

Final days

The exhausted 1st SS were pulled out of the line on 4 August and replaced by the 89th Infantry Division. The latter was right in the firing line when Operation Totalise was launched on the 7th. The 89th had only been raised in Germany in January and deployed to Norway for training before arriving in France in late June. Sent to Normandy at the end of July it had just been subordinated to Dietrich's I SS Panzer Corps on 3 August. Notably, elements of the division were in the Falaise–Bretteville area and moved into the line supported by thirteen Sturmpanzer IVs from Sturmpanzer Abteilung 217.

The 1st SS was withdrawn from the Caen sector and moved southwest toward Avranches, falling prey to Allied fighter-bombers en route. On the night of 5/6 August, the two tank *abteilungen*, two Panzergrenadier *abteilungen*, one self-propelled *abteilung*, one engineer kompanie and the flak kompanie deployed west to take part in the Mortain counterattack. Allied fighter-bombers helped ensure that the 1st SS Panzer Division's contribution to the Avranches counterattack was stillborn.

The 1st SS Panzer was halted just over a mile (2km) east of Juvigny-le-Terte at about 1300 on 7 August, after RAF Typhoons set about the panzers. It was not until 2200 that the remains of 1st SS, including twenty-five assault guns, were made available to continue the attack. Eberbach's 5th Panzer Army brought forward elements of the 331st Infantry Divisions to relieve pressure on 1st SS. Although the latter unit was a veteran of the Eastern Front, when it had been withdrawn in March 1944 it left behind all its combat-experienced officers and men who were distributed to other local units.

It was not until 28 July that the 331st had been ordered to join Panzergruppe West and it had only arrived on 4 August. A *kampfgruppe* was assigned to General Adolf Kuntzen's LXXXI Corps. The 1st SS were in the process of pulling out so they could renew the attack, when the Americans penetrated their left wing up to Hill 307 northeast of Mortain; those units that had withdrawn were required to seal the penetration. Within three days of the Avranches counterattack being launched it was clear that it was a lost cause and the 1st SS were withdrawn to defensive positions around St Barthelemy.

SS-Panzer Regiment 1 by 12 August was at Carrouges with just thirty panzers, eleven of which were lost during the fighting the following day. On the 13th, Wisch and his men arrived at Argentan on the Orne, southeast of Falaise. One of SS-Sturmgeschütz Abteilung 1's last assault guns was lost in the Orne at Putanges south of Falaise.

On the 16th, the division was forced to fall back and regrouped on the River Dives. The remains of the 1st SS, consisting of a weary *kampfgruppe*, broke out from the Gouffern Forest on the afternoon of 20 August, escaping from the Falaise Pocket via the St Lambert-sur-Dive corridor. Although free by the 22nd, the survivors had no operational panzers or artillery.

Chapter 10

Fighting Withdrawal –
9th SS Panzer Division *Hohenstaufen*

Like so many of the panzer divisions, the 9th SS suffered during its move to Normandy from Allied airstrikes, and did not arrive until 28 June, almost three weeks after the Allied invasion commenced. Fending off British attacks on Caen, the division endured heavy casualties and was pulled back into reserve in mid-July.

Returning to the line, the division fought during the bitter battle for Hill 112 and helped beat off Operation Goodwood. In the face of Operation Totalise, the 9th SS conducted a fighting withdrawal and escaped encirclement in the Falaise pocket, helping to keep the escape route open. Eventually it was withdrawn for a refit near the Dutch city of Arnhem, having lost almost half of its manpower.

Combat experience

Under the direction of SS-Obergruppenführer Wilhelm 'Willi' Bittrich, 9th SS Panzer Division *Hohenstaufen* was mainly formed from conscripts, many of them from the *Reichsarbeitsdienst* (RAD or Reich Labour Service), in February 1943. Bittrich, an able tank commander, controlled the *Deutschland* Regiment during the fighting in Poland and France in 1939–40; he then assumed control of the 2nd SS Panzer Division *Das Reich* for just three months in late 1941.

Before the 9th SS had finished its training, it was placed under Sepp Dietrich's I SS Panzer Corps, along with the remains of the 1st SS and the newly-raised 12th SS Panzergrenadier Division. However, in early 1944, along with the 10th SS, Panzer Lehr and the 349th Infantry Divisions, it became part of the II Panzer Corps under Paul Hausser. At the end of March 1944 the Red Army had surrounded the 1st Panzer Army and II Panzer Corps had been despatched to rescue it.

The 9th SS first saw action at Tarnopol in early 1944, where it took part in rescuing German troops from the Kamenets–Podolskiy pocket. On 9 April it successfully fought its way through to the 6th Panzer Division at Buczacz. Placed into reserve with Army Group North Ukraine, the 9th SS was refitting at Kovel when the Allies landed in Normandy. Hitler immediately ordered the division to join Panzergruppe West. Under Bittrich it was sent to Normandy on 12 June, though it was to have a series of commanders during the Normandy campaign. At the end of June it came under SS-Oberführer Thomas Müller.

SS-Obersturmbannführer Otto Meyer (not to be confused with Kurt Meyer of the 12th SS) commanded SS-Panzer Regiment 9. At the beginning of June the regiment mustered forty-eight Panzer IVs, seven of which were in repair and forty StuG III assault guns. The Panther *abteilung* was at Mailly-le-Camp undergoing training, which was hampered by the slow rate of new tank deliveries. Its full complement of seventy-nine tanks was not received until mid to late June. In addition, the division left SS-Panzerjager Abteilung 9 behind, which meant it had no tank destroyers and had to make do with towed anti-tank guns. However, the artillery regiment was equipped with twelve Wespe and six Hummel self-propelled guns for mobile artillery fire support.

As part of Paul Hausser's II SS Panzer Corps, the 9th SS moved to Normandy with its sister division, the 10th SS *Frundsberg*. It took them longer to reach Caen from the French border than it had taken to make the journey from Poland to France. All German reinforcements from the east were delayed by virtue of having to pass through the Chartres gap between the Seine and the Loire, this being vulnerable to air attack and French sabotage.

The division reached the French border on 16 June, but it was another four days before the lead elements were unloaded from their railway carriages between Paris and Nancy. It then deployed south of Aunay-sur-Odon with a total of 18,000 men, 170 panzers, twenty-one self-propelled guns, 287 armoured half-tracks, sixteen armoured cars and 3,670 trucks. This was a formidable array of hardware and the division knew how to employ it to best effect. Initially the 9th SS was deployed south of a line that ran from Falaise to Condé-sur-Noireau, but it then moved north between Caen and Villers-Bocage on a line between Tournay-sur-Odon and Neuilly-le-Malherbe.

Containing Epsom

Although the British VIII Corps' Epsom offensive toward Evrecy south of Caen in late June, against the 12th SS Panzer Division, was a tactical failure, the Orne was crossed, Hill 112 taken and a deep salient driven into the German defences west of Caen. The II SS Panzer Corps was ordered to strike the corridor created by the 15th (Scottish) Division from the southwest. The 9th SS was to attack towards le Valtru and the Cheux bottleneck supported by 2nd SS and Panzer Lehr, while the 10th SS would assault the Odon bridgehead and Hill 112. Elements of the 1st SS, 12th SS and 21st Panzer Divisions were also to be involved in attacking the other flank of the exposed corridor.

At a critical moment before this counterattack the Germans were forced to conduct one of their habitual command reshuffles. Willi Bittrich suddenly found himself directing II Panzer Corps after Hausser succeeded General Dollmann as commander of 7th Army when he dropped dead on 28 June of a suspected heart attack; though his Chief of General Staff, General Max Pemsel, suspected he may have poisoned himself. The senior regimental commander, SS-Standartenführer Thomas Müller, briefly took command of the 9th SS. To make matters worse, Rundstedt and Rommel were en route to see Hitler. On his own, Hausser, with II SS Panzer Corps, organised the counterattack using the 9th SS.

The western flank of the British corridor was the weakest point and the ridge that rose out past Rauray to Cheux offered a sheltered approach for the massing panzers. The division's SS-Panzergrenadier Regiments 20 and 19 were to be supported by I and II Abteilung of SS-Panzer Regiment 9 respectively. Unfortunately SS-Panzergrenadier Regiment 20, sheltering in the woods north of Noyers prior to attacking Cheux, was caught by the RAF.

Late in the afternoon of the 29th, III Abteilung, equipped with armoured half-tracks of SS-Panzergrenadier Regiment 20, had assembled for the attack together with Panther tanks from the panzer regiment. Preparing for action, it was not entrenched beneath the trees when about 100 Lancaster bombers struck. A huge pall of dust covered the area and it seemed certain that the battalion had been blown to smithereens; however, only about twenty men were killed and by the evening eighty per cent of the armoured vehicles, having been dug out, were operational again. The bombing also caught the panzer battalion but it pressed on to its assembly area.

The counterattack was scheduled for 29 June at 0700 with the 9th SS on the left of the Odon, but the attacks by the RAF delayed the preparations until 1430. In an additional stroke of bad luck, an officer from 9th SS with the plans for the coming attack was out early, reconnoitring the routes to Cheux, when he was captured.

The first group of SS captured Grainville-sur-Odon and the second group also reached Cheux, but everywhere else the British and Canadians held fast. Several flame-throwing tanks also assisted with the assault on Le Valtru, but although the panzers overran the British infantry, the latter held firm.

The 9th SS, who were used to the weak Russian air force and uncoordinated Russian artillery fire, found the resilience and firepower of the British forces something of a shock. The attack ground to a halt under a deluge of Allied air strikes, artillery and naval gunfire. Elsewhere, in the face of Allied firepower, the 10th SS got as far as Esquay and Gavrus on the southern edge of the corridor. The rest of the division was strung out along the road through Villers-Bocage.

Walter Harzer, then 1a (or Chief Operations Staff Officer) of the 9th SS, observed:

> As it was, our counter-offensive broke down under air attack and artillery fire, particularly the heavy guns of the battleships. They were devastating. When one of those shells dropped near a Panther, the 56-ton tank was blown over on its side, just from the blast. It was these broadsides from the warships, more than the defensive fighting of the enemy's troops, which halted our division's Panzer Regiment.

During the fighting against the Epsom salient the 9th SS suffered 1,145 casualties and lost sixteen Panzer IVs, six Panthers and ten StuG IIIs. Over the next few days the division's StuGs accounted for forty-nine enemy tanks, while its Panzer IVs and Panthers claimed another thirteen.

In July, SS-Brigadeführer Sylvester Stadler took command of the 9th SS, having previously commanded Panzergrenadier Regiment *Der Führer* of the 2nd SS Panzer Division. It was units of this regiment, under SS-Sturmbannführer Otto Diekmann, which conducted the massacre at Oradour-sur-Glane during the division's march northward to Normandy. Stadler was an experienced Eastern Front veteran, having gained the Knight's Cross for his part in the capture of Kharkov in 1943. He had then gained the Oak Leaves after his involvement in the massive Battle of Kursk. Thomas Müller, who had been acting commander of the 9th SS, subsequently assumed command of the 17th SS Panzergrenadier Division for a brief period in September, after SS-Oberführer Eduard Deisenhofer was wounded.

According to most sources Stadler replaced Müller on the 10th, however they may have been a handover period. Stadler recalls:

> My assumption of command of the Division was accomplished by 0800 on 3rd July 1944. During the preceding night, the last elements of SS-Panzergrenadier Regiment 19 had been pulled out of the main line of resistance (MLR) north of Esquay and replaced by the 10th SS Panzer Division. The combat units of the Division were assembled in the area of Maizet–Vacognes–Montigny – Division Command Post at Le Mesnil – so that they could be used as tactical reserves of the II SS Panzer Corps right behind the MLR and, if necessary, launch counterattacks.
>
> For this purpose, the Division was to investigate the possibilities of commitment in the sectors of the 10th SS Panzer Division and the

277th Infantry Division, determine routes of approach, and move the Artillery Regiment into such a position that it could support counterattacks in any direction and at any time.

Battle for Hill 112

Stadler quickly found his division being thrown into action and recalled the details of the battle at some length:

> Within one hour after the Division had been taken over, orders for a counterattack on Maltot, Eterville and on Baron by way of Hill 112, were received from the Corps by telephone, and a short time later confirmed in writing. So the attack on Baron was to be launched at 2000 and that on Eterville at 1200. Although the time was very short, the execution of this task was still possible thanks to the fact that the SS-Panzergrenadier Regiment 20 was not too far away and that a tank *abteilung*, together with the artillery, could support the operation from the positions they were in at the time. The units just mentioned received their orders accordingly by telephone and, after hasty assembly into position, were able to launch the counterattack at about 1300. Around Maltot a vigorous battle developed, in which reorganized elements of the 12th SS Panzer Division, which had been forced back early that morning from Eterville and Maltot – participated, on our side.
>
> At about 1500, Maltot was again in our hands. The enemy answered with increased air activity and concentrated very strong artillery fire on Maltot. In these circumstances, it was out of the question to continue the counterattack on Eterville by daylight, in spite of the support given by the entire Corps Artillery, which, however, consisted only of a few sudden concentrations. Therefore the Division ordered an attack on Baron to be launched at 2000, together with other elements. In the meantime, the Command Post (CP) had been transferred to the group of farmhouses, one kilometre northwest of Grimbosq. The advanced Division CP was located in the thicket one kilometre northwest of Bully [east of Esquay and Maltot].

Things did not run smoothly as the Allies did all they could to impede the massing of the 9th SS; in addition, its position was compromised by the loss of Hill 112. The latter was to become the scene of heavy casualties for both sides. Stadler discovered flexibility was an increasing prerequisite of such operations:

Concentration of the Division was greatly impeded and delayed by serious traffic jams on roads, harassing fire from the enemy artillery directed on villages along the routes of advance, and on road junctions, as well as by the strong enemy air activity. In addition to that, the enemy managed at about 1800 to capture height 112, which dominated the entire Corps sector. Thereupon the mission assigned to the Division was altered by the Corps, to the effect that only height 112, and later Eterville, had to be recaptured.

Having changed the combat plan accordingly, the counterattack was now launched at about 2100, (line of departure time). In spite of the extremely strong enemy artillery fire, our forces advanced toward Eterville and those operating in the area between Eterville and height 112, made good progress. Eterville was recaptured toward 0100. However, it was impossible to get near height 112 because of the concentrated artillery fire maintained for hours by all the enemy's heavy weapons. It was not until daybreak that the wooded strip of land – in other words, the southern edge of the plateau on this height could be taken. Thus the gap torn open in the MLR on the preceding day had been closed again and the mission assigned to the Division accomplished. Height 112 was no longer defended in the same way as before, i.e. on the northern edge of the plateau; the Division ordered the construction of a new MLR in the southern part of the plateau, near the northern edge of the wooded strip of land, continuing toward the west, a line which was not visible to the enemy.

The British quickly contested the 9th SS successes at Eterville and Hill 112 on the 4th, giving the division no respite from the bloodletting. The panzers managed to knock out a number of British tanks, for little loss, but the panzer-grenadiers suffered from the enemy's artillery. Stadler recalled, perhaps with some pride:

In the course of the forenoon the enemy, in turn, resumed his attacks and managed to take Eterville once again, whereas his attacks on height 112 were repelled with considerable losses. A counterattack launched immediately on Eterville succeeded and, by noon, the village was again in our hands. An extremely heavy and fluctuating battle ensued afterwards for the ruins of Eterville, which place changed hands repeatedly until, finally, it was firmly in our possession late in the evening of 4 July 1944. The losses suffered during these engagements in the rocky terrain offering almost no cover, were considerable (Grenadiers about 10%), and mainly caused, of course, by the excessively strong artillery fire, which could be countered by next to nothing from our side, since only some 700 rounds of ammunition were available for the entire attack on 4 July. Nevertheless, the panzer Abteilung operating near Eterville managed to destroy twelve–fourteen enemy vehicles, whereas they lost only two tanks. Thus, it could be figured out that the enemy losses were at least as high as ours.

During the night of 4/5 July the division was relieved on the eastern sector by elements of the 12th SS and on the western sector by the 10th SS. The divisional forces were reassembled in almost the same area as on 3 July. They were assigned the task of constructing prepared positions in the rear in the line along the course of a stream and along the heights south of it, and occupying the line with weak forces.

The Panzer Pioneer Abteilung was put in charge of the construction of this position, assisted by an *abteilung* from each of the SS-Panzergrenadier Regiments. The Artillery Regiment was then ordered to move into position to provide covering fire for the entire Corps sector. In the meantime the rest of the division was instructed to refit and rest up as best they could.

The British renewed their attacks on 6 July this time along the road running from Caen to Noyers. To help the 277th Infantry Division recapture Noyers, the 9th SS despatched its armoured reconnaissance battalion. The latter successfully retook the town and remained supporting the 277th.

The panzers' regimental HQ was established at Bully, about two and a half miles (4km) east of Point 112, between Caen and Evrecy, on 12 July. When the British attacked between Gavrus and Noyers-Bocage four days later, the division's tanks were undergoing maintenance. However, the 227th was ordered to counterattack, supported by the 9th SS. About twenty panzers were mustered to the right of Point 113 north of Evrecy, but the British put down smoke and they were forced to withdraw. While Point 113 remained unoccupied, the panzers took Bougy and reached Gavrus, moving up the Orne valley. During the various engagements they knocked out a total of forty tanks, including eighteen around Bougy and eight at Point 113, for the loss of just five panzers. Sylvester Stadler recalled the battle:

A serious crisis occurred only once on the occasion of a concentrated attack carried out by British armoured troops with some forty to fifty tanks late in the evening of 16 or 17 July 1944, on Height 113. All day, the enemy had pounded the hill with undiminished intensity and covered it with a smokescreen. Sometimes, the smoke was so dense that the majority of the troops felt sick and therefore believed that the enemy was using gas. An immediate investigation proved that this was incorrect. Besides the physical discomfort caused by this heavy smoke, the visibility was very bad, the result of which was that the troops became rather nervous and overstrained, as it was impossible to see what was going on ahead of the positions. With the duration of the smoke-shell firing, the situation naturally grew worse and worse. On the occasion concerned, the firing was maintained all day.

Stadler remembered the sudden British armed assault which came late in the day and threatened to overwhelm his men. The 9th SS though were quick witted and swiftly turned the tables on their attackers as their commander noted:

At about 2100, enemy forces all of a sudden appeared with tanks in the MLR and managed to break through on a width of 400–500 meters just east of Height 113. The Grenadiers committed on that part of the front (about fifty to sixty men) were all taken prisoner. Our own tanks, a battalion of about fifteen to twenty tanks, were located on the rear slope of the hill and noticed the enemy only at the very last moment, either on account of the dense smoke, or perhaps owing to the swift and surprising advance of his forces. During the ensuing tank battle, fifteen enemy tanks were destroyed with no losses at all on our side. Thereupon, the enemy quickly withdrew to his original position. At the same time, a smaller group advanced along the lane from Gavrus to Evrecy under cover of smoke, and darkness, which in the meantime had fallen. They managed to break through the forward elements, but then, also, ran right into our tanks on the rear slope, which overwhelmed them after a very short fire duel, or took them prisoner (two tanks and about twenty men).

By the 17th, the exhausted division could muster thirteen Panzer IVs, twenty-five Panthers and fifteen assault guns, while the infantry amounted to little more than a regiment. The 9th SS was called back from the left flank of the 10th SS at the height of the Goodwood battle and positioned in the Orne valley, guarding the southern suburbs of Caen. Over the next few days the 9th SS helped the 1st SS defeat Montgomery's Goodwood armoured offensive. Notably, on 18 July the division captured sixty-seven tanks, fifty-six of which were destroyed, the rest still running.

The 10th SS and the 272nd Infantry Division were instructed to retake St Martin, St André and May-sur-Orne east of the river and south of Caen on the 22nd, with support from the 9th SS. However, the Panthers of the 9th SS were still engaged around Bougy and could only be freed up slowly. Some were assigned to two companies of the 10th SS while the rest were to attack south of May. Few of the Panthers materialised except for those directed to take the high ground northeast of May.

Two of the division's Panthers led forward a panzergrenadier battalion. They surprised the British but, lacking armoured reinforcements, the infantry had to attack May-sur-Orne unsupported. The rest of the panzer battalion did not arrive until about midday and ran into heavy anti-tank gunfire. Three were caught broadside on and knocked out and the order was given to withdraw under a smoke screen. By the end of the day, nine of the division's twenty-four Panthers were out of action, but the key villages were secured. The division remained stalled north of Fontenay at Point 88.

Mont Pinçon

As Operation Spring got under way against the 1st SS on 25 July, the 9th SS was also hit hard by Canadian troops. When the enemy made a new large-scale attack in the sector of the 272nd Infantry Division and managed to achieve a deep penetration, the 9th SS launched a concentrated counterattack east of the Orne, which was successful and prevented a breakthrough by the Canadians. By the evening of the 25th, the 9th SS was able to muster eighteen Panzer IVs, eighteen Panthers and eleven assault guns; but, with their maintenance teams working full out, three days later the total stood at twenty-two Panzer IVs, twenty Panthers and twenty-two assault guns.

To restore the line, the division's panzer regiment and 102 SS Battalion's Tigers rolled forward on the 28th, inflicting heavy losses on the attacking tanks and stopping the Canadians in their tracks. At the end of July, General Eberbach, convinced that the British were attempting a big breakthrough, deployed the 9th SS into the woods west of Bretteville-sur-Laize and the 10th SS to Bretteville.

On 30 July, Montgomery launched Operation Bluecoat southwards towards Vire and Mont Pinçon, with the battered 7th, 11th and Guards Armoured Divisions in the lead. II SS Panzer Corps was now diverted to block this move that punched a hole in the thinly-held sector of the German line. By the 31st, the 9th SS had lost thirteen Panzer IVs, twenty Panthers, fourteen StuG IIIs, four armoured half-tracks, fifty-two trucks and six prime movers.

The 9th SS remained southwest of Caen until early August, when it moved northeast of Vire. British tanks got to within five miles (8km) of the town, the very heart of 7th Army's resistance against the Americans. Wanting to counterattack against the Americans, who were considered inferior fighters, the Germans first had to secure Mont Pinçon against the British to control the network of roads westwards. The division was relieved by 1st SS on 1 August and that night a *kampfgruppe* under Otto Meyer, including seventeen panzers and assault guns, moved west to take up positions on a line from Arclais to Montchauvet and Montchamp, to the west of Mont Pinçon and between Villers-Bocage and Vire. RAF Typhoons soon located the SS tank columns in the afternoon of the 2nd, launching 923 sorties, destroying thirteen tanks and seventy-six trucks, and holding up the deployment of the German panzers for most of the day.

The advance guard of the 9th SS Panzer *kampfgruppe* managed to engage the 11th Armoured Division near le Beny-Bocage on the afternoon of the 2nd, knocking out five Cromwells in the process. They fought furiously to regain the Périers Ridge and the bridge over the Souleuvre. The following day, the 9th SS successfully drove the British from Plesles, but the 11th Armoured Division countered their efforts at Périers.

The 9th then held the 15th (Scottish) Division with dug-in tanks, 8.8cm guns and Nebelwerfer rocket launchers. Those troops at Montchauvet were embroiled in heavy fighting round Point 170 and, although surrounded, managed to escape. On the 4 August, the 9th SS attempted to cut off the British breakthrough at Chênedollé, knocking out thirty-nine Allied tanks in the process. Otto Meyer, near Estry with thirty-two panzers and assault guns, had to block the road northwest of Chênedollé and went over to the defensive. From 11–12 August the division claimed another twenty-two enemy tanks in the unrelenting fighting.

Final days

The division was redeployed on the 13th to the Putanges area, where they were vulnerable. They then moved to the Vimoutiers area, having lost up to 5,000 casualties. The 12th SS commandeered some of their remaining tanks, but, along with the 2nd SS, the tired division attacked from outside the Falaise pocket to help some of those trapped escape.

Chapter 11

Point 112 –
10th SS Panzer Division *Frundsberg*

The 10th SS Panzer Division Frundsberg was formed in the winter of 1942–43 in southern France, initially as the 10th Panzergrenadier Division. It then moved north, but was sent to the Eastern Front the following year. In mid-June it was ordered back to France and went into action against the British VIII Corps bridgehead over the Odon on the 29th, along with the 9th SS. The following day they captured Hill 112, beating off a series of British counterattacks. Deployed between Domfront and Mortain, by 12 August the division, with just eight tanks left, was forced to withdraw toward the Falaise salient.

Combat experience

Under the command of SS-Standartenführer Michael Lippert, the 10th SS, like the 9th SS, was raised from conscripts drawn from the Reich Labour Service, or *Reichsarbeitsdienst*, in February 1943. Like the 12th SS, they were just teenagers; according to Reichsführer Heinrich Himmler, the average age of the recruits was eighteen years old. The division was redesignated the 10th SS Panzer Division on 3 October 1943 and named after Georg von Frundsberg (1473–1528), who had served the Hapsburg Monarchy during its many wars.

Subsequently, led by SS-Gruppenführer Karl Fischer von Treuenfeld, the division first saw action at Tarnopol in April 1944, where it took part in rescuing German troops from the Kamenets–Podolskiy pocket. In mid-June, Hitler cancelled a proposed offensive near Kowel and from his Rastenburg HQ ordered the division to be switched to the West, to help bolster the situation in Normandy. Under SS-Gruppenführer Heinz Harmel it was sent to France on 12 June, along with the 9th SS, to fight the Allied landings.

SS-Panzer Regiment 10's II Abteilung was loaded onto six trains in Russia and headed west from Sokol and Krystinowpol. It took five days to reach the assembly point at Saarbrücken. The first train reached Houdan, southwest of Paris on the 18th and the tanks took to the road, rumbling through Dreux, Châteauneuf, Digny and le Magne to Longy, where they dallied until the 25th.

SS-Obergruppenführer Paul Hausser, commander of II SS Panzer Corps, presented himself to Rommel on 23 June to inform him that the 10th SS had arrived in Northern France. By the following day most of the division, with an official strength of about 14,800 men, had reached the assembly area in Normandy, though fuel was a problem. These units consisted of SS-Panzer-aufklärungs Abteilung 10, SS-Panzer Regiment 10, SS-Panzerjäger Abteilung 10, SS-Panzergrenadier Regiments 21 and 22, SS-Artillerie Regiment 10, SS-Flak Abteilung 10, SS-Pionier Bataillon 10 and SS-Feldersatz Bataillon 10.

Harmel's command had the dubious accolade of being the weakest panzer division in Normandy. SS-Panzer Regiment 10, under SS-Obersturmbannführer Otto Paetsch, was only able to field a single tank battalion. The latter, under SS-Sturmbannführer Reinhold, which had come west, consisted of thirty-nine Panzer IVs, thirty-eight StuG IIIs and three Panzer III command vehicles, providing a tank force of just eighty panzers. Other divisional armoured fighting vehicles consisted of SS-Artillerie Regiment 10's six Hummel and eleven Wespe self-propelled guns. It seems it may have also had some Grille 15cm self-propelled guns.

The 10th SS suffered the same problem as the 9th SS, whose Panther battalion was still being worked up at Mailly-le-Camp. Both divisions experienced problems with tank deliveries. Although SS-Panzer Regiment 10's I Abteilung was already at Mailly-le-Camp, it only had training vehicles available and was unable to join its parent unit until 1945. Therefore, this battalion was not destined to see action in Normandy. The ten Panthers it did receive had to be handed over to Panzer Lehr and, by 1 August, I Abteilung had been assigned to Panzer Brigade 10, which out of an authorised strength of seventy-three Panthers only had seven. Similarly, the division's Panzerjäger *abteilung* was still forming and did not receive any Jagdpanzer IV tank destroyers until the end of August.

Containing Epsom

On the night of 25/26 June, just as the British were renewing their efforts, II SS Panzer Corps HQ and the 10th SS were instructed to move to the St Remy–Rousamps–La Bigne–St Symphorien–Les Buttes–Campeaux–Vire–Tinchebray area. The 10th SS was soon thrown into action against the British 2nd Army's Operation Epsom; enduring heavy fighting around the strategic Hill 112. Epsom launched on the 25/26th was a preventative strike to help tie down the newly-arrived II SS Panzer Corps west of Caen and stop it moving to the American sector.

Montgomery's intention was to push south over the Caen–Bayeux road on to the Fosse de l'Odon, before turning southeast to Bretteville-sur-Laize, 10 miles

(16km) south of Caen. On the 29th, the 9th SS, now formally assigned to II SS Panzer Corps, deployed facing Hill 112 along the Odon River, between von Funck's XLVII Panzer Corps and Sepp Dietrich's I SS Panzer Corps. Harmel's forces were deployed between Caen and Villers-Bocage.

The British XXX Corps had, by the 30th, reached Rauray and Tessel, but in the face of determined resistance from 2nd SS could not maintain its momentum and failed to reach the Odon. In contrast, VIII Corps forced its way over the river, creating a narrow bridgehead between Gavrus to the west and Baron to the east.

In countering Epsom, the 10th SS attacked the Gavrus bridgehead on the flank of the British 11th Armoured Division on Hill 112. The usual problem, shortages of fuel, greatly limited the number of panzers the division could initially throw at the British. Paetsch's and Reinhold's tanks and assault guns were committed to the fighting on the 29th, along with the 9th SS, when they attacked along the Odon. The two assault gun companies supporting SS-Panzergrenadier Regiment 22 took Gavrus, but could not reach Baron-sur-Odon. Near Evrecy the panzers took Point 113 and the division claimed twenty-eight enemy tanks for the loss of just two Panzer IVs.

Flanking fire from Avenay and St Martin hampered the push to Hill 112 and Esquay-Notre-Dame, that night the panzers and panzergrenadiers crossed the Guigne River between Avenay and Vieux, which enabled them to climb the southern slopes of Hill 112. The 12th SS attacked Hill 112 from the east and by midday on the 30th were on the summit. Hill 113 was attacked at the same time. During the period 30 June–1 July, elements of the 10th SS lost 571 casualties resisting Epsom and the division suffered badly from air strikes on 1 July, three miles (5km) south of Villers-Bocage.

Battle for Hill 112

On 3 July, the British counterattacked and the tanks of the 10th SS were moved up the hill. On the 10th the British, under the guise of Operation Jupiter, tried to wrest back control of the high ground around Hill 112. Major General G I Thomas' 43rd (Wessex) Division, consisting of the 129th, 130th and 214th brigades, were to attack positions held by the 10th SS, which were supported by Tiger tanks from Schwere SS-Abteilung 101, in what was to prove an extremely fierce battle.

The German defenders survived naval bombardment, air attack and artillery fire. The British then launched frontal attacks on Hill 112 and the village of Maltot on its northern slope, against the SS panzer troops, supported by dug-in and concealed Tiger tanks, holding an almost impregnable position. The British made some initial progress before being driven back by Tigers from the II SS Panzer Corps' heavy tank battalion, Schwere SS-Panzer Abteilung 102.

At the moment that it appeared twenty-five Churchill tanks were going to take the summit of Hill 112, I Abteilung arrived from its reserve position and knocked out almost all of them. In particular, the concealed Panzer IVs of the V Kompanie were confronted by twenty-five British tanks and were forced to attack a section at a time to avoid the Allied fighter-bombers. The British advance came to a halt to return fire, knocking out two panzers and killing two platoon leaders, SS-Hauptscharführer Borrekott and SS-Oberscharführer Leven. In the meantime, the remaining Panzer IVs and the StuGs advanced between Hills 112 and 113, catching the Allied spearhead in the flank, but the British had already reached the top.

The British attack on Maltot did not go well either, as the Tigers on Hill 112 opened up on the the British left flank, while the 12th SS Panzer Division's Panzer IVs and Panthers were to the attackers' front and elements of the 1st SS *kampfgruppe* were on the right. The British threw in a further attack and took the summit once again, but at nightfall the British tanks withdrew, leaving the infantry unsupported, to be thrown back yet again by a German counterattack undercover of darkness.

The 43rd Division alone lost more than 2,000 men in the first thirty-six hours of Operation Jupiter and it was reported that the Odon River was dammed with corpses. On 15 July the British launched Operation Greenline, holding the division west of Caen. When the 9th SS was withdrawn into reserve on the 15th, the 10th SS were left to cover the entire sector, and were driven off part of Hill 113, just north of Evrecy, by Major General G H A MacMillan's 15th (Scottish) Division.

Despite the commitment of Tiger tanks and the return of the 9th SS, the Scots held on to their gains, though the SS remained in possession of the lunar surface of Hill 112 until finally relieved by the 271st Infantry Division. The 10th SS, having now lost well over 2,200 men since the beginning of July, was withdrawn for a brief period of rest. The division had also lost a quantity of self-propelled guns and anti-tank weapons, including four Grille self-propelled guns, eight 7.5cm Leichtes Infanteriegeschütz 18s, six 7.5cm anti-tank guns and eighteen 8cm mortars as well as nearly a hundred machineguns.

In the face of such determined SS resistance, British casualties during 10–22 July amounted to approximately 25,000 men and 500 tanks. In particular, the 43rd Wessex suffered a total of 7,000 casualties. By the end of the month the 10th SS had lost seven Panzer IVs and three StuG IIIs, plus 168 other vehicles.

The 10th SS continued to fight southwest of Caen. In early August they halted the British 43rd Division, which, attacking from Dois du Homme, had driven 21st Panzer from Jurques and seized Hill 301. They also drove the British 7th Armoured Division almost back to Breuil.

On 1 August a *kampfgruppe* under Otto Paetsch headed for Aunay-sur-Odon about 18 miles (29km) southwest of Caen. The next day the *kampfgruppe* – with seven Panzer IVs and eighteen Panthers – entered the fray and successfully held most of Hill 188, claiming responsibility for destroying twenty British tanks. The remainder of the division arrived on the 3rd, threw back the British units that had established a foothold on Hill 188, and took nearby Hill 301 to form a defence line between the two high points.

This and other SS attacks brought British tank losses since the start of Operation Bluecoat on 30 July to a massive 200 vehicles. Bittrich's tired troops kept pressing forward until the battle reached a climax on 6 August. The 10th SS were switched from Aunay-sur-Odon to attack the British positions on the Périers ridge. They were then ordered to disengage, and on 6 August the division was committed to an attack on British units north of Chênedollé. They seized two prominent high points, Hills 242 and 224, only to be driven back by shellfire and air attacks. Having brought Bluecoat to a halt, Bittrich established a strong defensive line around Vire.

Mortain counterattack

For the German counterattack on Avranches on the American front, Field Marshal von Kluge had instructed that the 10th SS be available by 5 August in the Vassy area. However, 5th Panzer Army could not comply due to the tactical situation with II SS Panzer Corps. Army Group B informed 7th Army that 10th SS and 12th SS were to be brought up on 8 August under the direction of General Walter Krüger's LVIII Panzer Corps. The latter had only just assumed control of the sector southwest of Caen from Bittrich's II SS Panzer Corps.

Moving toward Mortain, Harmel's 10th SS became the Corps reserve for General von Funck's XLVII Panzer Corps. The division deployed to the Beauchene area, east of Mortain, to relieve elements of the 275th Infantry Division. During the night of 8/9 August the 10th SS found its extended frontline compromised when the enemy penetrated both sides of Barenton.

The SS launched a counterattack on the 9th along the road from Barenton to Ger, reaching the hill two and a half miles (4km) northeast of Barenton. The 10th SS was then committed to recapture Barenton, although they could only muster twelve panzers. Elements had to be committed to action near Barenton almost immediately, however, to block constantly probing American attacks.

The 10th SS launched their counterattack against the American penetration north of Barenton on 10 August and made some ground, although they could not reach the town. Heavy losses soon forced the division over to the defensive. Instead of being committed to the renewed Avranches/Mortain counter-offensive, the division was pushed eastwards, via Domfront and Frementel, as the Germans pulled back to defend Argentan.

Final days

By the 14th the division was in danger of being encircled and Domfort had fallen to the Americans. Its fighting strength stood at just 4,136 men. In stark contrast to all the British tanks it had accounted for, the division had only lost twelve Panzer IV and eight Sturmgeschütz since arriving in Normandy. SS-Brigadeführer Harmel mustered eight Panzer IVs and some panzergrenadiers in the hills to the north of Domfort and, with the assistance of the 2nd SS and 17th SS, prepared to attack the American forces.

They drove them back but this localised victory meant nothing. During the night, the remains of the division withdrew east on St-Bomer-les-Forges and then north of Argentan. Harmel and his men now faced the gauntlet of the Trun–Chambois bottleneck. Elements of the 10th SS, along with the 1st SS and 2nd Panzer, were trapped in the Falaise pocket.

Chapter 12

The Road to St Lô –
2nd SS Panzer Division *Das Reich*

The 2nd SS Panzer division arrived in southwest France in the spring of 1944 and was stationed near Toulouse; when the time came the French resistance harried it as it moved north toward Normandy. Das Reich fought both the British and Americans round Caen and St Lô respectively. It successfully recaptured Mortain during Operation Lüttich but had to withdraw. Then, along with the 9th SS, it was instrumental in helping large numbers of German troops escape from the Falaise pocket.

Combat experience

Formed in October 1939 from the *Deutschland*, *Germania* and *Der Führer* Regiments, the SS-VT-Division *Reich* was placed under the command of SS-Oberstgruppenführer Paul Hausser. It was involved in the campaign in the West in 1940 and after guarding the border with Vichy France was transferred to the Netherlands. The division then took part in the campaign in the Balkans, where a small detachment led by SS-Hauptsturmführer Klingenberg managed to get the Mayor of Belgrade to surrender the city without a fight.

Still under the command of Hausser, the unit took part in the invasion of the USSR and fought on the frontlines until August 1941, when it was withdrawn for refitting. It was sent back to the front in September and a few months later, now commanded by SS-Obergruppenführer Wilhelm Bittrich, it took part in the failed offensive against Moscow.

The division was sent to France in March 1942, with the exception of a small *kampfgruppe*, where it was upgraded to become SS-Panzergrenadier Division *Das Reich*. It was sent back to the Eastern Front in January 1943, where, under the leadership of SS-Obergruppenführer George Keppler, it took part in the capture and recapture of Kharkov, as well as fighting at Kursk.

In April 1944, under SS-Gruppenführer Heinz Lammerding, some 2,500 men from *Das Reich* were transferred back to France to the Bordeaux area, this time to be upgraded to a full panzer division designated 2nd SS. Lammerding had served as an infantry officer and was involved in anti-partisan operations on the Eastern Front. The subsequent actions of his division during its march through France may be partly attributed to Lammerding's experiences in the East.

In late 1943 he took command of those 2nd SS units on anti-partisan duties and assumed full command of the division on 25 January 1944. There were whisperings that he had been over promoted. It has been argued that he owed his appointment to his relationship with SS-Reichsführer Heinrich Himmler, indeed it was felt that Lammerding's position had more to do with his political allegiance to the Nazi Party rather than any real military aptitude.

Based around Montauban, one of the division's first priorities was to absorb about 9,000 new recruits as well as replenishing its vehicle stocks. The division took receipt of fifty-five Panzer IVs and thirty-seven Panthers toward a compliment of sixty-two of each, to supplement the existing thirty Sturmgeschütz, on 16 May. General Heinz Guderian arrived for an inspection tour and watched their exercises, particularly night movements. Lammerding and his men had already been warned that they would not enjoy the same level of freedom of movement that they had experienced in Russia, where the Russian air force was little more than a nuisance.

SS-Obersturmbannführer Christian Tychsen commanded the division's SS-Panzer Regiment 2. By the beginning of June he had fifty-four Panzer IVs, of which ten were in the workshops, thirty-nine Panthers and forty-one Sturmgeschütz III. Further deliveries of armour meant that the 2nd SS was to field a total of eighty-three Panzer IVs, eighty Panthers and forty-five StuG IIIs during the fighting in Normandy. Divisional self-propelled artillery consisted of five Hummels and six Wespe, along with the usual towed artillery batteries.

The SS-Panzergrenadier regiments also had 249 armoured personnel carriers, of which fourteen were undergoing maintenance. Despite this impressive inventory, spares and ammunition were a major problem for Lammerding, especially parts for the motor transport. The division had less than half the required number of trucks and out of the 1,821 it did have only 617 were operational. It was obvious that the division would have problems getting anywhere in a hurry. In May, SS-Obersturmführer Fritz Langanke was ordered to survey the local railways to assess their suitability for moving the panzer regiment.

While Lammerding grappled with getting his division up to strength and carrying out its training, in the run up to D-Day the French *Maquis* or Resistance, began to make its presence increasingly felt. By June Colonel René Vaujour claimed to have 5,000 men under his command. Three months earlier he had ordered his men, in the event of an Allied invasion, to cover the bridges over the Dordogne in south Corrèze and northern Lot. Vajour correctly assessed that the 2nd SS would move north to reinforce a German counter-offensive and it would fall to him and his men to obstruct it. The British SAS were also to conduct Operation Bulbasket with the same goal.

Lammerding's response to the Resistance was to treat them as a partisan army, with predictably brutal results. Throughout May the division conducted anti-resistance operations with units visiting Montpezat-de-Quercy, St Céré and Bagnac, Cardaillac and Lauze. This culminated on 2 June, when, following a *Maquis* attack, the village of Terrou was burned along with twenty-nine surrounding farms. When the SS discovered a resistance arms dump at Ggeac, a thousand townspeople were arrested and deported.

On 7 June, just a day after the start of the Allied landings in Normandy, Lammerding received the order to be ready to march. The 2nd SS, though, remained distracted by its own war against the local irregular French fighters. The following day some units were sent to the Limoges–Tulle area to conduct anti-partisan operations. The division was assigned to Army Group B on the 11th and the following day ordered to move to Normandy. Five days later, elements had reached the town of Mortain.

Troubled march north

Lacking equipment and with deficient training, the division's progress was not good. By 10 June Lammerding found his command scattered across the Lot, Corrèze and Haute-Vienne with broken-down panzers and StuGs stretching from Tulle to Montauban. Frustratingly for Lammerding and his men, the actions of the French *Maquis* ensured that what should have been a three-day journey for the 2nd SS took a fortnight.

On the 10th the situation boiled over at Oradour-sur-Glane, 12 miles (19km) northwest of Limoges. The male villagers were herded into the church and the village torched; in the mayhem 646 people were killed by members of Panzer-grenadier Regiment *Der Führer* under Sturmbannführer Otto Diekmann (he was killed in action on 30 June). The actions of the 2nd SS at Oradour-sur-Glane, and elsewhere during the march north, have been hotly debated ever since. What is clear is that the division acted heavy-handedly and the distraction of fighting the French Resistance was time consuming and clearly a tactical error.

Lammerding signalled General der Panzertruppen Walter Krüger's LVIII Reserve Panzer Corps in Toulouse with his catalogue of woes; he was under-standably annoyed that his panzer division was wasting its valuable time fighting the *Maquis*, which was a role that should be handled by the local security divisions. Large areas were under the Resistance's control, leaving local German forces surrounded and cut off.

On top of the *Maquis* problem, only forty per cent of Lammerding's panzers were serviceable and seventy per cent of his half-tacks and prime movers. Repeated calls for spare parts had fallen on deaf ears, which meant broken down vehicles could not be moved and therefore required infantry to guard them. Six depots had to be set up for the waifs and strays and efforts to commandeer local civilian vehicles produced few results.

In response, General Johannes Blaskowitz's Army Group G, also headquartered in Toulouse, requested OKW provide troops to replace the 2nd SS once it had left Corrèze and Dordogne. A *kampfgruppe* from the 11th Panzer Division, comprising two infantry *abteilungen*, an artillery *abteilung* and an anti-tank company, was assembled with instructions to contact the 2nd SS in Tulle. These forces arrived on the 11th and the 2nd SS rolled north to Limoges.

By this stage the division had suffered seventeen dead and thirty wounded, the *Maquis* fighting an uneven struggle had lost 500 killed and 1,500 prisoners. The French figures included civilian executions. On the 12th, von Blaskowitz finally took personal control of the anti-partisan operations and requested that OKW formally declare the southwest a battle zone. The French Resistance found itself at war with Army Group G.

On 13 June the *Der Führer* Regiment and the reconnaissance battalion crossed the Loire at Saumar and Tours, where the bridges remained standing. Due to the lack of transport, by the end of June some units remained stranded in the south of France and it was not until late July that the last elements began heading north. Only 11,195 men from 2nd SS's total manpower of 17,283 had reached Normandy by 1 July.

Arriving in Normandy, SS-Sturmbannführer Otto Weidinger, who had replaced Sylvester Stadler as commander of *Der Führer* three days after crossing the Loire, expected to take part in a major counterattack to drive the Allies back into the channel. Instead, his men were directed to plug a gap in the line beside Panzer Lehr. Fritz Bayerlein was amused when he heard they wanted to take the offensive remarking, 'It will be a miracle if we can stand where we are'.

Into action

During June, Kampfgruppe Weidinger, consisting of elements of Panzer-grenadier Regiments 3 and 4 along with the 9th SS, resisted the British Epsom offensive. Then, during July, elements fought in the American sector. Kampfgruppe Weidinger came under von Choltitz's LXXXIV Corps on 5 July, when it was tactically attached to the 353rd Infantry Division for the defence of La Haye Du Puits and Monte Castre.

They launched a counterattack against the Americans on the afternoon of the 7th, striking the American 79th Infantry Division on the recently-won Montgardon Ridge south of La Haye du Puits. The Germans inflicted 2,000 casualties, but American tanks, tank destroyers and artillery claimed three panzers and the attack died out. Such was the 79th's mauling that it had to be withdrawn to be refitted.

Holding a line Les Landes–Lemonderie, the V and VII Kompanies were attacked by the US 83rd infantry Division on 7–8 July. The US 9th and 30th Infantry Divisions pushed on Lé Desert after crossing the Vire–Taute canal. In the meantime the US 3rd Amored Division attacked northwest of St Lô. On the 9th, elements from the 2nd SS then ran into the 30th Infantry Division's right flank near Lé Desert. The SS, though, were driven back by American artillery fire.

However, The VII Kompanie caught a company of the US 743rd Tank Battalion pursing two Panzer IVs on the 9th near Lé Desert. The surprised American tanks reeled back with the loss of twelve Shermans. By the close of the 10th, the 2nd SS had claimed ninety-eight enemy tanks in the space of just eight days. On the 13th the division knocked out another thirty American tanks.

The SS *panzertruppen*'s morale was high, but the Americans' limitless resources dismayed them. The 2nd SS, like all the other panzer divisions in Normandy, was plagued by ammunition and fuel shortages. Due to the lack of supplies, by 11 July the 2nd SS had lost twenty-two tanks, seven guns and seven lorries.

On 8 July, SS-Unterscharführer Ernst Barkmann, commanding Panthers of SS-Panzer Regiment 2's IV Kompanie, knocked out his first Sherman and on the 12th claimed two more. The next day, American tanks hidden amongst the Normandy hedgerows almost surprised him. He recalled:

> First came a clattering noise; then, from behind the hedge, the rounded hull of a Sherman heaved into view ... and behind it, five more. The first *panzergranate* [armour piecing round] hit the leading tank in the hull. Smoke appeared from its open turret hatch. The other Shermans had come to a halt. A second round from the Panther knocked off one of the leading tank's tracks. The hedge behind which it had sought shelter had a hole in it as large as a man. The damaged Sherman was returning fire ... a third round hit its turret. The four tanks that were left opened fire with their machine guns which merely tore jagged holes in the Panther's Zimmerit [an anti-mine coating]. One of them was unwise enough to show its side.

A fourth round went right through it. Three of the crew got out, searching for a fold in the ground as they ran.

Although the Americans moved anti-tank guns behind Barkmann's Kompanie, he surprised them in a wood using high explosive rounds and his bow machine-gun. An anti-tank shell skidded off his turret and he hit the gun with his second shot. The Americans struck his turret again and a fire broke out. Although he and his crew were forced to bail out, they later got the tank back to the repair company. Throughout the 14th, Barkmann and his Panthers were heavily engaged against the Americans rescuing surrounded tanks and captured wounded.

Cobra strikes

By late July the 2nd SS was the only significant formation rated suitable for offensive operations within 7th Army. It had thirty-seven Panzer IVs, forty-one Panthers and twenty-five StuG assault guns available for combat. It was tasked with stopping the Americans seizing the main coastal road that led to Avranches, the best north–south route in the Cotentin Peninsula. At the time of Cobra the 2nd SS were supported by two 10.5cm artillery companies from Artillery Regiment 275, formally part of the infantry division of the same number.

On the 26th, the 2nd SS rushed to fill the gap left by Bayerlein's decimated Panzer Lehr Division, having deployed its panzer regiment to the St Aubin-du-Perron area south of the Périers–St Lô road the previous day. Some of those tanks south of Périers were sent southeast to Marigny. Two companies from 2nd SS counterattacked elements of the US 3rd Armored Division on the outskirts of the town that afternoon.

Barkmann's Panther, caught in the open, was attacked by four fighter-bombers and caught fire. Working through the night, his men had the tank up and running by the morning. At the village of le Lorey, north of the St Lô–Coutances road, they were confronted by comrades fleeing American Shermans driving from St Lô, where SS-Panzer Regiment 2 was supposed to be deployed. Barkmann decided to try and halt elements of the US 3rd Armored Division trundling down the Coutances road on the 27th, at the junction of the Lorey road and the N172 between Coutances and St Lô.

When the Americans drove into view, Barkmann's gun-layer, Poggendorf, opened fire at 200 metres. The Americans tried desperately to back off but soon the road was a twisted mess of smashed jeeps and half-tracks. Although the roar of the gun, the clang of the spent shell case and the hum of the ventilator sucking out the noxious cordite fumes deafened his crew, he kept a constant lookout. Two Sherman tanks advancing to the left of the road were dealt with, though not before his Panther took two shuddering hits to its armour. The Americans then called in fighter-bombers to shift the stubborn Barkmann, which damaged his tank's running wheels. Again, two more Shermans trying to outflank him found their guns had no effect and paid the price.

Halting 3rd Armored, he destroyed up to nine Sherman tanks, but his tank was damaged and had lost a track. Miraculously, although his driver was wounded, they managed to withdraw to Neufborg. Despite holding up the Americans the end result was still the same. Left behind by the rest of the division, Barkmann's Panther, with two others in tow, reached Coutances on 28 July, only to find the Americans already in the city. Two days later he had lost all three panzers and he and the crews made their way back to their own lines on foot.

Meanwhile, panzers of SS-Obersturmfüher Schlomka's II Kompanie, previously deployed east of Carentan, were instructed to hold the Americans west of Périers on the 27th. Following a briefing by SS-Obersturmbannführer Christian Tychsen, Fritz Langanke and his platoon moved into position to be greeted by heavy artillery fire. Langanke's tank then got stuck in a ditch and had to be towed out. The American advance, though, was brought to a brief halt and at nightfall the panzers withdrew. II Kompanie were then ordered to block the St Lô–Coutances road on the 28th. The ever present fighter-bombers did all they could to hamper the 2nd SS, as Langanke witnessed:

> As soon as we turned onto it, in the direction of St Lô, we were engulfed in the heaviest fighter-bomber activity I experienced during the war. The only thing similar occurred during the breakout from the encirclement at Falaise/Trun. The light coloured ribbon of concrete of this road was littered, as far as we could see toward Coutances, by wrecks of vehicles and other military equipment. Some of it was burning, smoking, entangled, or just abandoned. Here and there we saw dead or wounded soldiers. Once our small unit had been spotted driving on the road, fighter-bombers dove on us from all sides, dropping bombs and firing onboard weapons. To catch our breath, we pulled off the road to the right for a while into an orchard. That did not help very much as that area was being hammered as badly.

Like all German tank crews, they faced the dilemma of bailing out or staying inside their tanks, either option could be equally risky. In this instance Langanke's panzer drove on; passing a knocked out Panther, he observed:

> As far as we could see along the road, there were German and American vehicles of various types, cars, trucks, half-tracks, tanks, some of them burning and entangled. In between, German and American ambulances were driving back and forth, flying Red Cross flags, recovering dead and wounded who were strewn on the road or still in their vehicles.

There was a pause before the American armour opened fire amidst the chaos and Langanke's panzer beat a hasty retreat and took up an ambush position. That evening, Schlomka appeared and guided them back to the regiment in the Coutances area. On the night of 29/30 July elements of the 2nd SS, including Langanke, battered their way out of the Coutances pocket, allowing troops from a number of divisions to escape.

SS-Obersturmführer Otto Baum, assuming command of both the 2nd SS and the 17th SS Panzergrenadier Division, with his Corps commander's permission withdrew his troops towards Brehal, southwest of Coutances, to avoid the westward-moving American Army. This, however, was countermanded by General Hausser, 7th Army's commander, who ordered them towards Percy to the southeast.

Roncey Pocket

A major battle ensued at the crossroads southwest of Notre-Dame-de-Cenilly as the 2nd SS attempted to force a passage toward Percy on the 28th. One column of thirty panzers and 2,500 men, led by a Hummel 15cm self-propelled gun named *Clausewitz*, became trapped after the lead vehicle was knocked out. In the subsequent firefight the American 2nd Armored Division devastated most of this column. At La Pompe about fifteen Panzer IVs from 2nd SS and 200 paratroops successfully forced the Americans to fall back, but they could get no further.

Unable to get through, the bulk of the 2nd SS and 17th SS were trapped around Roncey, west of La Pompe. American fighter-bombers caught 122 tanks, 259 other vehicles and eleven pieces of artillery in the Roncey pocket on the 29th, reaping a cruel harvest of tangled metal. The 2nd SS Panzer's Panzerjäger Abteilung 2 lost some of its self-propelled guns, most notably a Panzerjäger 38(t) abandoned in the shattered streets of Roncey.

About 1,000 survivors and almost a hundred vehicles, including several dozen armoured vehicles, which escaped the Roncey pocket broke through at St Denis-le-Gast to the south. By dawn the town was back in American hands and the Germans had suffered 754 casualties and lost a further seven panzers and eighteen other vehicles. Only a battalion of Mark IVs from 2nd SS and elements of 17th SS managed to escape the chaos. Near La Baleine, to the southeast of St Denis, RAF Typhoons again caught those trying to flee, knocking out nine panzers, eight armoured vehicles and another twenty vehicles, leaving dead Germans strewn everywhere.

Christian Tychsen, SS-Panzer Regiment 2's commander, was killed at the crossroads near Cambry, southwest of Roncey, on 28 July, when the vehicle he was travelling in bumped into an American patrol. Rudolf Enseling, commander of I Abteilung succeeded him. Two days later the Americans reached Granville, about 11 miles (18km) northwest of Avranches, where Barkmann's Panther had retreated to. He and his crew abandoned their tank the following day.

To the south, the assault guns of Sturmgeschütz Brigade 341 were thrown into the fight to try and stop the US 4th and 6th Armored Divisions breaking out into Brittany and capturing the key Breton ports. This was one of only nine non-divisional panzer or Sturmgeschütz units to be involved in the Normandy campaign. Combined, these forces could theoretically field 363 tanks and assault guns, but they were committed piecemeal. Brittany was the responsibility of General der Artillerie Wilhelm Fahrmbacher's XXV Corps, comprised of entirely-infantry formations.

Brigade 341 had only been formed in late 1943 and by May of the following year was deployed near Narbonne in southern France. At the time of the invasion it was still incomplete and did not receive its full complement of thirty-three StuG IIIs and twelve Sturmhaubitze 42 (the latter were armed with a 10.5cm howitzer, rather than the regular 7.5cm anti-tank gun) until early July. By late June Sturmgeschütz Brigade 341 was still attached to General Wiese's 19th Army in southern France. It did not depart for Normandy until 25 July, just as Operation Cobra was commencing.

Two batteries saw combat against the Americans six days later, between Avranches and Brécey to the northeast, while the third battery remained in the Rennes area. Other elements of the brigade were caught up in the fighting in the Pontorson–St Malo–Dinan area along the north Breton coast, and in the Nantes area.

In the face of two American armored divisions, the fate of this inexperienced brigade was perhaps predictable: within the first few days the first battery lost twelve of its fourteen assault guns and by 1 August both batteries were largely destroyed. That day the US 4th Armored reached Rennes and by 5 August had pressed on south to Redon, where, three days earlier, elements of Brigade 341 had still been sitting on five railcars.

The Americans arrived at the well-defended Breton ports of Brest and Lorient on 6 and 7 August respectively. German forces in Brest would hold out until mid-September, while the garrisons in Lorient and St Nazaire did not surrender until the end of the war. This mattered little as by August Le Havre and Antwerp had much greater allure for the Allies.

Mortain counterattack

In order to close the gaping gap between the Vire and Avranches, Hitler fool-hardily decided to counterattack, a move that would force the panzers further into the noose. For the attack on Avranches on 6 August, the 2nd SS, with just twenty to twenty-five tanks, was to capture Mortain and the hills to the west. Elements of Panzer Lehr's reconnaissance battalion were assigned to the 2nd SS to screen their southern flank. It proved highly successful in its mission, though groups of Americans remained cut off in their rear.

Lammerding's men swept into Mortain, brushing aside elements of the American 30th Infantry Division by 0230, and attacked the high ground to the west. However, an American infantry battalion holding Hill 317 blocked further progress by 2nd SS toward Avranches. They could have bypassed it but would have been exposed to American fire from the hill.

General Hausser visited the 2nd SS command post at 1000 on the 8th and told them the attack would be renewed after the XLVII Panzer Corps had received additional tanks promised by Hitler. The 9th Panzer Division was to be diverted to Mayenne to seal up a breakthrough in the LXXXI Corps' front line. At 1400 the 2nd SS counterattacked the northern flank of the American 35th Infantry Division, which had moved south of Mortain between the 30th Infantry and the 2nd Armored at Barenton.

The Americans then broke through north of Mortain in 1st SS Panzer Division's area, threatening the northern flank of 2nd SS and the division came under heavy artillery fire. American Shermans were soon also pushing up from Barenton. The failure of Hitler's ill-advised Avranches/Mortain counterattack sealed the fate of Dietrich's Panzergruppe West (5th Panzer Army), Panzer-gruppe Eberbach and Hausser's 7th Army.

At 1800 on 10 August the 2nd SS came under the control of Krüger's LVIII Reserve Panzer Corps, having previously been under the operational direction of General von Funck's XLVII Panzer Corps. The division was then pulled back to the main line of resistance just to the east of Mortain.

Elements of the division were involved in heavy fighting and on 11 August alone destroyed nineteen American tanks. Despite all this fierce action, the division still had well over 13,000 men and was far from destroyed. Success-fully withdrawing east, the 2nd SS did not end up in the Falaise pocket and counterattacked against the advancing Allies to help some of those trapped to escape.

Final days

Tanks of the Polish 1st Armoured Division had taken up position on Points 262 and 239, at the foot of Mont Ormel, which dominates Chambois and St Lambert-sur-Dives on the 19th and were shelling the exit route from the congested Falaise salient. The following day, a number of 2nd SS Panzer IVs and Panthers stormed up Hill 239 from where they shelled Hill 262, knocking out five Polish tanks and gaining valuable time for the lucky survivors who were still streaming eastward.

When it was clear that all was lost, the 2nd SS made for the Seine. During the campaign the division claimed over 200 enemy tanks for a combat loss of seventy-five panzers, with another thirty abandoned around Falaise for the want of fuel and spare parts.

Chapter 13

Stabilising the Line –
116th Panzer Division *Windhund*

The 116th Panzer Division came into being in the spring of 1944, drawing on a cadre of battle-hardened panzergrenadiers from the worn out 16th Panzergrenadier Division and a fresh unit, the 179th Reserve Panzer Division. This was not to be a happy marriage and the division suffered severe teething problems. The 116th did not go into combat until 30 July and by 12 August had just twelve panzers remaining. It took part in the last gasp of Panzergruppe Eberbach, trying to hold open the southern lip of the Falaise pocket; however, the division managed to escape Falaise without too many personnel losses.

Combat experience

Initially the 16th Infantry Division had been split to create the 16th Panzer Division and the 16th Motorized Infantry Division in November 1940. The latter, nicknamed *Windhund* or Greyhound, fought in the Balkans and then on the Eastern Front with Army Group South in the Caucasus. In November 1942 the 16th Infantry was re-designated the 16th Panzergrenadier Division under General der Panzertruppen Gerhard Graf von Schwerin. The new unit incorporated the former's 60th Infantry Regiment and I Abteilung, Artillery Regiment 146; the infantry were drawn from the Rhineland–Westphalia region and this was to have a bearing on the division's involvement in Normandy. The 16th Panzergrenadier Division was committed to operations on the southern sector of the Eastern Front through November 1942 to March 1944.

In early 1944 the commander of Panzer Abteilung 116, Major Tebbe, visited the Reserve Panzer Abteilung 1 in France with a view to incorporating this unit to boost the 16th Panzergrenadier Division to panzer division status. The events on the Eastern Front derailed these plans. In February 1944 the Russians broke through on the bend of the Dneiper north of Nikopol and the exhausted 16th lost most of its motorised vehicles. Although awarded the Swords to his Knight's Cross, Schwerin initially refused them because the division was unfairly blamed for the collapse of the German line. When the division moved west some units were left behind with the 24th Panzer and 15th and 258th Infantry Divisions.

Particular ill feeling was caused when a regimental combat group was ordered to stay with the 24th.

Its move west and reorganisation as a panzer division (it adopted the number 116th to avoid confusion with the existing 16th Panzer) may in part have been due to von Schwerin writing to Hitler on 29 June 1943. He requested that, in light of the destruction wrought by the Allied strategic bombing campaign on their homeland, the division be given the opportunity to confront the Anglo–American forces. 'We have to settle the score with the English and the Americans in a special way', said Schwerin. The following month Schwerin wrote to Hitler's staff, again saying: 'We will take great pleasure in soundly beating the hell out of those fellows in everyway we can, according to the rules of warfare'.

General Schweppenburg's Panzergruppe West began to oversee the re-constitution of the division and the supply of new tanks and other vehicles. In late April 1944, 7,500 men arrived northwest of Paris from the Eastern Front. Boosted by 3,000 men from the 179th Reserve Panzer Division, plus other troops, the 116th soon stood at 13,500. However, there was no way the 1 May combat-ready deadline could be met and this was pushed back to 20 June.

The 179th Reserve Panzer Division, whose units included Reserve Panzer Abteilung 1, Reserve Panzerjäger Abteilung 9 and Reserve Panzergrenadier Regiment 81, were incorporated into the new units of the 116th. Its recruits must have looked on in awe at the battle-hardened former members of the 16th Panzergrenadiers, some of whom had survived almost a year and a half of fighting in Russia.

Initially, Panzer Division Nr. 179 under General Walter von Boltenstern, along with Nr. 178 and Nr. 155, had been formed in April 1943 in France, but was re-designated the 179th Reserve Panzer Division three months later. Boltenstern's main claim to fame was that he had commanded the 29th Motorised Infantry Division earmarked for the invasion of Britain in 1940, which was subsequently lost under Hans-Georg Leyser at Stalingrad in 1943.

While the the 179th helped create the 116th Panzer Division and the 155th supplemented the battered 9th Panzer Division, the Nr. 178 commanded by General Friedrich-Wilhelm Löper was also in France during May to August 1944, presumably providing replacements for the other panzer divisions caught up in the fighting.

The only other available reserve panzer divisions were the 273rd, stationed in France and the 233rd in Denmark. In May 1944 the men of the 273rd were sent to join the 11th Panzer Division in the south of France with Chevallerie's 1st Army and the 10th Panzergrenadier Division refitting in Germany after fighting on the Eastern Front.

The 116th came under the tactical control of Army Group B and Rommel on 29 April, though training and organisation remained the responsibility of Panzergruppe West. Confusingly, logistical support was provided by the I SS Panzer Corps, 15th Army and OB West; while immediate tactical control was assigned to General der Panzertruppen Hans von Funck's XLVII Panzer Corps in late May. The latter also eventually had responsibility for 2nd Panzer, as well as the 276th and 326th Infantry Divisions.

General von Schwerin's command was moved southeast of Rouen during 13–15 May, exhausting its available fuel supplies and leading to a request to Army Group B and Panzergruppe West for help. By 1 June the division was almost at full strength, but its combat training school for squad and platoon leaders did not start until 14 June and the first course was not completed until 25 July.

Equipped with Panzer IVs, Reserve Panzer Abteilung 1 was transferred over, though some of the artillery regiment were trained separately in Pomerania. Staff from Panzer Regiment 69 were also incorporated into Panzer Regiment 116, which, confusingly, was re-designated Panzer Regiment 16.

Initially, the division was provided with the Panther *abteilung* from the *Grossdeutschland* Panzergrenadier Division, while its own Panther battalion was still at Grafenwöhr in Germany. On 20 February Panzer Abteilung 116 was ordered to Grafenwöhr for refitting, where it was supposedly to be re-equipped with new Panthers. In the event, the *Grossdeutschland* battalion was ordered back to the Eastern Front before the 116th was directed to Normandy. An alternative Panther unit was then, ironically, provided by the 24th Panzer Division, although by the end of June this *abteilung* was not up and running either.

When the division did head for Normandy it had eighty-six Panzer IVs and seventy-six Panthers, while Panzerjäger Battalion 228 belatedly received twenty-one Jagdpanzer IVs in July. The division also had a range of other armoured fighting vehicles, including three Panzer IVs with the short-barrelled 7.5cm main gun, eight Panzer IIIs, six StuG IIIs and six self-propelled guns in early June. The Panzerjäger Battalion only had twelve anti-tank guns lacking prime movers, plus the six assault guns and six tank destroyers on loan from the 179th.

Like so many of the German armoured divisions in France, the 116th had the usual transport shortages. It was supposed to have 1,688 trucks but by 1 June only had two thirds of that number with some 1,065 vehicles and 163 armoured personnel carriers. Many of the trucks it did have were old and lacked spares. By 1 July the truck situation had not greatly improved though it could muster 252 armoured personnel carriers and its manpower stood a 14,358.

Just two days before D-day von Schwerin and his staff travelled to Army Group B's HQ at La Roche Guyon. There they learned from Rommel's Chief of Staff, General Hans Speidel, that an invasion was anticipated either side of the Somme and that in the event of this the 116th would thrust toward Dieppe. Eight days later, on 12 June, Rommel turned up at Schwerin's command post at Perriers and ordered him to move toward the coast behind the 348th and 245th Infantry Divisions to protect the Somme, even though the division formed General von Salmuth's 15th Army reserve.

Into action

Although the division was put on alert on 5 June, permission to commit the 116th was not granted until 19 July when 15th Army's last panzer division was ordered to march on Caen. The only remaining free panzer units were the 9th and 11th Panzer Divisions still in the south of France. When the 116th Panzer Division moved to Normandy it had to laboriously cross the Seine by ferries as all the bridges were down.

The 116th traversed the river on 20 July and four days later the II Abteilung Panzer Regiment 16, Panzerjäger Abteilung 228, Panzergrenadier Regiments 60 and 156 and the reconnaissance unit, Panzeraufklärungs Abteilung 16, were gathering in the assembly areas. When they took stock, just sixty-three tanks and twenty-five assault guns were combat ready. Last to arrive was I Abteilung Panzer Regiment 24 and the situation greatly improved, rising to 121 tanks.

Four days later the division moved into position behind Panzergruppe West. Graf von Schwerin and his men found themselves assigned the sector behind SS-Obergruppenführer Sepp Dietrich's I SS Panzer Corps southeast of Caen, supporting his 1st SS and 12th SS Panzer Divisions. The opening of American breakout efforts west of St Lô on the 25th drew the division onto the left flank of 2nd Panzer, deploying in the Vire area three days later. Despite being considered highly combat ready and having seen little action, available tank numbers had plummeted to just sixty-two. This may have been in part due to the loss of the Panthers of Panzer Regiment 24, which were allocated to the 2nd Panzer Division for the coming Mortain counterattack.

Someone had to take the blame for failing to hold Cobra, so General von Choltitz, commander of LXXXIV Corps, took the fall. General Elfeldt, his successor, was promised the 116th Panzer Division and recalled:

> It was on the 28th July, so far as I remember, that orders came to me to go at once to Field Marshal von Kluge's headquarters. On arrival he told me that I was to take over command of the LXXXIV Corps

from General von Choltitz. He said he did not agree with the defence policy of the latter, but did not say in what respect. The Corps, he told me, comprised the remnants of seven divisions. He also said that the 116th Panzer Division was to counterattack westward to relieve the pressure, and would be under my command. After spending the night with the Field Marshal I drove in the morning to Le Mans and on to tactical headquarters of the 7th Army, which was then 10 to 15kms [six to nine miles] east of Avranches. From there I was directed to my own Corps headquarters. I do not remember exactly where it was, as it was hidden in the trees, away from any village. Everything was confused, and the Allied air force dominated the area. The following day I went round my troops. They were very weak and there was no continuous front. Some of the divisions had only about 300 infantry left, and the artillery was much depleted.

The first order I gave was that all the troops south of the River La See, near Avranches, were to defend the south bank, while the troops from the east were to hang on where they were until the 116th Panzer Division arrived that night; they were then to join in its counterattack. But the 116th did not arrive, as it was diverted to another danger point while on the way.

Alerted to the movements of 2nd Panzer on 27 July, the Americans moved the 30th Infantry Division and 2nd Armored Division to Tessy-sur-Vire and Percy. The 2nd Armored, colliding with 2nd Panzer outside Tessy-sur-Vire, were unaware of the threat from the 116th Panzer.

Fully in position by the 29th, the 116th's first task was to help the 2nd SS trapped east of Coutances and then swing northwest of Villebaudon. This did not happen, though the 2nd SS managed to reach the 116th's left flank near Percy. Instead, von Funck ordered the 116th and 2nd Panzer to strike across the Vire while Panzer Lehr held the Americans at Percy. However, General Eugen Meindl, commander of the II Parachute Corps, was not happy about von Funck's plans. He wanted a limited attack to deny Percy to the enemy; otherwise his flank would be exposed. Meindl complained to General Hausser, commander of 7th Army, but it did him no good.

Schwerin's division had it within its grasp to retrieve the situation. He visited Meindl's command post south of Percy, only to be directed to Funck, who informed him 2nd Panzer had come to a halt. Next he pitched up at General Bayerlein's HQ and found Panzer Lehr desperately clinging on at Percy.

Bayerlein warned him that the ground to the east was not suitable for an armoured counterattack; the best place was to the north, striking due west.

Schwerin set his command post up near Courson and at this point von Funck turned up, saying 2nd Panzer needed help. This meant the 116th would have to attack south and not west.

On the morning of the 30th, the 116th pushed the Americans aside at Beaucoudray, north of Percy on the Bréhal–Tessy-sur-Vire road; but, as Bayerlein had predicted, the going was not good and Schwerin's panzers were confined to the roads and this resulted in traffic jams. They were ideal targets for air attack.

Sure enough, then came the swarms of Allied fighter-bombers and Schwerin called a halt to his ill-fated attack and waited for 2nd Panzer to withdraw east over the Vire. It was to cost him his command. He planned to resume the attack the following day, but pressure on 2nd Panzer caused Schwerin to abandon his plans. The bulk of the division was now forced onto the defensive.

Elfeldt recalled that despite the Americans rapid progress, all thoughts turned to counterattack rather than an orderly withdrawal:

> On the morning of the 31st American tanks dove towards Brescy [Brécey], on the River See, 10 miles (15kms) east of Avranches. At that moment my headquarters was north of Brescy, and was nearly cut off by this flank thrust. My headquarters personnel were in the fighting line all day. Luckily the Americans were not very vigorous in their thrust here.
>
> In the next two days I was reinforced by two new divisions which were nearly up to strength, as well as by the 116th Panzer Division. I formed the remnants of the other seven divisions into a single one. My orders were to stop a further break-through between Brescy and Vire, and to delay the expected American thrust south-eastwards from Avranches, as a powerful counter-thrust was to be made by a panzer corps, under General von Funk. This was subsequently reinforced, to provide a counter-stroke of bigger scale, by all the tanks that could be made available from Eberbach's 5th Panzer Army.

Elfeldt's task was a tall order in light of the inadequacies of his forces. Kampfgruppe Lueder, which had been placed at the disposal of Elfeldt's LXXXIV Corps was surrounded between Villedieu and Avranches after the Americans swung southeast. The battlegroup only just escaped by fleeing eastward and safely returned to the rest of the division.

By 1 August, 116th Panzer was fighting alongside the survivors of 353rd Infantry Division in the area of La Chapelle-Céceline. The following day elements of the division held onto Hill 290 and three *kampfgruppen* were then thrown into a counterattack with mixed results. Abteilung I, Panzer Regiment 16, alone accounted for nineteen American tanks, but the division then went back onto the defensive.

Mortain counterattack

On the night of 5/6 August the 84th Infantry Division relieved the 116th, though its divisional artillery remained in place to support the infantry. The 84th Infantry was a green unit and had to be bolstered with other units from the 116th, in particular the Panzerjäger Battalion. Stopping an American penetration at Sourdeval ensured that the two divisions were not cut off. Subordinated to von Funck's XLVII Panzer Corps, the bulk of the 116th's panzers were transferred to 2nd Panzer for the impending Avranches/Mortain counterattack.

For the attack on Avranches on the night of 6/7 August a panzer battalion from the 116th and 1st SS were assigned to 2nd Panzer. The 116th was ordered to support the attack north of Sée creek and to seize Chérencé-le-Roussel. Lacking its armour this was an impossible task, especially as the Americans had been in the town for a number of days.

The 116th, with just twenty to twenty-five tanks, was to attack north of La Sée to keep the enemy occupied, thereby protecting the northern flank of the counterattack. The 116th's right group was supposed to attack Hill 211 and its left La Mardelle, but in the event was unable to make any headway.

During the night of the 7/8th the left wing was able to reach the railway crossing 500m northeast of Chérencé. Elements of Panzergrenadier Regiment 156 reached Chérencé on 7 August and dug in. Unfortunately, word did not filter back that an old railway track was open and so no armoured support was pushed up it.

In the face of vigorous American counterattacks, the division was unable to hold its ground. Funck accused the 116th of dragging its feet, especially as its tanks had not reached 2nd Panzer in time, and he wanted Schwerin relieved. In fact, I Abteilung Panzer Regiment 24, forming the right attack group, successfully reached Le Mesnil-Adeleé, two and a half miles (4km) southwest of Chérencé. American firepower, though, soon drove it back and subsequent attacks by the panzergrenadiers met a similar fate. Nonetheless Schwerin was relieved of command and told to report to La Roche Guyon.

On 9 August the 116th, still under XLVII Panzer Corps, was strongly attacked by the Americans in the sector around Perriers-en-Beaufcel, but managed to repel these assaults. The division counterattacked southwest of Perriers-en-Beauficel the following day to alleviate the pressure before withdrawing. On the 11th it was sent to the Alençon area.

By 12 August, Panzer Regiment 16 was deployed north-south between Argentan and Sées with just fifteen tanks. After the liberation of Alençon on the 12th and the trapping of 9th Panzer in the Ecouves forest, the French 2nd Armoured Division drove back the 116th Panzer into Carrouges, south of the developing Falaise salient.

With the French in Argentan, Hitler's planned counterattack against General Haislip's XV Corps was rendered redundant. Instead of striking south from Carrouges towards Le Mans, the intention was to attack east through the Forêt de Ecouves to blunt the advance of the French 2nd Armoured and the US 5th Armored Divisions.

By late afternoon on the 13th, General Eberbach, commander of the grandly-titled Panzergruppe Eberbach, had gathered the remnants of the 116th, 2nd and 1st SS Panzer Divisions in the Argentan area with about seventy panzers. That day, elements of Panzer Lehr, en route to Argentan for the Alençon attack, bumped into strong enemy armoured units. Exhausted by all the fighting, it withdrew east of Argentan, heading for Fontainbleu.

Final days

On 16 August, Hitler finally authorised a withdrawal on the proviso that Panzergruppe Eberbach widened the exit by attacking the US XV Corps at Argentan. The Germans simply did not have the strength for such an operation. Nevertheless, the 116th and 2nd SS were thrown against the US 90th Division's roadblocks at Le Bourg-St Leonard with a view to driving the Americans off the ridgeline that dominated the escape routes to the north. This represented the last gasp of Panzergruppe Eberbach and the Americans were briefly dislodged.

The French, bypassing Mortrée where the Americans were blocked, were in the vicinity of Écouché, to the west of Argentan, by the evening of the 20th. The following day, at dawn, they took the Germans by surprise. In front of them were the remains of the 116th and 9th Panzer Divisions.

In the fighting that followed the French destroyed many vehicles of the 116th Panzer on the RN 24 bis and, liberating Écouché, they crossed the river Orne just to the north. The 116th Panzer Division remained in the Alençon–Argentan area until the 20th, managing to break out of the Falaise pocket, escaping across the Seine either side of Rouen. In total the 116th lost some 4,348 men during the campaign, its performance having been far from noteworthy.

Chapter 14

Stopping Patton – 9th Panzer Division

The 9th Panzer Division's efforts to stop the American break-out to the west and subsequent envelopment of German forces from the south were ill fated. The division was another exhausted unit pulled out of the Eastern Front and fleshed out with reservists. It was not ready for combat until almost the end of the Normandy campaign. Even then it did not fight as a coherent formation.

The US 3rd Army, consisting of seven armoured, fourteen infantry and two airborne divisions, became combat operational on 1 August. Ignoring General Bradley's orders to secure a wide corridor, Patton squeezed his armoured divisions down the coast in twenty-two hours. He was now ready to sweep southeastwards in order to trap the Wehrmacht in northwestern France.

Swinging toward Le Mans, Patton knew that if the Germans persisted with their Avranches/Mortain counterattack they would ultimately not be able to get away. Slowly but surely, the German 7th Army and 5th Panzer Army were being wedged in a giant vice. In trying to stop Patton, 9th Panzer went into action on 10 August and swiftly was reduced to a dozen tanks.

Combat experience

The 9th Panzer Division was created in January 1940 from the 4th Light Division. It took part in the attack on Western Europe, fighting in the Netherlands, Belgium and finally France before being transferred to Poland in September 1940. It was involved in the invasion of the Balkans before fighting on the southern sector during the invasion of the USSR. It was then transferred to the central sector in October 1941 and took part in the summer offensive of 1942 and later, like 2nd Panzer, in the fighting at Kursk. The division was transferred to the southern sector in the fall of 1943 and took part in the fighting on the Dnieper, suffering heavy losses. By this stage the formation was all but exhausted by the unrelenting combat.

In March 1944, desperately in need of a refit and rest, 9th Panzer, under Generalleutnant Erwin Jolasse, was sent to southern France, where it absorbed the 155th Reserve Panzer Division. The division's Panzergrenadier Regiment 11 remained on the Eastern Front and did not rejoin its parent unit until mid-June.

Jolasse had started the war commanding infantry units, until he took over the 18th Panzer Brigade in March 1942, followed by the 9th Panzer Division in late July 1943. He and his men found France a world apart from the bloodletting experienced fighting in Russia.

The 155th Reserve Panzer Division was a fresh formation, having only come into existence in the summer of 1943. Previously it had been designated Panzer Division Nr. 155, created in the spring of that year, largely as a training unit under General Franz Landgraf. The 155th, commanded by General Max Fremerey from October 1943 until late April 1944, included Reserve Panzer Abteilung 7, Reserve Panzergrenadier Regiment 5, Reserve Panzerjäger Abteilung 5 and Reserve Artillery Abteilung (motorised) 360. It must have been rather daunting for the relatively-new recruits and transferees joining the bloodied veterans of Kursk and the Dnieper; their stories cannot have greatly helped morale.

Unfortunately for Jolasse, on D-Day the 9th Panzer Division was far from combat ready; the II Abteilung Panzer Regiment 33, like so many other armoured units, was at Mailly-le-Camp, training and receiving shipments of much needed Panther tanks. In addition, the process of assimilating the 155th Reserve Panzer Division took time. It was not until late July that 7th Army began contemplating deploying 9th Panzer between Alençon and Domfront, with a view to it taking part in the proposed Mortain counterattack.

On 27 July the division was put on notice to be ready to march north from the Avignon area. Unfortunately for General Jolasse, when he received his marching orders the Panther battalion had already departed Mailly-le-Camp, heading south, and had to retrace its steps, wasting precious time. On the road between Mailly-le-Camp and Normandy they were caught in the open and a number of lorries were left as blazing wrecks.

Although earmarked for the Mortain counterattack, the Panther *abteilung* never arrived in time. In fact, all the travelling caused the tanks major mechanical problems. By 1 August, 9th Panzer and six infantry divisions of varying quality were heading for the Normandy battlefield now that it was clear to the Germans that Cobra represented a very real threat.

Rumbling north, 9th Panzer was set upon by the French *Maquis* and Allied aircraft. Nonetheless, despite numerous air attacks, the division seemed to escape largely unscathed as it moved north. After the war, Jolasse claimed that his division suffered no significant losses in men or equipment during its march to Normandy. It arrived at the front with a total of eighty-two Panzer IVs, seventy-nine Panthers, nine Marder self-propelled guns and five StuG III assault guns.

Mortain counterattack

Coming into the line on 6 August, the division deployed from Domfront in the north to Mayenne in the south, along with a mixture of other units. It ended up scattered, with elements of its panzer regiment, panzergrenadier regiments and artillery regiment east of Domfront, west of Alençon, and north of Angers, as well as in the Tours and Trun areas.

In fact, the division never got to fight as a whole, due to the destruction of the bridges over the Loire and the Allied landings in southern France in mid-August. Elements of the support services never reached the division in Normandy and were not reunited with the parent formation until it had retreated to Metz following the defeat. In the event, the Domfort–Mayenne defensive line soon became untenable once the Americans reached Alençon, way to the east in the Germans' rear.

For the Mortain attack Field Marshal von Kluge had to make do with what troops he had available, although Hitler did authorise the release of a new corps and two divisions. General der Panzertruppen Adolf Kuntzen's LXXXI Corps, based in distant Rouen, was due to assume command, with 9th Panzer ordered north from Avignon and the 708th Infantry Division redeployed to Royan.

Kuntzen was an experienced Panzer Corps commander who had fought in Poland and on the Eastern Front. He had been sent to take charge of LXXXI Corps in April 1942, where he had languished ever since with the Dieppe raid being the high point of his deployment to France. However, neither of his assigned divisions made it to Mortain in time as General Patton's forces obstructed them. The 708th Infantry managed, with some difficulty, to deploy only 5,000 men in the Laval–Le Mans area, right in the path of Patton's US 3rd Army.

Therefore, for the Avranches counterattack in early August, although the 9th Panzer along with the 708th Infantry Division were placed under Kuntzen's direction, they were simply instructed to protect the flank of 7th Army at Domfront–Mayenne, north of Montsurs, and to prevent an American armoured attack in the Alençon area.

The division could muster just fifteen combat-ready Panzer IVs of the I Abteilung Panzer Regiment 33, its two panzergrenadier regiments, 10 and 11, the reconnaissance and pioneer battalions and most of its artillery regiment. The wayward Panther battalion was assigned to the II SS Panzer Corps on the 9th, but in the event was sent to Krüger's LVIII Panzer Corps and five days later was placed under operational control of Gerhard Graf von Schwerin's 116th Panzer Division.

Patton's newly-formed XV Corps, under Major General Wade H Haislip, reached Le Mans on 8 August, outflanking Krüger's LVIII Panzer Corps and

Kuntzen's LXXXI Corps, the latter consisting of little more than 9th Panzer and some ad hoc units. By the 10th it was clear that strong American forces, including the US 5th Armored Division, had successfully pivoted from Le Mans northwards, with the US XV Corps striking toward Alençon. The 9th Panzer, with just seven combat battalions holding a thirty-one mile (50km) front, was able to do little more than delay the advance of the American Army.

In desperation, a *kampfgruppe* drawn from the 352nd Infantry Division was deployed to the east and northeast of Le Mans. At the time of D-Day this division had its own mobile anti-tank force in the shape of Panzerjager Abteilung 352, equipped with fourteen Marders and ten Sturmgeschütz IIIs. The division suffered heavy losses in the subsequent fighting against the American landings and by the end of July was no longer combat capable, with less than 100 combat-ready men supported by just two Sturmgeschütz, four heavy anti-tank guns and four artillery batteries. Under such circumstances little could be expected of the 352nd.

It also had operational control of elements of five other infantry divisions. Understandably, at the beginning of August the remains of the 352nd were withdrawn from the front. It had spent barely a week refitting southeast of Alençon before it became embroiled in the desperate rearguard actions along the axis Le Mans–Dreux. Inevitably the 9th Panzer, 352nd and 708th were too weak to hold off the fresh American armour. The battle that followed was to be desperate and confused.

Battle for Beaumont-sur-Sarthe

At 0300 on 10 August, orders were received that General Haislip's US XV Corps would attack at 0800 to seize the line Sees–Carrouge, north of Alençon. German defences consisted of elements of 708th Infantry Division on the left, with 9th Panzer Division in the centre, and Panzer Lehr Division on the right. The American 5th Armored Division was to attack in the east with 2nd French Armoured Division to the west.

The Americans crossed the startline and by 1100 were meeting strong German armoured and artillery resistance. About fifty panzers were encountered and several counterattacks were repulsed in securing the Sarthe river crossings. German anti-tank units were discovered deployed at road junctions and critical points and nine American tanks and two armoured cars were lost to combined ambushes.

Jolasse's 9th Panzer encountered the American's in the Beaumont-sur-Sarthe area, roughly midway between Le Mans and Alençon, and the division's two *kampfgruppen* were engaged in heavy fighting on both sides of the River Sarthe. Despite their best efforts, the Americans swarmed round the division's flanks.

The command post of both the 9th and Panzer Lehr Divisions came under attack and were forced to retire. With the 9th Panzer outflanked, the French seized the bridges over the Sarthe and in fierce fighting the division was shattered, losing 100 tanks.

In the late afternoon on the 10th, elements of the 9th counterattacked and drove back the Americans who had advanced via Rouessé-Fontaine. By the end of the day, 9th Panzer and the 352nd Infantry Division had claimed thirty-six American tanks. Nonetheless, by the evening the American Army was in Beaumont, Ballon, Marolle-le-Braukts, Bonnétable, La Ferté-Bernars and beyond Nogent-le-Rotrou. Oberst Max Sperling replaced General Jolasse and the division was increasingly involved in the heavy fighting south of Alençon.

The following day, the 9th's two *kampfgruppen* were almost decimated in the futile and heavy defensive battles. Whilst the 352nd's *kampfgruppe* was able to establish a new defensive position near Huisne, a gap formed either side of Mamers, into which poured Allied armour, including the newly-arrived French 2nd Armoured Division under General Leclerc. German armoured forces were appearing in greater number in an effort to stop the advance, with as many as 200 panzers reported in the area, though such a number seems unlikely. It was also notable that panzers were now tenaciously contesting the roadblocks.

After the French 2nd Armoured Division liberated Alençon on 12 August, the 9th Panzer lay in ambush in the Forêt d'Écouves south of Tanville. Leclerc's forces skirted east and entered Sées, but became tangled with the American 5th Armored Division. By mid-afternoon the French were northeast of Tanville, which was liberated the following day, although the forest remained full of Germans.

During the afternoon and early evening of the 12th, a column from the French 2nd Armoured blocked the supply route through Sées, three miles (5km) east of the boundary between themselves and the American 5th Armored Division. Refuelling of the 5th Armored was delayed six hours by this traffic jam. Consequently, its attack towards Argentan was not launched until just before dark and was stopped short of the town. Remarkably, German aircraft strafed the Americans three times during the day. That night, American patrols did enter the town.

German casualties suffered fighting the Americans to date amounted to 301 killed, 362 captured; vehicle losses were seventy panzers, eighty-eight motor vehicles, two armoured cars and seven pieces of artillery. The German defences were now in chaos, units identified being not only 9th Panzer but also elements from the 2nd SS, 6th Parachute, 9th SS, 10th SS, 12th SS, 17th SS, and Panzer Lehr, as well as scattered service and GHQ units.

Final days

Kuntzen's LXXXI Corps, including 9th Panzer, Panzer Lehr and 708th Infantry Division, were tasked to take part in the aborted Alençon counterattack on 13 August, though in reality Kuntzen's only effective force was a small combat group from Panzer Lehr.

The 9th Panzer's II Abteilung was pulled out of the line on the 15th to fight on the lower Seine. The rest of the division escaped being trapped in the Falaise pocket after it was ordered to withdraw southwest of Paris, having lost about 3,500 men in the fighting. By this stage the Americans were completing their wider envelopment toward the Seine.

By the end of August, the French 2nd Armored Division claimed to have killed 4,500 Germans and captured another 8,800, as well as accounting for 117 tanks, seventy-nine guns, and 750 wheeled vehicles. Many of these were from 9th Panzer. However, the uncharitable have assessed that the French, being road-bound, 'claimed' all casualties they came across.

Major General Walton H Walker's US XX Corps reached Chartres on 16 August and four days later was at Fontainbleu, just short of the Seine. Just to the north, Haislip's US XV Corps was at Dreux, west of Paris, while way to the south Major General Gilbert R Cook's US XII Corps had liberated Orleans on the 17th. Sperling's 9th Panzer could do no more. The German defeat in Normandy would be complete within three days.

Chapter 15

Falaise – The Killing Grounds

Army Group B's weekly situation report on 14 August 1944 noted that since 6 June they had destroyed 3,370 tanks and 475 aircraft. In this war of attrition it had not been enough to halt the impending encirclement. After two long months, Panzergruppe West, in the face of OKW's insistence that no ground must be given up, even to regain the initiative and escape the Allied naval guns, had done all it could to stave off defeat.

North of Falaise, Lieutenant General G G Simonds' Canadian II Corps could muster nearly 700 tanks by 10 August. The remains of Panzergruppe West and 7th Army facing them had just thirty-five panzers. Southeast of Falaise at Argentan, the Germans had just seventy tanks with which to fend off 300 American Shermans. The reality of pitting 105 panzers against 1,000 enemy tanks meant the Falaise salient was now a panzer killing ground.

The Falaise salient

Major General Wade Haislip's US XV Corps drove on Alençon and Argentan on 12–13 August, with its spearhead formation, the French 2nd Armoured Division, seizing the bridges over the Sarthe in a night attack. The US 5th Armoured Division burst into Sées on the Orne on the 12th and headed north for Argentan, tightening the noose. Both Alençon and Sées fell on the 12th, despite resistance from the remains of the 9th Panzer Division and 708th and 352nd Infantry Divisions.

By the 13th, XV Corps was less than 25 miles (40km) south of the Canadian 1st Army, which was struggling to take the town of Falaise and close the gap. General Patton instructed Haislip to take Argentan and then push on Falaise. However, General Bradley ordered Haislip to remain at Argentan. It was this decision that partly ensured Falaise was a flawed victory. Criticism was later heaped on Montgomery for not urging the Canadians and Poles on, but what more could they have achieved in the face of such dogged German resistance?

On 13 August, 1st SS and 2nd Panzer were thrown piecemeal into the fight. The 10th SS launched a counterattack against the Americans the following day. It was supposed to have included 1st SS between Carrouges and La Ferté-Macé, 2nd Panzer in the Écouché area and 116th Panzer in Argentan, but with only seventy panzers remaining these kept being siphoned off to plug emerging gaps along the southern front. The 10th SS met an American attack on the 14th with a small and short barrage followed by a counterattack deploying just eight panzers supported by panzergrenadiers north of Domfort. The following day, this weak force was driven back, but not without a fight and the exhausted 10th SS was finally removed from the line.

Trapped in the Falaise salient was the cream of the German tank forces, including elements of the 9th, 21st, 116th, 2nd SS, 9th SS, 10th SS, and 12th SS Panzer Divisions. By now, 116th Panzer was down to only fifteen tanks, 1st SS had just nineteen tanks, the 10th SS eight and 12th SS about twenty. The 116th Panzer Division tried to hold up the Americans, but the Germans had lost 100 armoured fighting vehicles.

By mid–August, along the northern shoulder of the pocket were the 21st, 1st SS and 12th SS Panzer Divisions fending of the British, Canadian and Polish forces. To the south the 10th SS, 9th, 1st SS, 2nd, 116th, 2nd SS Panzer Divisions and 17th SS Panzergrenadier Division were deployed from west to east respectively, resisting the Americans

The western end was defended by elements of seven infantry and one parachute division lying north to south: 326th, 3rd Fallschirmjäger, 363rd, 331st, 353rd, 243rd, 84th and 275th. Notably the 363rd was holding positions east of Flers, 22 miles (35km) west of the Falaise–Argentan Road. Behind these forces were the 2nd SS and 9th SS Panzer Divisions.

On the northern edge of the pocket also lay the 276th, 277th, 271st and 89th Infantry Divisions. The commander of the 276th, perhaps sensing all was lost, ordered all those men not needed, some 4,000 soldiers from an original strength of 13,500, to withdraw on 14 August. The only infantry to the south with the remains of the panzers were weak elements of the mangled 708th Infantry Division. About a half of the rapidly-contracting pocket lay west of the Orne, while the other half lay west of the Dives.

The various Corps staffs found themselves scattered throughout the salient, unable to maintain effective control of their formations. At the western end, deployed north to south, were General Meindl's II Parachute Corps and Elfeldt's LXXXIV Corps. Along the southern edge, west to east were Krüger and von Funck's LVIII and XLVII Panzer Corps, while to the north was Straube's LXXIV Corps with Priess' I SS Panzer Corps lying east of Falaise. In reality, many of the radio trucks had been lost and staff members were cut off from their HQs; those HQs that did retain any cohesion found it extremely difficult to get through to the divisions under their command. Only Bittrich's II SS Panzer Corps in the middle of the pocket was able to withdraw while still exercising control of its divisional assets.

Beyond the northern shoulder of the Falaise salient, resting on Morteaux-Coulibuef, was the German 85th Infantry Division, struggling to hold the Polish 1st Armoured Division at bay; north of them, Hans von Obstfelder's LXXXVI Corps was facing three British divisions. The 51st (Highland) Division was pushing toward St Pierre-sur-Dives, while the 7th Armoured and 49th (West Riding) Divisions were pushing on Mézidon. They were over the Dives and the Vie, driving toward Lisieux by 19 August. This sector was held by the German 272nd Infantry Division, which was able to withdraw from Normandy in good order.

General Bradley, fearing his troops might be trampled by the fleeing enemy, refrained from driving on to Falaise. This meant the two German armies trapped in the Falaise pocket were able to struggle eastward for another week. To the north, the German defenders held up the Canadian advance, known as Operation Tractable, for two days before they reached Falaise. There, 1st SS was on its last legs and similarly 12th SS had only fifteen tanks left. Canadian soldier Duncan Kyle recalled the carnage:

> Germans charred coal-black, looking like blackened tree trunks lay besides smoking vehicles. One didn't realise the obscene mess was human until it was poked at. I remember wishing the Germans didn't have to use so many horses. Seeing all those dead animals on their backs . . . The road to Falaise was nauseating. I felt like puking many times, what butchery. The air force did its job well.

Fighting retreat

On the night of 14/15 August, Army Group B ordered all anti-aircraft artillery to be withdrawn from the pocket. Lacking support from the Luftwaffe, 5th Panzer Army (as Panzergruppe West had been known for the past week) was on its own and at the mercy of Allied fighter-bombers. Panzer Lehr had withdrawn on the 13th, but had left behind Kampfgruppe Kuhnow, consisting of a tank company, a howitzer battery and elements of Panzergrenadier Regiment 902. This crossed the Orne at Mesnil-Jean on the night of 16/17 August and joined the 12th SS. The German position became completely untenable on the 15th when the Allies landed in the south of France. The 11th Panzer Division, conducting defensive combat, withdrew to Alsace to defend the Belfort Gap in September.

Officer-cadet Kurt Misch and his comrades of 12th SS soon realised that, after all their tough resistance to the advancing Canadian and Polish forces, they were surrounded. Misch remembered the sense of apprehension:

> On the night of 15 August we were marching in an unknown direction. During the night we suddenly saw Verey lights [flares] on three sides;

we looked at each other knowingly – surrounded? Next day, we were sure. We tried to keep it from the men as long as possible. But they realised it as soon as the field kitchen did not turn up and the rations got smaller. Something new, unknown, takes possession of us. All the usual joking is silence. We are all inwardly preoccupied, wondering how to meet the situation, as individuals. If it does not mean death, being taken prisoner will mean a long separation from home. We 'old' ones stick together. Our Chief leaves no doubts in our minds about the gravity of the situation, and I come back from the conference deep in thought. The Verey lights hang like great signs in the heavens. The front lies beneath them in a breathless silence. Low-flying German planes drop rations, and a large container of chocolate lands near me. A nice surprise, and a greeting from the outside world. We have not yet been abandoned.

The truth was that Panzergruppe West, Panzergruppe Eberbach and 7th Army were well and truly trapped. The French *Maquis* were also active in the pocket, blocking roads with felled trees, harassing stragglers and, where possible, negotiating the surrender of isolated pockets of troops. Tired and hungry columns of Germans would often be greeted by a new roadblock with locals nonchalantly hanging around.

Those comanders that could make it, including von Kluge, Hausser and Eberbach, assembled at Nécy in the early hours of the 16th. All talk of a decisive counterattack was now completely forgotten; there was no way the Avranches/Mortain operation could be resurrected. Eberbach recalled the grim reality of the situation now engulfing the senior German command:

Each of us told him [Kluge] that an attack with divisions now bled white, without air forces, and without a safe supply service, was unthinkable. Only a quick withdrawal from the encirclement could, perhaps, avoid catastrophe. Kluge was now ready to give all orders for evacuation of the 'finger', as we had proposed, but only after having communicated with Hitler's headquarters. Without its approval, he did not dare to make such a far-reaching decision. The people there, he said, lived in another world without any idea of the actual situation here, as he knew from our reports and what he had experienced himself in the last 24 hours.

Hitler grudgingly agreed to let the German Army withdraw through the Argentan–Falaise Gap. The II SS Panzer Corps (2nd SS, 9th SS, 12th SS and 21st Panzer Divisions) were to hold the northern flank against the British and

Canadians and XLVII Panzer Corps (2nd and 116th Panzer Divisions) were to hold the south against the Americans while the remains of 7th Army, 5th Panzer Army and Panzergruppe Eberbach conducted a fighting retreat.

Field Marshal Walther Model replaced von Kluge as C-in-C West on 17 August, the latter committing suicide the following day. Model gained a reputation as Hitler's 'fireman', being sent to stabilise various areas of the vast battlefield. He had fought in Poland, France and Russia, most notably he commanded the 9th Army on the Eastern Front. While von Kluge got permission to retire beyond the Orne, his replacement ordered a withdrawal behind the Dives. He also launched the 2nd SS Panzer against the British moving southward towards Trun on the eastern side of the Dives, just north of the main crossing point at St Lambert.

Model arrived at La Roche Guyon on the evening of the 17th, bumping into Bayerlein, commander of Panzer Lehr. 'What are you doing here?' enquired Model. 'I wish to inform Field Marshal von Kluge of my departure, for what's left of my division is to be withdrawn from the front to rest and refit, replied Bayerlein. Model was not amused: 'My dear Bayerlein, in the East divisions are rested at the front, and in future that will be the practice here'.

It would take three nights to get the westernmost troops over the Orne and at least one night to complete the withdrawal over the Dives. In other words, the mouth of the pocket had to be kept open for at least four days, at all costs. This had to be done under constant Allied artillery and fighter-bomber bombardment and *Maquis* attack.

The Americans and British were slowly heading for each other and the Falaise salient was steadily squeezed from all sides as the Germans valiantly held open the neck. By the 17th, the pocket was only twenty miles (32km) wide by ten miles (16km) deep, containing about 100,000 men, remnants of fifteen divisions with elements from at least twelve others, all trying desperately to extricate themselves from the developing chaos. While the panzer divisions managed to hold the Americans and Canadians at bay, the vast columns of retreating Germans were decimated by the fighter-bombers and artillery, the roads becoming choked with burnt out vehicles, adding to the confusion.

Flying Officer J G Simpson, RAF 193 Squadron, recalled that it was tricky picking friend from foe:

> We turned out to stop the German Counterattack at Mortain when the Germans tried to cut off the Americans and we were involved in the destruction of a lot of transport etc, during the Falaise Gap operation.

This involved quite tricky map reading as it was essential to know exactly where you were. The battlefield was pretty fluid and you didn't get a lot of time to identify the tank you were attacking. Being a bomb squadron we did not do so much of this although quite often we bombed a nominated target like the edge of a wood or the end of a village. Then did a range around with our cannon which could do a lot of damage. Our chief problem was that the Germans were pretty good at camouflage – they even re-routed roads so that [they] sat under the cover of the apple orchards and you thought the roads were empty. Of course, all their tanks were under the trees. It was quite revealing how much of the German Army relied on the old horse rather than the famous Panzer. We chased them all the way across the River Seine; had some fun trying to catch them going over this river.

SS-Untersturmführer Herbert Walther, 12th SS, experienced the full terror of being trapped in the pocket:

My driver was burning. I had a bullet through the arm. I jumped on to a railway track and ran. They were firing down the embankment and I was hit in the leg. I made 100 metres, then it was as if I was hit in the back of the neck with a big hammer. A bullet had gone through beneath the ear and come out through the cheek. I was choking on blood. There were two Americans looking down at me and two French soldiers, who wanted to finish me off.

The Americans took him to an aid station and he eventually had thirteen bullets removed from his leg.

For three days sixty members of the 12th SS clung on in Falaise in the face of repeated Canadian attacks; when the town fell only four wounded prisoners were taken. When the Canadians finally entered on 17 August they found three Tigers from SS-Sturmbannführer Weiss's Schwere SS-Panzer Abteilung 102 waiting for them. After fighting in the area of the cathedral, the panzers retreated with two assault guns covering their retreat toward Necy the following day. One immobilised Tiger was towed to the southern edge of Abbaye, while the northwest exits were blocked by the assault guns. The Canadians were beaten off and its crew destroyed the broken-down Tiger before they withdrew.

It was every man for himself now as Abteilung 102 abandoned its rearguard role and made for the assembly area at Vimoutiers, way to the west on the River Vie. The remaining Tigers made for Trun to the southeast and were harassed all the way by artillery and fighters. Finding St Lambert choked with vehicles and under low-level attack, they bypassed the village and sped for Chambois further south. Just outside the town, Will Fey's Tiger had to be destroyed after it spluttered to a halt. Shortly after, SS-Sturmbannführer Weiss, having been wounded twice, was captured when the ambulance half-track he was travelling in came under fire.

When Falaise fell, the Allies had two options; a short hook or a long envelopment, the latter requiring a blocking force along the Seine. The Americans opted for the short hook, although Patton's 3rd Army was already sweeping toward the Seine. At this point the Polish 1st and Canadian 4th Armoured Divisions had crossed the River Dives to the east of Falaise. Both were poised to strike for Argentan but were now directed to Chambois, about 10 miles (16km) northeast of Argentan.

Closing the gap

Montgomery now sought to block the corridor further east by blocking the narrow valley between the villages of Trun and Chambois. He demanded the Trun–Chambois gap be closed and on 17 August ordered:

> It is absolutely essential that both armoured divisions of II Canadian Corps, i.e. 4th Canadian Armoured Division and 1st Polish Armoured Division, close the gap between 1st Canadian and 3rd US Army. 1st Polish Armoured Division must thrust past Trun and Chambois at all costs and as quickly as possible.

The Canadians and Poles were soon pressing hard on the Germans flanks. The Poles occupied Mount Ormel, the high ground east of Chambois. Although the Germans cut them off for three days, they kept shelling the fleeing troops below. This became known as 'the corridor of death'.

The RAF were already doing Montgomery's bidding; Wing Commander Johnnie Johnson was in the thick of it:

> When the Spitfires arrived at Falaise, over the small triangle of Normandy bordered by Falaise, Trun and Chambois, the Typhoons were already hard at work. One of their favourite tactics against the long streams of enemy vehicles was to seal off the front and rear of the column by accurately dropping a few bombs. This technique imprisoned the desperate enemy on a narrow stretch of dusty lane, and since the transports were sometimes jammed together four abreast, it made the subsequent rocket and cannon attack a comparatively easy business against the stationary targets. Some of the armoured cars and tanks attempted to escape their fate by making

detours across the fields and wooded country, but these were soon spotted by the Typhoon pilots and were accorded the same treatment as their comrades on the highways and lanes.

The Germans did everything they could to escape the pocket. Major-General Sir Francis de Guingand, Monty's Chief of Staff, found that Allied pilots were presented with a dilemma:

> During this time pilots reported a large proportion of the enemy's vehicles were carrying Red Cross flags and emblems. It was obvious that this was merely a ruse to avoid having their transport attacked. I believe these flags were even seen on tanks. What were the pilots to do? The decision was to avoid attacking them, for it was thought that the Germans in their present mood might well take reprisals against our prisoners and wounded. A difficult decision, but probably the right one.

The Free French forces fighting alongside the Americans were given a bloody nose by rearguard units of the 9th and 116th Panzer Divisions, but Patton was driving all out for the Seine. His US 3rd Army was on the line of Orleans–Chartres–Dreux, facing little or no opposition, by the 16th. The drive was continued, hoping to swing north to seal off the Germans trapped against the river. US XV Corps, though, was held up by determined resistance as the retreating Germans fought desperate rearguard actions along the Seine. Nonetheless, the US 79th Division from XV Corps managed to secure a bridgehead over the Seine at Mantes-Gassicourt on 19 August. That day, supported by Sherman tanks, the Canadians seized St Lambert-sur-Dives, right in the path of the fleeing Germans.

On the night of 16 August, Eberbach had transferred his wholly inadequate command post to the staff of II SS Panzer Corps in Montabard, north of Argentan, while the staff of 7th Army shifted to Nécy. The following day, when Falaise fell, 116th Panzer reported that its forces east of Argentan had been driven off, the enemy had taken Le Bourg-St Léonard and Chambois was now impassable due to very heavy artillery fire.

Eberbach recalled:

> During the night, I received a wireless message stating that Field Marshal Model, who had relieved Kluge, would like to meet the Commanding Generals of both Armies and me next morning at 0900hrs at 5th Panzer Army headquarters in Fontaine-l'Abbé. The distance was 47 miles (75km). I needed from 1500hrs until 2300hrs for the trip, primarily because I got caught up in II SS Panzer Corps'

movements. We saw grievous pictures. Bittrich's attempt to reach his divisions and lead them against Trun failed. . . .

Model wanted to withdraw behind the Seine and use the panzer divisions to hold open the bottleneck at Trun and Argentan. Eberbach goes on:

> Instead of SS-General Hausser, Chief of Staff of 7th Army, Colonel von Gersdorff was present at the conference. With him, we came to an agreement that I should immediately leave for the Staff of II SS Panzer Corps near Meulles, in order to lead Corps to the combat area near Trun. The distance to Meulles was 22 miles (35km). I was, however, so often attacked by fighter-bombers and my car pierced through by bullets that I contrived to arrive at the staff of II Panzer Corps at 2200hrs. There I was informed that the British and American troops had met south-east of Trun, and had thus completed the encirclement of 7th Army.

Hausser, 7th Army's commander, was shot through the jaw and Eberbach, taking charge, ordered Bittrich to get his troops either side of Vimoutiers ready to strike southeast of Trun to help the break-out, knowing full well that this was unlikely to happen. Bittrich had been unable to contact his divisional staff and in any case his men lacked ammunition, food, fuel and radio equipment. Eberbach then made his way to the HQ of 5th Panzer Army to get his decision confirmed by Sepp Dietrich, coordinate efforts with 7th Army and get II SS Panzer Corps supplies.

In the meantime, Otto Henning's Panzer Lehr reconnaissance battalion did what they could to help their comrades escape:

> We had to rescue a large troop contingent because it had been surrounded. Their commanding officer wanted to break through in a westerly direction but this was impossible and we took them to the north. There were so many people on the roads, whole headquarters units, medical staff, even ordinary cars with French civilians in them. During the day they didn't dare show themselves but chose instead to travel at night. The retreat moved towards Falaise and we also drove in that direction; the roads were very crowded and the attacks constant. Oberfeldwebel [Staff Sergeant] Keichel told me: 'We are pretty much surrounded, only one road is still open but under heavy fire, we will try tonight to break out along it.' We tried and came under heavy artillery fire but we pressed on and managed to get out at the last moment.

SS-Brigadeführer Theodor Wisch, commander of 1st SS Panzer Division, suffered a terrible wound and was only just rescued by one of his staff officers, SS-Hauptsturmführer Hans Bernhard. The latter recalled:

> We were at the edge of a wood with the Corps commander – a Wehrmacht General – Freiherr Hans von Funck [XLVII Panzer Corps]. There was a big discussion – they were shouting at each other, everybody wanted to be right but nobody knew what was going on. Then the commander of the division [Wisch] and I set off across a field – eastwards – towards a village. There was an old stone bridge across the river there and I had an instinct that the enemy would fire on it. I told the commander, if I was in charge of the guns, I would fire in this direction. He didn't pay any attention and then suddenly there was an explosion. He was hit and his leg gone. There I was – he was much bigger than me – he weighted 90 kilos or more. I was helpless. A *Schützenpanzerwagen* [armoured half-track] drove by – I knew the driver and ordered him to help us, 'the divisional commander is wounded and we have to get him out of here.' So we drove the SPW to the edge of the village where there was a big barn with a hayloft. I put him there and the staff doctor came to look at him and then we put him back in the SPW and set off toward the east.

A unit of the 9th SS then helped them escape the pocket.

On the night of the 17/18th, the 353rd Infantry Division, which had been acting as a rearguard, crossed the Orne. It then gathered in the Forêt de Goufferns with some 5,000 troops, less than half its strength, successfully escaping. Late on the 18th, the 271st Infantry Division broke contact with the British and its combat elements gathered northeast of Chambois, escaping with in excess of 5,000 men before the pocket was finally closed. In June its manpower had stood at 12,600.

Also on the 18th, the British were poised to drop the Special Air Service into the open mouth of the Falaise pocket by glider to seal the trap. Operation Falaise was to harass those units, especially the transport, that were escaping. Four gliders were actually in the air when the mission was called off. This may have been part of Operation Transfigure, which proposed dropping American, British and Canadian airborne troops in the Paris–Orléans Gap as a blocking force. The SAS were to form the reconnaissance element, but these plans were overtaken by events on the ground.

Schwere Panzer Abteilung 503's I Kompanie, trapped in the pocket, destroyed four Tigers on 18 August and two more two days later. Near Chambois, the last few Tigers of SS-Panzer Abteilung 102 found the town under a 'dome of fire'. Reports also indicated that the road to Trun had been cut and that there was no escape.

Coming under enemy fire, the tanks loaded up as many fleeing troops as they could and drove clear. Everyone's fighting spirit was now all but broken as Will Fey recounts on the 18th:

> Our mood was completely depressed. No one spoke anymore, and a gloomy silence covered us. In Chambois we had to push a burning vehicle aside just to get through. Our soldiers in field grey streamed north, with dry throats and sweat dripping faces. We stopped on a hill and contemplated the situation before setting up a small *kampfgruppe* at a large farm. Our commander took over the command panzer, and we felt better again. An Oberst of the paratroops contributed a handful of men, and so the afternoon passed. The noise from the tanks on the road nearby got louder. This caught our interest and made us want to take some action, but we could not endanger the last Tiger of our small Kampfgruppe.

Instead, the commander and his radio operator crept forward with panzerfausts and knocked out a Churchill tank, thereby holding up the advancing column. Withdrawing at nightfall, they bumped into elements of the reconnaissance battalion from the 2nd SS, confirming that they had escaped the Falaise pocket.

The escape route was just five miles (8km) wide by 19 August, though it would not be completely sealed for another two days, and the rapidly-shrinking pocket measured just seven miles (11km) by six (9km). Under pressure from German paratroops within the pocket, the Poles were forced to relinquish control of some of the roads and up to 4,000 paratroops, supported by three tanks from 2nd SS, escaped. Kluge left La Roche Guyon at dawn on the 19th and after lunch, having failed Hitler, took his own life using cyanide.

Canadian armour probed the German defences at St Lambert-sur-Dives, losing two tanks on the 18th. The next morning they attacked, seizing half the village and then held on for thirty-six hours in the face of dogged counterattacks by the remains of 2nd Panzer to dislodge them. Germans fleeing over the river came under constant fire and at one point the Canadians called artillery fire down onto their own positions.

Escape from the cauldron

Jupp Steinbüchel from the 1st SS remembered the desperate drive to cross the Dives via the ford at Moissy, which, although in German hands, was under heavy Allied artillery fire, becoming a 'corridor of death.' His experiences encapsulated those of many of the men trapped in the Falaise salient, witnessing the horrifying death throes of the German forces as they sought frantically to escape the Allies deadly embrace:

> After we had crossed the Falaise–Argentan road, the whole mess descended on us. Artillery fire, the likes of which we had never known, rained down upon us. We raced forward, trying to escape this area. Here and there panzers took hits and burst into flames. We just kept driving. Stopping meant certain death. Right next to us, the air was full of planes. The roads were jammed. We drove straight off through the fields, not caring what happened to the vehicles. Infantry fire alternated with artillery, only to be replaced by anti-tank guns. The horse-drawn units raced through the area. Horses hitched to driverless wagons went wild and ran, dragging everything behind. Wounded men groaned and screamed.
>
> We loaded some onto our vehicle. One died on it. After that, he protected us from countless pieces of shrapnel.
>
> On our route between Ville-de-Dieu and Tournai-sur-Dives, the enemy artillery had a direct shot at us. I need hardly describe what that felt like. Shells fell just in front of us, beside, or behind our panzer. We coursed over that road as fast as we could.
>
> We reached a village. The town was a traffic jam of horse-drawn wagons, panzers, and automobiles. The enemy tanks were now firing into that mess with high-explosive shells. One can hardly imagine the chaos which reigned. Guns without crews. Panzers without drivers. Everyone trying to flee. Men running around and finding no way out. Fire from all sides. Our retreat was stuck; the enemy forces were too strong. Then someone found a new way. On we went. Enemy guns fired at us from six hundred metres away, but they missed. We saw the Canadians standing at their guns wearing white gym shorts.
>
> The number of vehicles abandoned or burning kept on growing. One could barely move forward on the road. Off we went again through the fields. If we had not been in tracked vehicles, it would have been all over for us.
>
> Then came the last step, the so-called 'Road of Death.' It was the most terrible part of the whole trip. No one can describe what we saw and lived through here.

Eberbach returned to Bittrich on 19 August, to find he had received no fuel and what ammunition had arrived was insufficient. Fuel did arrive the following day and the 9th SS and 10th SS were finally ready for action, though between them they could only muster twenty panzers. The II SS Panzer Corps found their way impeded by the debris of war. Eberbach noted: 'One road of advance was packed with burned-out vehicles to such an extent that the tanks had first to clear an alley before passing'.

The 10th SS was right in the middle of the Falaise pocket. It was comparatively fortunate in being one of the formations which managed to escape over the River Dives before the rapidly narrowing gap at Chambois was finally closed by the US, Canadian and Polish armour. By the end of the third week of August it was everyman for himself in what seemed to be a state of increasing bedlam.

Nevertheless, German discipline held; rarely did whole units bolt and stragglers and units cut off from their parent formations were willingly welded into the ubiquitous battle groups or *kampfgruppen*. Members of 2nd, 12th SS and 116th Panzer found themselves fighting alongside each other. In the meantime, elements of the withdrawing 277th Infantry Division were east of Falaise by the 19th, enabling 2,500 men to break out to reach the rest of the division outside the pocket. The 363rd managed to withdraw 19 miles (30km) to the east and head south of Trun, escaping with 2,000 men.

Although wounded, General Freiherr von Lüttwitz resolutely led a *kampf-gruppe* of 2nd Panzer through the chaos. Oberfeldwebel Hans Erich Braun was with them:

> That night of 19 August, we heard our passport for escape from the cauldron. It was, simply 'Forward'. Forward with a mixed battle group of tanks, self-propelled guns, flak and mounted artillery, scout cars, light tanks, and armoured troop carriers packed with Grenadiers, Paratroopers, and soldiers of all kinds of units. Forward through hell, but also towards the enemy, past the dead and the wounded. We had been tempered, like the steel plating of our tanks, and inside us now there was hardly any human feeling left. We were alive, but inside we were dead, numbed by watching the horrible scenes, which rolled past on both sides, just like a film. The Grenadiers sitting on their vehicles cowered low, grasping their weapons and holding on to the wounded. Anyone dying on top of these rolling steel coffins was just pitched overboard, so that a living man could take his place. They were sitting behind their tank guns, their flak guns, behind their automatic weapons, with one thought in their minds – to destroy the enemy who would soon appear now, to be without mercy, just like him.

The road taken by the remnants of 2nd Panzer and its grateful hangers-on was like a scene from hell; civilisation had abandoned them to the industrialised killing of the twentieth century. Braun felt numb as they drove by the wretched creatures that had once formed Hitler's invincible Wehrmacht; members of the Heer, Waffen-SS, Luftwaffe and Fallschirmjäger. Braun watched:

> The never ending detonations – soldiers waving to us, begging for help – the dead, their faces screwed up still in agony – huddled in trenches and shelters, the officers and men who had lost their nerve – burning vehicles from which piercing screams could be heard – a soldier stumbling, holding back the intestines which were oozing from his abdomen – soldiers lying in their own blood – arms and legs torn off – others driven crazy, crying, shouting, swearing, laughing hysterically – and the horses, some still harnessed to the shafts of their ruined wagons, appearing and disappearing in clouds of smoke and dust like ghosts – and the horses, again, screaming terribly, trying to escape the slaughter on the stumps of their hind legs. But also there were civilians lying by the roadside, loaded with personal belongings, often of no value at all, and still clinging to them in death. Close by a crossroads, caught by gunfire lay a group of men, women and children. Unforgettable, the staring gaze of their broken eyes and the grimaces of their pain distorted faces. Destroyed prams and discarded dolls littered the terrible scene.

Oberst von Gersdorff, 7th Army's Chief of Staff, having lost contact with the Panzergruppe, was completely lost on the night of 19/20 August. Arriving at the southern entrance to St Lambert at around 0400 he found a column of vehicles and quickly took charge. Enemy armour and anti-tank guns were dominating the Trun–St Lambert–Chambois road, destroying anything that attempted to use it.

Gersdorff rallied two Mark IV Jagdpanzers from 2nd Panzer to clear the route. Following in his Kubelwagen, Gersdorff led a column of panzers, assault guns, self-propelled guns and half-tracks. The enemy anti-tank gunners were taken by surprise and surrendered but the advance was held up after the lead panzers were knocked out.

In a nearby orchard, Gersdorff took stock and found he had a *kampfgruppe* of six to eight tanks, four to six assault guns, twenty-five to thirty armoured personnel carriers and a number of Hornisse 8.8cm self-propelled anti-tank guns and Hummel 15cm self-propelled artillery under Major Bochnick, commander of Panzerjäger Abteilung 228, 116th Panzer. There were also about 1,000 infantry under SS-Sturmbannführer Brinkman from the 12th SS or 17th SS.

Elements of all the units controlled by XLVII Panzer Corps were involved in the breakthrough groups. Between 0600 and 0700 on the 20th, the corps staff, 1st SS and 2nd Panzer Divisions reached the Chambois–St Lambert area. Following the breakout of the 353rd Infantry Division and its successful escape over the Dives, the Allied artillery fire intensified, causing a great loss of men and material in the Chambois–St Lambert zone.

Gersdorff was determined to fight his way to safety, noting:

> After brief preparations, the battle group thus formed set out at 0600hrs from the area approximately less than a mile (1km) north of St Lambert to attack and drive northwestward. Again and again, enemy tanks attempted to obstruct the advance, or to attack the flanks of the assault group from the hills, but were effectively taken under fire by our own armour-piercing weapons, ten–fifteen enemy tanks being set afire. Without any delay worth mentioning, the attack reached the elevated terrain around Goudehard [Coudehard], so that a breach had been laid in the enemy-encircling ring. Upon returning at about 0900hrs, as far as circumstances permitted, to search for the Army Commander, and to arrange for protection of the flanks in the gap created, the Chief of Staff found that the entire region between Chambois and St Lambert was now under terrible intense artillery fire. Nevertheless, the enemy, who was preoccupied with attacks by other breakthrough groups which were taking effect at Chambois as well as at and north-west of St Lambert, for the time being made no attempt to close the gap again. An endless line of infantry and vehicles now flowed along the road through the gap.

On the night of 19/20 August, General der Fallschirmtruppen Eugen Meindl and his Chief of Staff, Oberst Ernst Blauensteiner, each led a *kampfgruppe* of survivors from the II Parachute Corps, 3rd Fallschirmjäger Division (which had been decimated), 7th Army HQ staff and some SS tanks in a final effort to escape.

Battle for St Lambert

Inside the corridor, 2nd Panzer with their remaining fifteen tanks attacked toward Canadian held St Lambert and found the bridge intact. Their commanding officer recalled: 'The crossing of the Dives bridge was particularly horrible, the bodies of the dead, horses and vehicles and other equipment having been hurled from the bridge into the river formed a gruesome tangled mass'. The 10th SS and 116th Panzer managed to cross the river Dives via the

St Lambert bridge and drove the encircling Allies away. The 116th escaped with just fifty vehicles.

Notably, at St Lambert Lüwitz's 2nd Panzer met fierce resistance in the form of enemy tank, anti-tank and infantry fire. The tanks of 2nd Panzer had to renew their efforts to break out, while from midday enemy armour resumed trying to penetrate the town. Lüttwitz, now wounded, ordered his men to break out in separate groups. In particular they discovered an open road between Chambois and St Lambert heading northeast.

Panzer Lehr's Kampfgruppe Kuhnow broke out on the 20th and the following day gathered at Senlis, north of Paris. Elements of the 1st SS, with the 277th Infantry and 3rd Fallschirmjäger Divisions, also escaped the pocket. However, the staffs of the controlling LXXXIV Corps, including General Otto Elfeldt, Oberstleutnant Friederich Creiger and Major Viebig, and those of the 84th Infantry Division were not as lucky. Remarkably, these were the only two staffs out of twenty higher-level staffs that did not escape. The 84th, which was valiantly acting as a rearguard, suffered some 5,500 casualties.

General Elfeldt mustered some of Panzergruppe West's last remaining panzers for a final escape attempt:

> By the time we had got back to the Orne the whole front had become much narrower than before, so my Corps headquarters had become superfluous and was temporarily withdrawn from the line. But the following morning the Canadians broke through southwards to Falaise and I was at once ordered to form a front to check them. The available troops were very scanty and we had no communications. The Canadian artillery fired all day into my headquarters, but fortunately did no damage at all although they fired about a thousand shells. These fell all round the small house in which I was, but no one was hurt. During the day I was able to re-form a continuous line, but beyond my right flank I could see the British tanks driving down the other side of the River Dives towards Trun. Thus our line of retreat was blocked.
>
> The next day I was ordered to break out northeastward, behind the backs of these armoured forces. It was soon clear that this was not possible, as the British were now there in strength. So I proposed to the Army commander General Hausser, that my troops should be placed at the disposal of General Meindl, who was commanding the parachute forces, to help the latter to break out near St Lambert, southeastwards. It seemed to me that one strong thrust might have a better chance than a number of small ones. Meindl succeeded in

breaking out, but when I reached St Lambert myself next morning the gap was again closed. I tried an attack with all I had left – a couple of tanks and two hundred men. It started well but then ran into part of the 1st Polish Armoured Division. After a two-hour fight our ammunition began to run out. Then the troops which were following behind me surrendered, thus leaving me with a handful of men at the cut-off tip of the wedge. So we had to surrender in turn. The commander of this Polish division was a fine-looking man and a gentleman. He gave me his last cigarette.

Outside the mouth of the pocket on 20 August, II SS Panzer Corps finally attempted to reach the trapped remnants of 7th Army. Directing the attack from its HQ at Vimoutiers, the corps launched the operation at 0400 hours. To the south of Vimoutiers two *kampfgruppen* of the 2nd SS struck toward Neauphe-sur-Dive and St Lambert. The much weaker 9th SS, which had lost an entire battalion fighting the Poles, was launched along the Champeaux road toward Trun.

For the counterattack Will Fey and the last Tiger tank joined men from the 9th SS and 12th SS equipped with nothing heavier than panzerfausts, holding defensive blocking positions on the Vimoutiers–Trun road. He recalled how they bumped into the Polish 1st Armoured Division near Champosoult; knocking out two Shermans and forcing the rest to retreat, they pressed on. The *kampfgruppe* broke through almost to Chambois, reaching some of those trapped. Fey noted:

At full speed, we fired salvos from our MGs [machineguns] at the transport convoys of the enemy, joyfully welcomed by German soldiers who already had one foot in the prisoner of war camp. Our enemies stared at us with fearful faces as we broke into the encirclement of Falaise, a wild and daring chase. We experienced things we never had before, such as knocking out a Sherman that suddenly showed up from a side street, at a distance of eight metres! We had achieved our mission to open up the encirclement. The whole staff of our Panzer Army with its Commander-in-Chief, Hausser, which was still inside the encirclement, was able to escape being taken prisoner! But then we had to get back if we did not want to lose contact with the withdrawal operation!

The 2nd SS, with just twenty panzers, were unable to achieve much and the Polish 2nd Armoured Regiment halted the 9th SS. The counterattack came to a stop before a series of hills: 258, southwest of Les Champeaux; 240, east of

Ecorches; 239, west of Champosoult and 262, northeast of Coudehard. The SS could get no further and at Hill 239 the 2nd SS were counterattacked by sixty enemy tanks and a bitter tank battle followed; 9th SS panzergrenadiers, lacking tank support, got as far as the heights of Les Cosniers.

Nevertheless, II SS Panzer Corps' efforts were an unwelcome distraction for the Allies and eased the pressure on some of those inside the pocket. A gap was forced and 2,000 men streamed through as well as twenty-five tanks and fifty guns. Having completed its mission of briefly opening up the pocket, Fey's Tiger, covered in panzergrenadiers, drove west toward the Seine.

In the meantime, General von Schwerin's 116th Panzer, covering the rear of the XLVII Panzer Corps during the afternoon of the 20th, had got as far as Hill 168 without being molested. In St Lambert the 116th was greeted by abandoned and destroyed debris strewn everywhere. At dusk on 20 August the brave Canadian defenders in St Lambert-sur-Dives, calling down artillery fire, were able to destroy the gathering German forces before they could even mount their attack.

During the bitter two-day battle for the village the Germans suffered 300 dead, 500 wounded and 2,100 captured, including some of the officers and men from 2nd Panzer Division, who laid down their arms under the watchful eye of Canadian Sherman tanks. During the close-quarter fighting seven panzers, forty other vehicles and twelve 8.8cm guns were destroyed.

Clearing a way through the choked roads between 2300 and 0100 on the night of 20/21 August, the survivors of the 116th Panzer Division, with about fifty combat vehicles, broke through without notable loss. The division managed to escape with eleven Panthers, four Panzer IVs, three StuGs, and two Wespe and one Hummel self-propelled guns.

One group were not so fortunate. A *kampfgruppe* at Argentan found itself left behind and tried to fight its way through at Trun, but was not successful and surrendered. Elements of Panzer Lehr, supporting the 331st Infantry Division, also remained behind north of Gráce, defending the Gráce–Vimoutiers road.

The 9th SS vainly tried to break through again on 21 August, using two massive King Tiger tanks, but these were swiftly knocked out. The Allies now began to mop up the remaining Germans trapped west of the Dives and about 18,000 troops went into the 'bag' that day. The Allies found the surrounding countryside a charnel-house, the air fouled by the stench of rotting corpses, cattle and horses. Incredibly, despite the desperate situation, in less than a week between 14 August and 21 August, the German Army and Waffen-SS claimed to have destroyed 293 Allied tanks. Liquidating the pocket had come at a terrible cost in men and matériel.

Horrendous destruction

Second Lieutenant Stuart Hills, Nottinghamshire Sherwood Rangers Yeomanry, 8th Armoured Brigade, followed the British 11th Armoured Division
through the Falaise pocket via Chambois to L'Aigle. There he witnessed the
devastation:

> The scenes in the Falaise pocket, where Allied air power had wreaked
> such destruction, were horrendous. The various German divisions
> had a terrible pounding in the Normandy battle, Panzer Lehr, for
> instance lost all its tanks and infantry units, while about 50,000 of the
> enemy had been killed and some 20,000 taken prisoner. Thousands
> still lay unburied within the pocket: the roads and fields were littered
> with German dead in various stages of decomposition. Then there
> were the carcasses of cows and horses, the smashed vehicles and
> abandoned carts laden with loot. Many of the human and animal
> bodies had swelled grotesquely in the summer sun, and the stench
> was awful. 'Who in God's name will do what about this lot?' asked
> Padre Skinner. It was a fair question.

Similarly, *The Times'* war correspondent was aghast at the destruction wrought
in the Falaise pocket. He recalled:

> Nearly every yard of ground must have been pin pointed by batteries
> of all calibres: coming down from Trun there is hardly a yard of road,
> along which sporadic fighting was still going on yesterday, that does
> not tell its grim tale. The ditches are lined with destroyed enemy
> vehicles of every description ...
>
> For four days the rain of death poured down, and with the road
> blocked with blazing tanks and trucks little can have escaped it.
> Nothing can describe the horror of the sight in the village of St
> Lambert-sur-Dives, an enemy graveyard over which his troops were
> struggling yesterday in an effort to break through the cordon
> hedging them off from the seeming escape lanes to the Seine.

Lieutenant Hills was staggered by it all and recorded that the public back home
were perhaps rightly spared the full reality of the butchery:

> Press and news photographers certainly recorded the grisly scene,
> although I myself have never seen the results of their efforts: I can
> only surmise that the sheer horror of it all may have placed
> constraints on the publication of such material. For this was strong
> medicine, even for those of us who were more accustomed than those

at home to the hideous visions of war. For my part, I was simply dazed and dumbfounded at what I had witnessed. If it had not been before my eyes, I would have felt it to be utterly unreal.

The Times reporter observed Hitler's armoured forces were completely spent: 'Within an area of about a square mile hundreds of tanks and armoured cars, great trucks and guns and horse-drawn wagons, lie burned and splintered in hideous disarray.' Anything salvagable was quickly retrieved as the correspondent witnessed: 'All manner of enemy vehicles that had escaped the destruction were being driven back to our own lines under white flags or hastily designed white stars.'

General de Guingand, like many senior Allied officers, went to view the scene at first hand:

> The destruction caused to the enemy was terrific. I have never seen it equalled before or since. The tens of thousands of prisoners, the wounded and the dead. Thousands of tanks and vehicles lying all over the countryside. Some burnt out, some abandoned. The roads that were still open to them were packed with transport, nose to tail. Our aircraft had got to work and record bags had been obtained by our pilots. There were hundreds of dead horses rotting in the hot sun. Never have I seen such a scene of desolation. I flew over the area once or twice in a puddle jumper. It was an unforgettable sight, and the smell of decay was strong in the air above. It seemed difficult to imagine how any army could survive a defeat of this sort.

General Dwight Eisenhower, Allied Supreme Commander, was also taken on a tour:

> Forty-eight hours after the closing of the gap I was conducted through it on foot, to encounter scenes that could be described only by Dante. It was literally possible to walk for hundreds of yards at a time, stepping on nothing but dead and decaying flesh.

He was rightly pleased with the crushing defeat of the Nazi war machine and recalled in his memoirs:

> German commanders concentrated particularly on saving armoured elements, and while a disappointing portion of their panzer divisions did get back across the Seine, they did so at the cost of a great proportion of their equipment. Eight infantry and two panzer divisions were captured almost in their entirety.

During this final battle the Wehrmacht lost approximately 10,000 killed and 50,000 captured, though Eberbach estimated the number killed during 10–22 August at about 20,000. The Americans counted in their zone of the pocket 380 tanks and 160 self-propelled guns as well as 5,000 vehicles. In the British, Canadian and Polish areas were littered 344 armoured vehicles. The 2nd Tactical Air Force claimed to have destroyed or damaged 190 tanks and 2,600 vehicles during its sorties over the battlefield.

Typhoon pilot Flight Lieutenant H Ambrose, 175 Squadron, was amazed by the coordination of the air attacks and disgusted by the smell of death:

> [Wing Commander] Charles Green was absolutely brilliant about the Falaise Gap. He had sorted it all out. He saw what was going on and warned the AOC [Air Officer Commanding] and the Army that this was a situation that had to be arrested pretty quickly. Some of the German Army did escape, of course, but the Typhoons and some Spitfires, made mincemeat of the German Army at Falaise. They just blocked roads, stopped them moving and just clobbered them. You could smell Falaise from 6,000 feet in the cockpit. The decomposing corpses of horses and flesh – burning flesh, the carnage was terrible. Falaise was the heyday of the Typhoon.

The Germans claim that 40,000 troops escaped, although many of them were killed before they crossed the Seine and, crucially, they only took twenty-five panzers with them. Eberbach thought less than half this number of men escaped the pocket. The Germans had lost all their equipment and it was seen as their worst defeat since the Battle of Stalingrad.

Colonel David Belchem, Head of Montgomery's Operations and Planning Staff succinctly summed up the desperate nature of the battle:

> The stubborn Falaise pocket was finally closed on 19 August, when American troops driving from the south towards Chambois met 4th Canadian Armoured and the Polish Armoured Divisions converging on the town from the northwest and northeast. As the noose tightened, this tiny area of Normandy contained the shattered remnants of some eighteen German Army formations. The battle for Falaise lasted for nearly two weeks. Initially the beleaguered enemy retained some degree of organisation – the infantry units fighting in the west while the remnants of the panzer divisions battled desperately to keep open the narrow escape route at the neck: but by 16 August the situation was chaotic. For some time after 19 August, the Allied formations were fully occupied in rounding up

the dispersed groups of confused enemy survivors – each group containing, perhaps, members of up to a dozen different units. The wreckage and confusion within the 'pocket' is difficult to describe: enemy transport vehicles, guns and tanks were found packed nose to tail in a landscape of total devastation.

In contrast, Colonel Ralph Ingersoll, historian of General Bradley's 12th Army Group summed up Falaise with an air of deep regret:

The failure to close the Argentan–Falaise gap was the loss of the greatest single opportunity of the war. The news would have come hard on the heels of the attempted assassination of Hitler ... and would have been accompanied by the news of the liberation of Paris [less than a week later]. But as long as any of the German Army escaped, Hitler had a chance to cover up the extent of the disaster.

This he would do in spectacular fashion.

Chapter 16

The Flawed Victory

Despite the Allies snapping at their heels all the way to the Seine, thousands of German troops would escape to fight another day. Gefechtsschreiber (headquarters clerk) Rolf Munninger, a 23 year old Swabian who had served Rommel, was one of the last to leave Army Group B's HQ: 'I was in La Roche [Guyon] with the rearguard, the main body of troops had left two days earlier. We realised that tanks were preparing to storm our HQ so we decided to leave during the night'. He found himself despatched on a fool's errand to collect champagne from Reims, noting tartly: 'under Rommel I would certainly not have been sent to organise champagne'.

The Rouen bridgehead

The Germans were fully aware that they had suffered a catastrophe at Falaise, St Lambert, Chambois and Trun, but there was no time to reflect as they had much more pressing matters. Once the Falaise gap was closed, British I Corps, under the command of the Canadian 1st Army, pushed along the coast to Honfleur, while on its flank the Canadian II Corps headed for Rouen and the Seine River.

Model, Dietrich and Eberbach knew they must hold the west bank stretching north from Paris, through Rouen to the coast and Le Havre, in order to allow their retreating forces to escape over the river. This would provide a new main line of resistance, or, if it came to the worst, as seemed likely, they could withdraw behind the Somme. Providing a fighting screen for the retiring forces meant no rest for the shattered panzer divisions, which Model described as little more than 'torsos'.

While the destruction of the Falaise pocket seemed a deathblow from which the German Army could never recover, numerous units had not been caught. On the Allies' immediate eastern flank were elements of the 85th, 272nd, 331st, 346th and 711th Infantry Divisions, numbering about 32,450 men. Behind them were another nine infantry and parachute divisions, eight of which had come from von Salmuth's 15th Army.

In fact there were an estimated 250,000 German troops and 250 panzers still west of the Seine, consisting of men outside the pocket, those who had escaped the pocket and units withdrawing from Army Group G's area. In mid–August

Hitler, finally grasping the gravity of the situation developing in Normandy, had ordered all non-combatant troops under Army Group G in western and southern France to commence withdrawing beyond the Seine.

The staff of 5th Panzer Army found that from each of the panzer divisions on average 3,000 men had escape the shambles of Falaise, while each of the infantry divisions could only muster up to 2,000 men. It took command of the entire sector west of the Seine, ordering that Elbeuf, laying on a huge west-facing loop in the river south of Rouen, should be held. This was the nearest crossing point for those troops fleeing from Falaise and represented their primary escape route. In the meantime, the exhausted staffs of 7th Army, no longer capable of directing anything, were ordered to collect all available infantry units beyond the Seine.

The Americans achieved a bridgehead over the river north of Paris at Mantes-Gassicourt, just south of Army Group B's HQ at La Roche Guyon, on the 19th, posing a threat to 5th Panzer Army's left wing. If Patton had been instructed to exploit this with a rapid thrust north along the east bank instead of the west, fewer Germans would have escaped.

Model instructed Dietrich to counterattack with four of his panzer divisions. Four days later a few weak panzergrenadier units and about thirty panzers were launched into a feeble attack that was swiftly halted. This was repeated on the 24th, with similar results.

Further north, the remnants of three panzer divisions, 2nd SS, 21st and 116th Panzer, were melded into Group Schwerin, with about twenty battle-worthy tanks and assault guns. On the night of 23rd/24th, 21st Panzer and 2nd SS moved to reinforce the eastern flank of 5th Panzer Army between the Seine and the Risle in an effort to protect the Seine crossings near Rouen. The 21st Panzer was subordinate to 116th Panzer, while 2nd SS were to hold blocking positions south and southeast of Elbeuf. By the evening of the 24th a line had been established between Elbeuf and the Risle north of Brionne. The withdrawing 9th SS were also ordered to join Group Schwerin.

The Germans did all they could to hold up the US 2nd Armored Division attempting to cross the River Avre at Verneuil. Suffering heavy casualties, the Americans crossed upstream, swinging north toward Elbeuf. They penetrated the town on 24 August but were expelled by the 2nd SS the following morning. German resistance was so aggressive that one American column attacking from the southeast was cut off for two days and nights. Holding the high ground on the east bank opposite Elbeuf was the 17th Luftwaffe Field Division, blocking the crossing and the way to Rouen.

Further north, Kuntzen's LXXXI Corps also soon found themselves at risk, necessitating moving the 9th SS to the Montfort area on the 25th. East of Rouen the British 43rd (Wessex) Infantry Division crossed at Vernon and three days later the 11th Armoured Division was over and swinging northward toward Amiens and the Somme.

Withdrawal across the Seine now became an imperative and Model gave the order. Priority of crossing was armoured fighting vehicles, motorised transport and then horse-drawn. By 25 August, as the retreat got underway, 5th Panzer Army was able to muster just 18,000 men, forty-two tanks and assault guns and 314 guns, essentially a single panzer division. These forces were pulled back to the Seine bridgehead, formed by three large river loops, to protect the crossings at Caudebec-en-Caux, Duclair, Elbeuf and Rouen.

Those who escaped the Allied encirclement still had to get over the river. Now that the frontline had vanished, for the retreating troops there was a constant air of uncertainty, driving through villages unsure if they would bump into enemy patrols, hostile *Maquis* or simply indifferent locals, and with the ever-present fighter-bombers circling menacingly overhead. One anonymous German soldier writing home recalled that even after escaping the Falaise pocket his ordeal was far from over, as it became a case of every man for himself:

> I was in the Argentan–Falaise pocket and I still don't know how I got out of it. We were running in wild fiery circles with artillery and aerial bombs dropping around us. After I got out of there I had to fight partisans and our own soldiers to get on the ferry across the Seine.

The retreating Germans made for the crossings at Elbeuf, Oissel and Rouen, which were under constant air attack. The main crossing point was at Rouen, so holding the wooded river bulge became vital, though with the river unfordable and with all the bridges down they had to rely on boats and rafts. The pontoon bridge at Rouen could only take wheeled vehicles and the bridge at Oissel, having been brought down in May, was likewise makeshift. Many surviving tanks and other vehicles that had been so painstakingly coaxed eastward were abandoned on the dockside. On the 25th bombers attacked the German transport massed on the quayside twice; the following day the fires were still burning both sides of the river.

Outside Rouen, Will Fey and his comrades from Schwere SS-Panzer Abteilung 102 witnessed the fate of the surviving panzers:

> All the panzers and artillery had to remain on the west bank of the Seine. They were driven out of the columns, and some were blown

up. Some of the Panzers that were still mobile were driven into the stream and sunk or blown up in the woods. We had dragged the panzers, artillery, and valuable equipment away from the front for days across long distances to this river; then we had to leave them there. The crews drifted across the river without panzers and guns. But we could not leave our panzer so easily.

Driving their Tiger into the docks, a boat came to Fey's rescue:

Just then a navy barge came put-putting across the Seine to solve our problems and take our Tiger to the other shore. Our Tiger with the 001 on the turret, ready for action, rolled onto the barge without problems, and we set out. Was it the 001, the number of the command Panzer, that helped us get across? We were sitting on our Tiger with anticipation and had almost reached the shore when a formation of two fighter-bombers firing from all barrels, came flying at us across the Seine.

This meant that all possible speed was needed, and our driver started the engine before the barge reached the shore. The navy men were jumping off to secure the boat when the next attack by the fighter-bombers began. Full cover was the only answer to the well-aimed fire from a low-level attack. Before the ropes were fully fastened, the Tiger set out slowly and the tracks were already getting a hold on the harbour wall when the sixty tons of our panzer pushed the barge away from the wall. Our 001 rolled from the deck into the Seine. The stern of the barge stuck out of the water, and there was just enough time for the crew to jump off before Tiger 001 sank into the waters of Rouen harbour like a submarine.

The lacklustre 116th Panzer scored a minor success at Bourgtheroulde, briefly driving the Americans back on the 26th with a combination of tanks and artillery. On the night of 26th/27th the 116th's Panzergrenadier Regiments 60 and 156 were deployed along the Seine loop near Moulineaux to the north and the Forêt de la Londe in the centre respectively, with 2nd SS holding the left wing near Orival, thereby blocking off the approaches to Rouen. The three self-propelled guns of I Battery, Panzer Artillery Regiment 146, 116th Panzer, rendered inoperable after air attack were pulled out of the line and withdrawn over the Seine on the night of 26th.

The 116th Panzer and a *kampfgruppe* from the 2nd SS were given the task of holding the Americans at bay at Elbeuf, but on the 26th 2nd Armoured overran the town's southern outskirts. Having pinned down the Americans, the

116th withdrew at midnight under the cover of fog and rain. Members of the 2nd SS, including Fritz Langanke, escaped by swimming across the river. At daybreak the Americans mopped up resistance and handed the town over to the Canadians.

Some surviving Tigers of Panzer Abteilung 102 reached Elbeuf on 25 August only to find the bridge down, so headed for Oissel to the northeast. There the crews found the area clogged with an estimated 5,000–7,000 vehicles all waiting to cross. Reluctantly the order was given for the remaining panzers to be destroyed. Panzer Abteilung 503 is believed to have lost the last of its Tigers west of the Seine near Rouen at la Bouille. There were no ferries that could take their massive weight and they had to be abandoned. The 10th SS crossed at Oissel on 25–27 August by means of two bridges they had seized, selfishly fending off attempts by other retreating units to use them until all their own troops had crossed.

A withdrawal to the three Seine loops south of Caudebec-en-Caux, south of Duclair and south of Rouen was ordered on the night of the 27th/28th, with the 331st Infantry Division taking over the Duclair and Rouen loops and the dense forest in between.

While the Canadian 3rd Armoured Division crossed at Elbeuf, the Canadian 2nd Infantry Division was required to push through Forêt de la Londe, whose wooded hills stretched northward all the way to Rouen. They suffered almost 600 casualties in three days of bitter fighting. By nightfall on the 28th the Canadian 3rd and 4th Armoured Divisions had taken possession of the hills about a mile inland from Elbeuf, having put the 17th Luftwaffe Field Division to flight. The Polish 1st Armoured Division also crossed at Elbeuf on the 29th.

SS-Flak Abteilung 17 crossed the Seine on the 27th, upstream from Portejoie, and made its way to Metz to join the rest of the 17th SS. The battalion's I Battery at Saumur, although lacking transport, managed to commandeer local vehicles and headed for Tours on the 24th. After defending the bridge there and covering stragglers, the unit finally reached Metz on 20 September.

The remaining survivors of 2nd Panzer managed to cross the Seine on 28 August. Ironically, Otto Meyer, commander of SS-Panzer Regiment 9, having survived all the fighting in Normandy, was killed on 30 August crossing at Duclair. In the early hours that day the 331st Infantry, acting as rearguard, finally pulled back across the river and the Canadian 3rd and 4th Armoured liberated Rouen.

Model decided that 7th Army would cover the withdrawal of 5th Panzer Army toward Arras, northeast of Amiens and behind the safety of the Somme, where it could be refitted. At Amiens, Dietrich was supposed to hand command of 5th Panzer Army back to Eberbach on the afternoon of the 31st. Dietrich left early and Eberbach, commanding 7th Army in Hausser's absence, and his staff were surprised by British tanks rumbling into their midst and compelled to surrender. His Chief of Staff, von Gersdorff, escaped but 5th Panzer Army's guard company, drawn from 116th Panzer, were not so lucky. Eberbach's only reserves were just five Tiger tanks and they could achieve little in the face of the British 11th Armoured Division. The last remaining operational unit of Panzer Abteilung 503, III Kompanie, finally lost its Tiger IIs near Amiens.

This drove a wedge between 15th Army west of Amiens and 5th Panzer Army to the east. Any hopes Model had of holding the Somme as a main line of resistance were dashed. He was now forced to retreat yet again and the British were soon pushing on Brussels and Antwerp. In the meantime, Dietrich made his way to Model's Army Group B HQ at Havrincourt and was briefly appointed commander of 7th Army.

Also on the 31st a team of *panzertruppen*, including Will Fey, bravely slipped back across the Seine to destroy the abandoned Tiger tanks on the dockside, as he relates:

> Our VW took us into the city and to the harbour, and a boat of the pioneers took us across ... A wild chaos awaited us at the crossing point ... It was covered with burning and smoking wrecks of vehicles ... We comforted the moaning and begging wounded ... We spotted the first three Tigers, undamaged, very close to our crossing point. They had been abandoned by their crews.
>
> We pushed the explosive charges, which every panzer carried in case they were needed, into the breech of the 8.8cm gun, poured gasoline from a jerry can into the interior, activated the detonator charge, and threw a hand grenade into the engine compartment to set the fuel on fire. Then we jumped off and took full cover. The explosion followed. All this took only a few seconds, and one Tiger after the other burned with bright flames.

Then, using panzerfausts, they took out two Panthers commandeered by the local *Maquis* who were trying to operate them, before escaping back over the Seine in a rowboat.

There had been no second Falaise pocket. Frustratingly for the Allies, the bulk of those German forces west of the Seine, some 240,000 troops, 30,000 vehicles and 135 panzers, escaped over the river. German armoured vehicle losses were modest considering the rapidity of the Allied advance, only sixty panzers and 250 other armoured vehicles being left on the west bank. About

10,000 troops seem to have been caught. The surviving staffs of 5th Panzer Army and LVIII Panzer Corps were pulled out of the line and responsibility assumed by 7th Army once more.

Fall of Paris

Hauptmann Helmut Ritgen found himself in Paris overseeing the refitting of elements of Panzer Lehr and missed being trapped at Falaise. There was an air of unreality in the French capital as the occupiers drank champagne and danced. The Allies had hoped to bypass Paris, but this was made impossible by the actions of Charles de Gaulle's Free French Forces. He was concerned that the French Communists would liberate Paris and got an undertaking that General Leclerc with the French 2nd Armoured Division could enter the city. At this stage, the Supreme Allied Commander, General Eisenhower, felt it best to bypass Paris to avoid being sucked into costly street fighting with General Dietrich von Choltitz's garrison. Once the Allies were over the Seine, Paris had become a strategic irrelevance.

General von Choltitz, former LXXXIV Corps commander in Normandy, was under strict instructions to deny Paris to the Allies, even if it meant razing it to the ground. Hitler told him the city 'must not fall into the hands of the enemy, if it does, he must find there nothing but a field of ruins'. Choltitz fortunately had no intention of going down in history as the one who torched Paris.

His garrison was weak, consisting of the 325th Security Division, a company of tanks from Panzer Lehr, and twenty batteries of 8.8cm anti-aircraft guns with inexperienced teenage crews, supported by sixty aircraft. This amounted to just 5,000 men, fifty guns and perhaps twenty tanks. The force was about adequate to contain any insurrection, but nothing else. Now that German forces in France were in disarray, help was unlikely to be forthcoming. Hitler had promised two skeleton panzer divisions from Denmark, but they had not materialised.

Since early August, von Choltitz had found the city ungovernable, though the Resistance were under instructions from de Gaulle not to rise up until the arrival of Leclerc's armour. While 5th Panzer Army and 7th Army were in their final death throes, the Parisians had risen up on 19 August, launching numerous attacks on the German garrison. Securing a one-day truce, it withdrew to the east of the city.

On the 21st Leclerc, ignoring orders, sent a reconnaissance group, consisting of ten tanks and ten armoured cars, toward Paris. Furious, US V Corps commander, Major General L T Gerow, ordered Leclerc to recall them;

he refused. However, the Communist resistance had also already risen up a few days earlier, forcing Eisenhower's hand. On 22 August he authorised the French 2nd Armoured and the 4th US Infantry Divisions to drive on Paris the following day.

Outlying German defences consisted of small numbers of tanks supported by anti-tank guns holed up in the villages and at the crossroads. At Jouy-en-Josas three French Shermans were lost in tank-to-tank engagements. Stiff resistance was also met at Longjumeau and Croix de Berny. German 8.8cm guns at Massy and Wissous accounted for more of Leclerc's tanks. Similarly an 8.8cm sited in the old prison at Fresnes, blocking the Paris road, held off three Shermans. The first was knocked out, but the second destroyed the gun and the third ran over it. The French lost another four tanks to German anti-tank guns trying to outflank Fresnes. Despite the demoralised state of the Germans, the push on Paris cost the division 296 casualties, thirty-five tanks, six self-propelled guns and eleven assorted vehicles disabled or destroyed.

A French patrol slipped into the city on the evening of 24 August. By nightfall their tanks were within a few hundred yards of von Choltitiz's HQ at the Meurice. The next day, during five hours of street fighting to clear the German defenders from the foreign office building on the Quai d'Orsay, another Sherman tank was lost. At the Arc de Triomphe a French tank silenced its German counterpart at a range of 1,800 metres. Unfortunately, von Choltitz felt honour dictated he put up at least token resistance before surrendering. In the Place de la Concorde three Shermans were lost after they drove in with their turret hatches open and each received a German grenade.

When von Choltitz finally capitulated there were still 2,000 Germans in Paris and fighting was still going on in the suburbs. Gerow ordered Leclerc to clear them from the northern suburbs and de Gaulle wanted to keep the division in Paris to counter the Communists. He then wanted the division to join the French 1st Army pushing up from the south of France, instead Leclerc got his force reassigned to US XV Corps moving towards Alsace. Unfortunately, Leclerc's actions in liberating Paris helped prolong the war, for the delay round the city enabled a greater part of Army Group G's 1st Army to escape over the Rhine.

Counting the cost

The fallout of the Falaise pocket went beyond 5th Panzer Army and 7th Army. General von Salmuth was relieved of his command of 15th Army by Hitler in late August following the disintegration of the German front line. Infantry General Gustav-Adolf von Zangen, fresh from Italy, replaced him. To add to

German woes, in the south of France on 26 August Toulon, followed by Marseilles two days later, was liberated with the loss of several thousand dead and 37,000 troops captured. The Allies secured the region between Nice and Avignon as far north as Briançon via Grenoble to Montelimar, effectively destroying General Wiese's 19th Army, mainly through artillery and air strikes.

The remains of Wiese's command streamed north to join Chevallerie's 1st Army, which was evacuating southwestern France and heading for the Belfort Gap. The latter forms the pass between the Jura and Vosges mountains and the Germans knew that if they lost control of it Strasbourg and all Wurtemberg would be exposed. It did not fall until 25 November. Meanwhile, the retreating Germans conducted delaying actions, notably in the Autun and Dijon regions, but ultimately they were now being driven from the whole of France. On 3 September Lyon was liberated and another 2,000 Germans captured.

The situation on the Western front appeared irretrievable for Hitler and the Third Reich. While the Germans had barely 100 serviceable panzers, the Allies could muster 6,000 medium and 1,700 light tanks. It seemed as if nothing would stop their armoured juggernaut; by 4 September they were 200 miles (320km) east of the Seine and in control of the vital port of Antwerp. They were seven months ahead of their schedule.

The Wehrmacht had lost forty-three divisions by September, roughly thirty-five infantry and eight panzer, two more than were originally stationed in northern France. They suffered a total loss of 450,000 men; 240,000 killed and wounded and 210,000 prisoners, as well as losing most of their equipment: 1,500 panzers, 3,500 pieces of artillery and 20,000 vehicles. Some 58,412 are buried in Normandy in the main German cemeteries at Huisnes-sur-Mer, La Cambe, Lisieux (Saint-Désir), Marigny and Orglandes; the largest is La Cambe, which holds 21,400. For the Allies the price of victory was dear, approximately 84,000 British and Canadian, and 126,000 American casualties, consisting of 36,976 killed and 172,696 wounded.

In total the Germans lost about 1,500 tanks and assault guns from an accumulated strength of 2,248 armoured fighting vehicles deployed to Normandy by mid-August. The latter figure includes all the General Headquarters panzer formations and the armoured fighting vehicles of the Infantry Divisions and the Luffwaffe Field Divisions. From 1 June–31 August the Germans had lost a total of 4,050 panzers and assault guns on all fronts. The exhausted panzer divisions lost all their tanks in northern France; in fact, from an accumulated tank force of 1,804 just eighty-six remained. Similarly, the independent tank battalions and assault brigades, from an accumulated strength of 458, could scrape together forty-four vehicles.

Scrutiny of German panzer losses produces some startling results. In the Roncey pocket 122 tanks were accounted for and another forty-six were lost during the Mortain counterattack. Of the 380 found in the Falaise pocket, eighty per cent had been abandoned or destroyed by their fleeing crews. Another 150 tanks were found west of the Seine. Therefore in total some 638 tanks, tank destroyers and assault guns lost west of the Seine are accounted for. This, though, is far from the total figure; around another 900 were lost in Normandy during June, July and August.

While they remained in range, naval fire support from the Allied warships in the Channel could produce devastating results against the massing panzers. Few members of the German High Command seemed to have fully considered the implications of this; once the effects became apparent Rommel had been swift to call for a withdrawal out of harm's way, but to no avail. In contrast, the sustained and often very heavy attacks by the Allied bombers and fighter-bombers produced surprisingly mixed results against the armoured fighting vehicles of Panzergruppe West and 7th Army. In fact the bomber raids preceding the Allies' major offensives often proved more fatal to their own men and hampered the advance because of the damage caused.

Subsequent analysis showed that RAF Typhoon rockets had not caused as much destruction as first thought or indeed claimed. It has been assessed that only about 100 armoured fighting vehicles were actually knocked out by air strikes during the entire campaign; in stark contrast the Allies lost a total of 1,726 aircraft.

According to subsequent British analysis, two of the main causes for the defeat of the Panther tank were abandonment and self-destruction by the *panzertruppen*. These two categories accounted for nearly half the Panthers left on the battlefield during August and constituted eighty per cent of all the Panthers lost. Air power only accounted for about six per cent of all the lost Panthers investigated.

Rockets and free-fall bombs were highly inaccurate when trying to hit vehicles and the Germans were masters of camouflage. The Allied air forces' real contribution was the sense of panic their attacks caused, with vehicle crews quickly taking to the fields at the onset of an air strike.

One of the divisions that appeared to have suffered the most was the 2nd Panzer. On 24 August it assembled fifteen tanks near Meaux, east of Paris, four days later less than 1,200 men and five tanks managed to cross the Seine. At the end of August Panzer Lehr, which had also suffered heavy casualties, mustered barely 6,000 men near Fontainbleu and the repair units were able to provide just twenty tanks. The 9th Panzer Division was not encircled at Falaise and was able to muster about 11,000 men, though few, if any, tanks. The 21st Panzer

Division was also one of those that suffered heavy losses in Normandy and by late August had just ten combat ready tanks, but also had about 11,000 men available. Similarly about 10,600 men of the 116th escaped along with fifteen tanks, three assault guns and three self-propelled guns.

The 1st SS lost about twenty-five per cent of its manpower and had no combat-ready tanks. Parts of the 10th SS were encircled along with the 1st SS and 2nd Panzer and lost all their armour. The 2nd SS had just six tanks, but it was not surrounded and by the end of September had mustered 12,357 men. Likewise, the 9th SS escaped the trap and was able to muster twenty to twenty-five tanks, though in early September ten of these were handed over to the 11th Panzer Division.

A major element of the 12th SS was outside the Falaise pocket and was able to gather 12,000 men and possibly a handful of tanks. The division received twelve Panzer IVs on 5 September, which had been despatched to it in Normandy but had not arrived in time. Kurt Meyer, their highly-capable commander, having escaped Falaise, was captured at Amiens on 6 September. Likewise the 17th SS Panzergrenadier Division had a strength of 16,832 by mid-September.

Remarkable recovery
The panzer divisions' manpower totalled about 160,000 men during the campaign and they had lost almost 62,000; yet, crucially, 98,000 men were still available to rebuild these formations – all they needed were replacement tanks. The Allies strategic bomber campaign may have severely hampered German armaments production, but it had not brought it to a standstill, nor was it able to completely prevent equipment being shipped to the front.

German industry pulled out all the stops and in August a record number of 869 tanks and 744 assault guns came off the assembly lines. Most notably, in the first week of September the German tank factories churned out sixty Tigers, which were delivered to Field Marshal Model on the morning of 24 September. These were to cause the Allies real problems during Operation Market Garden. The panzer divisions, once fleshed out by new recruits and transferees led by veteran officers and NCOs, were to obstruct the Allies at every turn right until the very end of the war.

Most of the survivors of Panzergruppe West, XLVII and LVIII Panzer Corps and the I SS and II SS Panzer Corps were withdrawn to Germany behind the relative safety of the long-neglected Siegfried Line. The latter had been built in the late 1930s along the pre-war border formed by the Saar River. Some units, however, had to remain behind to help stabilise the front and buy Rundstedt much-needed time.

The tattered remnants of 2nd and 116th Panzer were reformed in Germany, ready for operations on the Western Front. The 9th withdrew to the Aachen area for refit and became embroiled in the attempts to halt the American advance there. Conducting a fighting retreat, the 21st Panzer was engaged in the Saar and Alsace before being shipped to Germany for refit; the division was destined for the Eastern Front. The Panzer Lehr was also sent to the Saar and then on to Paderborn in Germany for rebuilding.

The Waffen-SS panzer divisions were also moved out of harms way for refit. The 1st SS, 2nd SS and 12th SS fell back to the Eifel region in Germany, and in November the 1st SS were refitted in Westphalia and the 12th SS refitted in Bremen. Both the 1st SS and 2nd SS went into reserve near Aachen. The 9th SS and 10th SS were withdrawn to the Netherlands to a place called Arnhem. In September the 12th SS was posted to the Aachen area and the 17th SS Panzergrenadier Division withdrew to the Metz area.

Panzergruppe West's smaller armoured formations suffered varying fates. The 503 Schwere Panzer Battalion was refitted and eventually sent to Hungary. The 101 SS and 102 SS Schwere Panzer battalions were re-equipped with Tiger IIs in September and re-designated the 501 and 502 respectively; both were also to end up on the Eastern Front. In contrast, the 506, which had been fighting with Army Group Centre on the Eastern Front, was sent to the West in August for refit.

Panzer Abteilung (Funklenk) 301 suffered heavy casualties during June and July 1944 and was withdrawn for rebuilding. On 19 August it was ordered to reorganize and re-equip as Schwere Panzer Abteilung (Tiger/Fkl) 301. Each of the three companies was to have ten Tiger Is and the HQ was to have two Tiger Is. Ten of these Tiger Is were acquired from an SS-Panzer *abteilung*. Some thirty-six Borgward IV remote-controllable demolition vehicles were issued to each company. The 301 were swiftly brought back up to strength and received twenty-one Tigers between 25 August and 15 September and another ten from Abteilung 103. The unit reported to LXXXI Corps in November with thirty-one Tigers (four were inoperable) and sixty-six BIV (five of which were inoperable).

The independent Panzer Abteilung 100 and 206, equipped with French tanks lost in the chaos of Normandy, were not rebuilt. Similarly, the majority of Panzerjäger Abteilung 657, armed with a mixture of inadequate French and Czech equipment, was lost in the St Lô area and the survivors were disbanded in mid-October.

In contrast, the assault gun units remained in a salvagable condition. By early October, Sturmgeschütz Brigade 341 had twenty-three assault guns, about half of which were in short-term repair. Sturmgeschütz Brigade 394 lost all but one of its assault guns in the Falaise pocket, but by early September had been despatched to the Aachen area to pick up thirty-one new vehicles. It was soon assisting 9th and 116th Panzer, resisting the Americans.

Sturmgeschütz Abteilung 902 in early September was with 19th Army and had ten assault guns; this number had doubled by the beginning of the following month. Sturmpanzer Abteilung 217, which variously served with the 89th Infantry Division, 12th SS Panzer Division and the 271st Infantry Division during the Normandy campaign, received twenty-four replacement Sturm-panzer IVs in September; however, by 1 October the battalion only had fourteen combat ready with another five in repair.

Not all the panzerjäger battalions of the mauled infantry divisions could be retrieved, for example Panzerjäger Abteilung 243's parent division was disbanded on 12 September. Similarly Panzerjäger Abteilung 352 saw the remnants of its parent division merged with the 581st Volksgrenadier Division in late September to create the 352nd Volksgrenadier Division. The 346th Infantry Division escaped southeast of Falaise and over the Seine with just three of its ten assault guns. Although the 353rd Infantry Division broke out of the Falaise pocket, it is unlikely that it was able to save any of its Marder self-propelled guns or Sturmgeschütz assault guns.

Fighting withdrawal

On 7 September, Rundstedt sent a situation report to Keitel spelling out just how grim the situation was:

> All our forces are all involved in battle, badly bruised, partly burned out. They lack artillery and anti-tank weapons. No reserves worthy of the term are available. The numerical superiority of enemy tanks compared to ours is indisputable. At this time, about 100 tanks are combat ready in Army Group B. Enemy air force dominates the battle area and the lines of communication deep into the rear echelon. The pressure of the enemy toward Lüttich (Meuse Valley) with a clear direction of advance via Aachen toward the industrial region of Rhineland–Westphalia has developed into a serious danger. The immediate addition of strong forces (five to ten divisions), as requested several times, seems an urgent necessity to me.... In agreement with Generalfeldmarschall Model, I recognise (near Aachen) the acute danger to the rear of the Westwall connecting toward the south. ... Our task is to fight with available forces to gain time, to make the western positions and the Westwall completely

capable for defence.... A time period of six weeks is forecast for completion of the western positions. This time has to be won through combat.

The ramifications of the failure to entirely destroy the panzer forces in the west soon became apparent. The 9th and 116th Panzer Divisions remained constant thorns in the side of the advancing Allies' sides. By 4 September the 116th was northwest of Namur, with orders to enter Charleroi, but American tanks were already there. It had a combat strength of just 600 panzergrenadiers, twelve tanks and ten pieces of artillery. Four days later Count Schwerin reported:

116th Panzer Division and Group Fiebig execute exchange of river banks on 8 September until dawn. The Division takes up position on the east bank of the Meuse at the southern edge of Argenteau– southern edge of St Remy–southern edge of Trembleu, in such a way that expected attack out of Lüttich (Liege) along east bank of Meuse can be repelled.

On 3 September, the 9th SS and 116th Panzer Divisions were ordered to pick up thirty Panzer IVs each from the Luttich area, but in the event the 116th only received fifteen tanks. The 9th and 116th Panzer attempted to fend off an enemy attack at Limbourg on 11 September but were thrown back toward Henri Chapelle. At this stage the 116th only had three battle-worthy tanks, but Henri Chapelle was secured by Sturmgeschütz Brigade 394.

The Americans though were able to exploit a gap between 116th and 9th Panzer forcing them back. On 12 September elements of the French II Corps pushing up from the south of France met the French 2nd Armoured from Patton's US 3rd Army at Châtillon-sur-Seine thereby linking up the southern and northern invasion forces.

In mid-September the 9th and 116th Panzer Divisions were given responsibility for the defence of Aachen. The 9th, which was bolstered by Sturmgeschütz Brigade 394, destroyed twenty-six American tanks on 13 September, and the following day a penetration south of Aachen was countered by the 116th. By 17/18 September the American 2nd Armored Division had reached the Siegfried Line north of Aachen. However, the attack on the line was postponed because during the Arnhem operation a gap had developed between the British and American Armies. In October, the Tigers of Abteilung 506 took part in the defence of Aachen, having fought at Arnhem.

The 17th SS Panzergrenadier Division was to play a key role in denying Metz to the Americans. Elements of the division arrived in the city with just ten assault guns on 1 September. SS-Panzergrenadier Brigades 49 and 51, which had arrived from Denmark and SS-Panzer Brigade 'Merzig', reinforced the 17th SS Panzergrenadiers, refitting west of Metz along the Abbeville–Mars La Tour road.

Eight days later the division was engaging French Sherman tanks and the US 5th Infantry Division. The Americans crossed the Mosselle River at Dornot on 8 September and came under immediate counterattack by SS-Panzergrenadiers. The following day American crossings between Noveant and Arnville received a similar reception. Heavy fighting continued throughout October and into November as the 17th SS helped hold up the American advance.

It was not long before the 2nd SS made its presence felt at Wittlich. Both the 2nd SS and Panzer Lehr were to be instrumental in halting Allied thrusts into the Eifel region west of the Rhine. On 14 September the US 4th Infantry Division, attacking the 'Black Man' ridge and the hamlet of Brandscheid, which had been incorporated into the Siegfried Line, came up against Kampfgruppe Kuehne. This consisted of young recruits rushed to the front from Wittlich in half-tracks of the 2nd SS.

The Americans were brought to a halt with 800 casualties. To the south, the US 28th Infantry Division attacking out of Luxembourg also came up against elements of the 2nd SS. Although they broke through the Siegfried Line it was at the cost of 1,500 casualties and losses for both divisions were such that the offensive was called off.

At Wallendorf the US 5th Armored Division, crossing the Our and Sauer Rivers, pushed aside a weak company of Panzer IVs from Panzer Lehr and pierced German defences to a depth of six miles (10km). Field Marshal von Rundstedt counterattacked with two infantry divisions and the remaining twenty-five tanks of Panzer Lehr. The Americans were driven back with the loss of sixty Sherman tanks, though the last of Panzer Lehr's tanks were also knocked out. The shaken US 5th Armored withdrew back over the Sauer on 22 September. Thanks to the assistance of the 2nd SS and Panzer Lehr, an entire US Corps had been successfully thrown out of their positions on the Siegfried Line.

To the north, to stop the Allies push across Holland and Belgium, were 80,000 men of General Gustav-Adolf von Zangen's 15th Army, which lacked tanks, and the 18,000 men of Colonel-General Kurt Student's 1st Parachute Army, equipped with just twenty-five panzers. Once the British were in Antwerp the 15th Army fell back to a bridgehead at the mouth of the Scheldt estuary, thereby blocking the approach to Antwerp. It would take the Allies almost two months of heavy fighting to secure it and the Scheldt estuary, in the meantime much-needed supplies had to rumble across Europe from the French ports.

Although the 2nd, 116th, 9th SS and 10th SS were ordered to replenish in the area of Eindhoven, the combat-worthy elements of these divisions were to remain in continual contact with the enemy. The 1st SS, 2nd SS and 12th SS were to return to Germany for a complete refit. Understandably these plans did not run smoothly.

Chapter 17

The Reckoning in the West

The escape of II SS Panzer Corps was to have dire consequences. Just three weeks after the liquidation of the Falaise pocket Montgomery launched Operation Market Garden, intended to take the Allies across the mighty Rhine and into the Ruhr. Designed to swiftly bring Germany to her knees, Montgomery's plan was ill-conceived, especially as the British 1st Airborne spearhead came up against the recuperating 9th SS and 10th SS Panzer Divisions at Arnhem. Although the SS were extremely under strength, the outcome of pitting lightly-armed paratroops against the panzers was inevitable.

Three months later, all the panzer divisions, now fully recovered, would be thrown into a surprise offensive against the Allies in the Ardennes, designed to cut them off from Antwerp. This was to fail and most of the panzer divisions were to end their final days trapped in the Rhur pocket.

Victory at Arnhem

Following Falaise and the liberation of Paris, Montgomery reasoned:

> The Germans are now completely disorganised as a result of their defeat in Normandy. If we can prevent their recovery, there is a good chance of the war being won in the autumn of 1944. We should, therefore, stage a powerful thrust, preferably up the coastal plain, which must keep on and on without pause, so that the Germans never get time to draw breath. We shall then be able to bounce a crossing of the Rhine before they get their defences organised. We can encircle the Ruhr from the north, cut it off from Germany, and the war will then be over.

Montgomery's logic was sound but failed to take account of two very depleted SS panzer divisions that had escaped the chaos of Normandy. After II SS Panzer Corps' failed counterattack at Falaise, it had withdrawn eastward through Evreux and Soissons. On 4 September Bittrich and his staff were directed north to Eindhoven in the Netherlands to oversee the refit of the 9th SS along with the 2nd and 116th Panzer Divisions. The latter and the 10th SS were ordered to the Venlo–Arnhem–Hertogenbosch area, also in the Netherlands, and began moving the following day.

The 9th SS, under SS-Obersturmbannführer Walter Harzer, numbered about 6,000 men with just twenty Panther tanks, though not all were serviceable; however, it did have a large number of other armoured fighting vehicles such as self-propelled guns and armoured cars, along with forty armoured personnel carriers. Its sister division, still under SS-Gruppenführer Heinz Harmel, could muster barely 3,500 men and hardly any tanks.

According to Bittrich, his instructions from Model were verbal and he only ordered the 9th SS and 10th SS north. The 2nd Panzer Division, in fact, withdrew to the Wittlich area in September; the 116th Panzer was sent to Aachen or Dusseldorf for refitting and was transferred to the Cologne sector two months later, where it resisted the Allied Rhine crossings.

Major Winrich Behr serving General Krebs, Model's Chief of Staff, recalled on 17 September:

> All round Arnhem the Germans had set up a series of field workshops and transit camps where the stragglers and survivors of the long retreat could be collected together. Many divisions had been reduced to a fraction of their original strength and were now being regrouped into operational units. Every day specialised freight trains brought back the battered tanks and mobile guns which had stubbornly held back the Allied advance, allowing the infantry and other troops to fall back towards Germany. Here in relative peace the fitters and engineers worked on urgent repairs and refitting: the weapons were repaired or replaced and crews re-equipped and retrained. Then, as soon as the tanks, self-propelled guns and fighting vehicles were ready for action, they were sent eastwards without delay to help in the defence of Germany.
>
> There was an enormous concentration of heavy armour in all stages of preparation, from cannibalised wrecks to fully battle-ready Tigers. Some of these were the updated Royal Tigers, with much thicker armour plating and larger guns, which had proved a match for the Russian T-34s. Among its armament was the 8.8cm gun (originally an anti-aircraft weapon) that had wrought such havoc among the British tanks in North Africa.

German intelligence judged that the Allies would strike toward Arnhem, which lay on the northern bank of the Rhine. By the middle of the month the 9th SS was located in a triangle formed by Arnhem–Zutphen–Apeldoorn. They were scheduled to withdraw to Germany and had been ordered to hand over their vehicles to the 10th SS, though Harzer used every trick in the book to not surrender his precious equipment. The 9th SS had also despatched some forces south to support Kampfgruppe Walther, part of Student's 1st Parachute Army, which numbered twenty-five armoured vehicles, including some Panther tanks and assault guns.

Montgomery, a usually-careful general showing uncharacteristic boldness with his narrow-front thrust, chose to ignore the intelligence about the two SS panzer divisions. Besides, what threat could these exhausted units pose? The 1st Airborne Division landed at Arnhem in ignorance of their presence on 17 September. Glider Pilot Alexander Morrison recalled the pre-briefing: 'A tall, dapper-looking officer then moved to the centre of the platform and gave a brief summary of the known troops in northern Holland which, incidentally, made no reference to the two depleted divisions of German armour in the Arnhem area!'

Bittrich and II SS Panzer Corps learned of the British landings five minutes after they started. Following some initial confusion, his two divisions quickly cobbled together various *kampfgruppen*. The 9th SS, although preparing to transit home, quickly sent its reconnaissance battalion south, over the Arnhem highway bridge toward Nijmegen, and another battle group westward toward Oosterbeek, which would prevent reinforcements reaching those British paratroops in Arnhem itself. Harzer had removed the tracks and wheels from some of his vehicles and deliberately reported them unserviceable, so it was not until late afternoon that sufficient numbers of tanks were battle ready.

The following day the 9th SS reconnaissance battalion, leaving a few self-propelled guns to guard the southern approaches of Nijmegen bridge, headed north to Elst. A column of twenty-two vehicles then attempted to force a crossing of Arnhem bridge, the northern end of which was now firmly in British hands; half were destroyed and the Germans were driven off.

Glider Pilot Louis Hagen was grateful that the 9th SS were not up to full strength:

> If there had not been a sprinkling of first-class and fanatical officers and NCOs in this division, no fight would have been possible. But even with the present state of affairs, it was ridiculous that they did not wipe us out within a few hours. This panzer division, with tanks, mobile guns, flame-throwers, very close Focke-Wulf support and the heaviest and most concentrated ack-ack seen by any of the RAF pilots whom I met later on at the 'drome', and even mobile loudspeakers with trained German propagandists spouting English never

dared to change over to direct assault or succeeded in penetrating our perimeter. No body of men, with only small arms as we had, could possibly have withstood a German panzer [division] of the old material.

The 10th SS was despatched to Nijmegen to hold the main bridges against the advancing British armour moving to link up with 1st Airborne, this was key to isolating and destroying the paratroops at Oosterbeek. However, with Arnhem bridge in British hands, the bulk of the 10th SS was obliged to use the ferry at Pannerden, eight miles (13km) southeast of Arnhem. Twelve Panthers reached the Nijmegen area and Arnhem Bridge was finally secured on 20 September.

Major Behr recalls the attack on the 20th:

> At dawn the heavy SS *Frundsberg* Mortar Section moved into position and blasted the Arnhem bridgehead. This was followed by a frontal attack by ten somewhat elderly tanks firing wildly but continuously, and supported by infantry keeping up a steady pounding of heavy machine-gun fire. The tanks were met by the very accurate fire of the British 6-pounder anti-tank guns; they slowed to a stop and then began to go back away. The barrage quietened and the machine-gunners slipped back with the tanks. But, from a safer distance, the SS mortars kept up a continuous fire.

For three days Harmel's SS slowed the British armoured advance and to the south the Panthers of Kampfgruppe Walther attacked toward Veghel, between Eindhoven and Nijmegen, on the 22nd. The 9th SS, reinforced by Schwere Panzer Battalion 506 consisting of some sixty King Tigers, set about eliminating the defenders at Oosterbeek. Luckily for the paras, these attacks were not very well coordinated. The 10th SS were eventually forced back toward Arnhem, so Bittrich sent forty-five Tigers and a company of Panthers to reinforce them following the landing of the Polish 1st Parachute Brigade at Driel south of Oosterbeek.

The British armoured forces pushing north along a single exposed road, under constant counterattack, could simply not get through and on 26th the decision was taken to evacuate the exhausted paratroops trapped at Oosterbeek. The SS lost 3,300 casualties, including 1,100 dead in the fighting. The British 1st Airborne Division at the start of the operation had numbered just over 10,000; only 2,163 escaped back across the Rhine. The 9th SS and 10th SS had helped thwart Montgomery's attempt to swiftly end the war with a single thrust into the Rhur and the Allies reverted to their plodding broad-front strategy across the whole of western Europe.

Military historian Max Hastings notes:

> The battles in Holland and along the German border so often seem
> to belong to a different age from those of Normandy that it is startling
> to reflect that Arnhem was fought less than a month after Falaise;
> that within weeks of suffering one of the greatest catastrophes of
> modern wars, the Germans found the strength to halt the drive
> of Horrocks XXX Corps in its tracks, and to prolong the war until
> May 1945.

In the meantime, following the Arnhem landings, Model wanted to attack from
the west of Venlo and the 9th and 116th Panzer was selected for this. They
arrived near Arnhem just as the remaining British paras were surrendering. On
1 October, along with the 10th SS, they were thrown into a counterattack
toward Elst, halfway between Arnhem and Nijmegen.

The 9th Panzer only achieved modest gains and the 10th SS to the south lost
eight Tiger tanks. The 116th got to within a mile and a quarter (2km) north of
Elst, but the attack was called off six days later and the division despatched
back to Aachen. The division was exhausted by this needless operation that
did little to alleviate pressure on the 15th Army. Nonetheless, it continued to
obstruct American efforts north of Aachen. During early November the 116th
resisted the US 28th Infantry Division in the Hurtgen Forest, destroying fifty-
three tanks.

On 8 November two squadrons of fighter-bombers from the US 9th Air
Force's 405 Group attacked the 17th SS Panzergrenadier Division's command
post located at Peltre, France, two miles (3km) east of Metz. Two buildings
were destroyed, killing most of the occupants. Within a matter of weeks of
this incident the full impact of the flawed victory at Falaise and the failure at
Arnhem was to be felt by the Allies.

Masterly effort

Despite the German defeat at Falaise, by the end of the summer Adolf Hitler
began to plan a massive counter-stroke against the Allies. He intended to
punch his armour through the lightly-defended Ardennes region in Belgium
and grab the port of Antwerp. This would strangle the Allied supply lines. His
anxious generals wanted to restrict their goal to Liege, but Hitler ruled the
panzers must reach Antwerp.

This was not to be some feeble counterattack like Mortain, or indeed every
counterattack that had been characterised by it since. This was to be a full-
blown counteroffensive using two whole panzer armies. Most of the generals

who had escaped from Normandy were to play key roles. At Army and Corps level they knew that this was an all or nothing gamble. At divisional level some hoped that they could unbalance the Allies' momentum, regain the initiative and recapture the heady glory of the *Blitzkrieg*.

Astoundingly, despite the losses inflicted on them in Normandy, just four months later all the panzers divisions (except the 21st) were to be involved in Hitler's major counterstroke. Army Group B was allocated the strategic reserve of 2,168 tanks and assault guns, some 700 were held with the 15th Army for the proposed supporting attack, leaving 970 for the opening of the offensive with a follow-on force of about 450. Some 2,500 tanks had been committed to the German attack through the Ardennes in 1940, but by this stage of the war these numbers must be viewed as quite remarkable. During the last half of 1944 Hitler was able to refit the tattered remains of thirty-five divisions, which had been shredded on the Eastern and Western Fronts, as well as forming fifteen new divisions.

Considering the disaster of Falaise and the ongoing efforts of the Allied bomber fleets, the regeneration of 5th Panzer Army, now under General der Panzertruppen Hasso von Manteuffel, is little short of a miracle. The 2nd and 9th Panzer Divisions were successfully reorganised after their heavy losses in Normandy and by December each division had over 100 tanks. The 9th included Tigers of the attached Schwere Panzer Abteilung 301. Two of 5th Panzer Army's three panzer corps commanders were familiar faces. General von Lüttwitz found himself in charge of XLVII Panzer Corps, which included his old command, 2nd Panzer, as well as 9th Panzer and Panzer Lehr. General Krüger, still commanding LVIII Panzer Corps, had responsibility for the 116th Panzer. General Karl Decker's XXIX Panzer Corps would be brought up to direct 1st SS and Panzer Lehr at the end of December.

The two SS Panzer Corps of SS-Oberstgruppenführer Sepp Dietrich's 6th SS Panzer Army were also swiftly rebuilt. The two panzer divisions of SS-Gruppenführer Herman Priess' I SS Panzer Corps were each brought up to about 22,000 men; the 1st SS Panzer Division was supplemented with Tiger tanks of SS Schwere Panzer Battalion 502 and 12th SS, now under SS-Brigadeführer Hugo Kraas, was rebuilt, though it lacked experienced junior officers. The 2nd SS, re-assigned to SS-Gruppenführer Heinz Lammerding, and 9th SS, re-assigned to SS-Brigadeführer Sylverster Stadler, formed SS-Obergruppenführer Willi Bittrich's II Panzer Corps and were similarly rebuilt with better than average recruits, though the 9th SS lacked transport.

In late September the Allies became aware that the Germans were withdrawing their armour from the front in order to build up a panzer reserve. Signals intelligence indicated that Normandy veterans the 1st SS, 2nd SS,

9th SS and 12th SS Panzer Divisions along with the 17th SS Panzergrenadier Division were being pulled back for rest and refitting. Following its perform- ance at Arnhem, the 9th SS had moved to Paderborn for a well-earned break and to be re-equipped. In early October the I SS Panzer Corps withdrew to Westfalen for refit. German tank strength on the Western Front steadily expanded to 2,600, compared to 1,500 on the Eastern Front, by December.

Throughout September–December the Panzer Lehr, 2nd SS and 10th SS Panzer Divisions helped hold the Siegfried Line while Hitler built up his counterattack force for the Ardennes offensive. After three months the Americans had been unable to punch though the Siegfried Line between Geilenkirchen and Aachen. After Arnhem the 10th SS were to wreak yet more havoc. While trying to eliminate the German salient at Geilenkirchen on 15 November, elements of the British 43rd (Wessex) Infantry Division were trapped by the 10th SS around Hoven.

On 12/13 November the 17th SS and 21st Panzer, with its last seven tanks, counterattacked at Sanry-sur-Nied, driving the Americans back, though they were themselves forced to withdraw for fear of encirclement. The 17th SS was ordered to retreat and escaped being trapped in Metz, which finally fell on 17 November. By the beginning of December the division was down to just 4,000 men and twenty tanks.

The Panzer Lehr, all but destroyed in Normandy, was in the process of being rebuilt when it was committed to the counterattack against the US 3rd Army in the Saar region. Unable to replace its losses in time for the Ardennes attack the division was bolstered by the attachment of Sturmgeschütz Brigade 243. The 116th Panzer Division was given very little time to recover as it was committed to the fighting in the Hurtgen Forest during the end of 1944, but even so was able to muster over 100 armoured fighting vehicles.

General de Guingand was in awe of the German efforts: 'We must acknowledge that the re-equipping of these Panzer Armies during the difficult autumn was a masterly effort by such a hard pressed enemy'. Three things had made this possible, the escape of the panzer divisions from Normandy, German industry going flat out and the Allies struggling at the end of their supply lines. The Germans had gathered twenty-eight divisions, including eight panzer divisions, numbering 275,000 men, 950 armoured fighting vehicles and 1,900 field guns.

These forces consisted of: 6th SS Panzer Army with the 1st SS, 2nd SS, 9th SS and 12th SS Panzer Divisions and the 501 and 506 Schwere Panzer Battalions, equipped with 450 tanks, assault guns and self-propelled guns; 5th Panzer Army, including the 2nd, 9th, 116th and Panzer Lehr Panzer Divisions, with about 350 armoured fighting vehicles; 7th Army, now under General der

Panzertruppen Erich Brandenberger, which lacked armour except for the 5th Parachute Division's Sturmgeschütz Brigade 11 and the panzer units of the 15th Panzergrenadier Division.

Three other Normandy veterans that took part in the Ardennes offensive were the 341 and 394 StuG Brigades assigned to 15th Army's LXXXI and LXXIV Army Corps respectively. Brigade 394 was reassigned to 19th Panzer Army's XXXIX Panzer Corps in the New Year. Abteilung 301 reported to LXXXI Army Corps in November with thirty-one Tigers (four were inoperable) and sixty-six BIVs (five of which were inoperable). It served in the Ardennes with Army Group B. At the start of the attack the battalion had twenty-seven tanks but less than half were available; by 30 December it had twenty-one operational Tigers.

Everything that the Germans had striven so hard to rebuild now stood on the very brink of victory or destruction. Elements of the 1st SS and 12th SS Panzer Divisions launched the 6th SS Panzer Army's main thrusts to the north, along the line St Vith–Vielsalm, on 16 December 1944. They did so under dense cloud, thereby avoiding the unwanted attentions of the Allies' troublesome fighter-bombers. Perhaps not surprisingly after its losses in Normandy, the 12th SS was only able to field one mixed tank *abteilung* for the Ardennes offensive, consisting of two companies of Panzer IVs and two companies of Panthers. The other *abteilung* remained in Germany where it was being reconstituted. The division also committed its two panzergrenadier regiments and its anti-tank battalion to the struggle.

Kampfgruppe Peiper, drawn from 1st SS, consisted of 100 Panzer IVs and Panthers, forty-two formidable King Tigers and twenty-five assault guns. Unfortunately, desperately short of fuel, SS-Obersturmbannführer Peiper, instead of pushing west, turned north to seize 50,000 gallons of American gasoline at Bullingen. His force was eventually surrounded and destroyed, leaving forty-five tanks and sixty self-propelled guns north of the Amblève River. The 12th SS, following-up the *kampfgruppe*, was unable to budge the Americans from the Elsenborn Ridge and had to swing left, nor was Panzer Lehr able to get to Bastogne before the Americans reinforced the town.

On the northern shoulder, the 9th SS headed northward after breaking through the Losheim Gap. Initially only the artillery regiment and reconnaissance battalion were committed, though once St Vith was captured, the rest of the division was brought in. On 18 December the 9th SS reached their official start line and fought their way toward Manhay and Trois Ponts before being replaced by the 12th Volksgrenadier Division. They got as far as Salmchateau, less than halfway to the Meuse.

Meanwhile, 116th Panzer drove between Bastogne and St Vith, but the Americans holding out in Bastogne delayed 2nd Panzer. Failing to take Bastogne greatly slowed 5th Panzer Army's drive on the Meuse. St Vith fell on 21 December, though American artillery fire forced 6th SS Panzer Army to become entangled with the 5th Panzer Army. Hitler felt that even if Antwerp were not taken, keeping his panzers in the hard won bulge created in the frontline would slow the Allied push on the vital Ruhr. To secure the bulge, Bastogne had to be taken and the 12th SS was shifted south to help capture the town.

By 22 December 9th SS had been committed to the southern flank of 1st SS, but they were unable to reach Kampfgruppe Peiper. At the end of the month the 9th SS were replaced by the 12th Infantry Division and also moved south to help with the assault on Bastogne. Once the weather cleared, however, Allied fighter-bombers began to attack the panzers in a repeat of the Falaise battle. Exposed on the snow-covered landscape many were easy targets.

Lacking fuel, 2nd Panzer got as far as Celles, just four miles (6.5km) short of the River Meuse before American armour moved in for the kill. Celles was not far from Dinant on the Meuse, where Rommel's 7th Panzer had crossed the river in 1940, heralding France's defeat. American tanks also halted the 2nd SS, and 116th and Panzer Lehr were stopped short of Marche.

Even in the face of defeat, the 2nd SS continued to inflict heavy losses on the Americans. Normandy survivor SS-Obersturmführer Fritz Langanke, taking his Panther tank into battle just before Christmas, recalled:

> I climbed back into my seat and watched the slope in the direction of La Fosse. Obersturmführer Veith, who would later die in the Ardennes and be awarded the Knight's Cross after his death, stood in front of my vehicle next to the muzzle break of the gun.
>
> Suddenly, American tanks appeared. They came down the slope from La Fosse in a spread-out formation and obviously wanted to drive forward the III Kompanie. I yelled at Veith to get out of the way, we had to fire. He did not hear it over the noise of the engines. In a very short time the Americans were at the points we had test fired at earlier; and we had to fire our first shell.
>
> Despite the sad situation I could not suppress a grin when Veith's cap was blown off by the air pressure from the shot. He was completely confused for a moment until he grasped what was happening when our second shell was fired. Thanks to our preparations, we knocked out the first five Sherman tanks in quick succession despite the poor visibility. They moved at a steep angle to us, down the slope,

half-right. The firing distance between us was 500 and 700 metres. The other tanks then turned around and drove back. Thereafter it was quiet and dusk set in soon.

On Christmas Eve the reconnaissance battalion of 2nd Panzer reached Foy-Nôtre-Dame just three miles from Dinant. Pushing on to the river they ran into five British Shermans from the 3rd Royal Tank Regiment guarding the crossing. Losing two panzers, the Germans fell back. General Bayerlein was ordered to help 2nd Panzer near Celles.

At midnight, Unteroffizer Otto Henning of Panzer Lehr's reconnaissance battalion met some stragglers from 2nd Panzer:

Our unit was supposed to reinforce 2nd Panzer Division but the enemy's artillery fire was so intense we didn't dare move out of the forest. All this happened on Christmas day and, of course, we knew that the Ardennes offensive had failed.

Panzer Lehr's efforts to rescue 2nd Panzer were thwarted by Allied air power. On Christmas morning the Americans launched an all-out assault on the tip of the German bulge, seeking to trap those forces at Celles. The 2nd Panzer reconnaissance battalion was surrounded at Foy-Nôtre-Dame on Christmas day and 148 men surrendered. Their achievement of getting the furthest in Hitler's Ardennes offensive had got them nowhere other than a prisoner of war camp. In three days fighting in and around the Celles pocket the 2nd, 9th and Panzer Lehr lost eighty-two tanks and 2,500 casualties.

The US 6th Armored Division launched an attack near Bastogne on 2 January 1945. Although the tanks were driven off, their infantry broke through the positions of the 26th Volksgrenadier Division, reaching Michamps. Under Normandy survivor von Ribbentrop, the 12th SS escort company and I Abteilung, SS-Panzer Regiment 12, was sent to counterattack. They recaptured Michamps and Obourcy and, along with the fighting at Arlencourt, 12th SS accounted for twenty-four American tanks. The 12th SS were then thrown at the northeast outskirts of Bastogne on the 4th, but the Americans turned back every attack. Shortly after, the 12th SS were withdrawn to Cologne. By now the 9th and 12th SS Panzer Divisions only had fifty-five tanks left between them.

Rundstedt counselled Hitler to withdraw the two battered panzer armies east of Bastogne, ready for the inevitable Allied counterattack. To the south in Alsace, to distract attention from the Ardennes, the Germans launched Operation Northwind, involving ten divisions, including the Normandy veterans 21st Panzer, 10th SS Panzer under XXXIX Panzer Corps and 17th SS Panzergrenadier

Division, on 31 December. At the crucial moment Edgar Feuchtinger was again absent from 21st Panzer and was at home in Germany. On the 26th, the 17th SS had received fifty-seven new assault guns; a Panther tank company from 21st Panzer also reinforced it. Along with the 36th Volksgrenadier Division, the division attacked the US 44th and 100th Infantry Divisions near Rimlingen on 1 January. Within a week Northwind had been thrown back and the Americans recaptured Rimlingen on the 13th.

The 10th SS achieved some modest success in its attack from Offendorf to Herlisheim on 17 January, avoiding a mauling by American armour. Although the attack petered out, SS-Obersturmführer Bachmann, adjutant of the 1st Panzer Abteilung, SS-Panzer Regiment 10, remembered:

> Everything went according to plan. The two panzer crews cooperated in a first-rate fashion. Panzer 2 opened fire while Panzer 1 raced into the junction and knocked out the first Sherman. More US tanks were knocked out, and a white flag appeared.
>
> I stopped the fire and walked forward. An American officer offered to surrender. I requested that his men put down their weapons in front of me. When sixty Americans had put down their weapons, twenty Germans who had been in US captivity were added. I asked the Americans if they were the crews of the knocked-out tanks. The US officer explained that they were the crews of tanks that had not been knocked out and pointed to a farm to the left of the road where four Shermans sat, their guns facing the road. He said the other tanks were a little farther down. That was a surprise to us. We had to keep calm. I demanded speedy action. I had the American tank drivers step forward and ordered them to drive the Shermans to Offendorf, accompanied by one of the rearmed German soldiers. I felt better when the tank column set off. I advised the Abteilung in Offendorf of the approaching captured Shermans and requested more of our Panzers to come to Herlisheim and pick up another forty-eight prisoners. The total was twelve captured Sherman tanks and sixty prisoners. I deployed my own two Panthers forward to the edge of Herlisheim. From there they covered in the direction of Drusenheim and knocked out two Shermans on their way to Herlisheim. Thus my two Panthers achieved nine kills.

Bachmann's tanks crews were rewarded with Iron Crosses, with Bachmann gaining the Knight's Cross. While Northwind caused a crisis, it also wasted away Germany's already-meagre reserves. After the Allies counterattacked in the Ardennes on 8 January, Hitler finally ordered a partial withdrawal. The 6th SS Panzer Army was needed on the Eastern Front, following a major Russian offensive. The 9th SS moved to the Longchamps area to help maintain communication with the 5th Panzer Army to the south and the 116th Panzer was moved to the Kleeve sector on the Rhine.

By the 28th the German bulge had gone, for the loss of 100,000 casualties and most of their armour; 5th Panzer Army and 6th SS Panzer Army lost up to 600 tanks. Although the offensive was stopped, it showed how the defeat at Falaise had singularly failed to crush the panzer divisions on the Western Front. Hitler's great gamble had not paid off, although in five weeks of fighting twenty-seven US divisions suffered 59,000 casualties thanks to his reconstituted panzer divisions. However, Hitler had achieved what Falaise had failed to do, the near total destruction of his panzer forces in the West. This time there could be no miraculous recovery.

Holding the Rhine

General von Manteuffel's 5th Panzer Army was redeployed to help defend the Ruhr. In preparation for the advance of Montgomery's 21st Army Group (Canadian 1st, British 2nd and US 9th Armies), the Allied air forces sought to disrupt communications within the Ruhr and between the Ruhr and the rest of Germany with Operation Bugle. This was followed by Operation Clarion, a major bombing offensive designed to destroy German communications and morale at the end of the month. Significantly, Bugle helped to ensure that much of Model's Army Group B, consisting of 5th Panzer Army and General Gustav von Zangen's 15th Army, remained trapped in the Ruhr.

Following the counterattacks into the Ardennes and Alsace, German reserves were now completely depleted. The remaining mobile panzer reserve comprised the XLVII Panzer Corps, consisting of the 116th Panzer Division and the 15th Panzergrenadier Division. These sounded formidable but they could scrape together just thirty-five panzers. Units of 9th Panzer were also despatched to defend Cologne.

The Americans launched Operation Lumberjack on 1 March, employing Lieutenant Courtney H Hodge's US 1st Army and General George S Patton's US 3rd Army attacking between Koblenz and Cologne. The plan was to drive Army Group B back through the Eifel region to the Rhine. Six days later, Hodges met his VII Corps commander General Collins on the Rhine at Cologne. The US 3rd Armored Division drove the remnants of the 9th Panzer Division from the city, but the Hohenzollern Bridge was destroyed before it could be secured.

These operations served to distract the Germans southward. Lieutenant General Fritz Bayerlein, commanding the German LIII Corps, wanted to gather three divisions before counterattacking at Remagen, but Hitler gave orders for immediate attacks with everything to hand. On 10 March the newly-formed Schwere Panzer Abteilung 512 was thrown at the bridgehead. It was one of only two units equipped with the Jagdtiger, which, although armed with a formidable 12.8cm gun, weighed a colossal seventy tons and was not easy to operate. The 512 were unsuccessful, as were elements of 9th Panzer, and covered the German withdrawal.

Montgomery's preparations for the crossing of the Rhine took two weeks, which many felt unnecessary. The Americans were particularly unhappy with his cautious preparations and meticulous planning. While they were getting ready, the XLVII Panzer Corps was able to regroup in the Netherlands and the Germans improved their defences, particularly at Speldrop.

General Brian Horrocks, commanding the British XXX Corps, had a good picture of what to expect:

> According to my intelligence staff whose information was always astonishingly accurate, we were opposed by the 8th Parachute Division round the small town of Rees with part of the 6th and 7th Parachute Divisions on its flanks. Behind in immediate reserve were our old friends, or enemies, 15th Panzergrenadier Division and 116th Panzer Division.

On the whole, the stunned Germans defending the Rhine were brushed aside on 23 March and by dawn the Allied bridgehead had been firmly established. However, the Germans were quick to recover their wits and the *fallschirmjäger* began to fight back. At midnight on the 23rd the 15th Panzergrenadier Division was directed toward Rees near the German II Parachute Corps sector, while the 116th Panzer Division was ordered across the Lippe to attack the Americans. It found itself having to take control of the frontline from the 180th Infantry Division, which had disintegrated.

At 1800 on the 25th, the Americans drove 116th Panzer from Hunxe. The following day the panzers initially found themselves holding the entire XLVII Panzer Corps front until assisted by the 180th and 190th Infantry Divisions. To the south LXIII Corps, consisting of the 2nd Parachute and 'Hamburg' Divisions, struggled to hold the line. The latter was made up of staff and communications personnel supported by some *fallschirmjäger*. During the night of 27/28, the 116th Panzer withdrew under covering fire from the divisional artillery, two days later it was strengthened with just fourteen new Jagdpanthers.

With the Allies swarming over the Rhine, there was very little the Germans could do to contain them. Within a week of the crossing Montgomery had amassed twenty divisions with 1,500 tanks, and 30,000 German PoWs went into the 'bag.' General Schlemm's 1st Parachute Army was forced northeastwards toward Hamburg and Bremen, which opened a breach with the German 15th Army defending the Rhur. Schlemm was wounded and command fell to General Günther Blumentritt, who, along with his superior, General Johannes Blaskowitz, was under instruction to hold fast at all costs. Both knew in reality that this was a pointless exercise, the situation was a shambles, there were few panzers or artillery and no air cover or reserves. Those reinforcements that did arrive were deemed all but useless, comprising frightened old men and boys.

Blummentritt, feeling it his duty to save the men under his command rather than throw them away in the defence of the Reich, withdrew behind the Dortmund-Ems Canal, toward the cover of the Teutoburger Forest. During April both geographical features were assaulted by the British 7th and 11th Armoured Divisions, which had pushed over the Rhine.

At Glissen west of the River Weser, the 2nd Fife and Forfar Yeomanry 11th Armoured Division, captured weeping, ill-equipped youngsters from the 12th SS. They had been reduced to bicycles and panzerfausts to fend off British tanks. The 7th Armoured found itself enduring a feeble counter-attack southwest of Harburg from members of the 12th SS Reinforcement Regiment and other Hitler Youth supported by just two self-propelled guns on 26 April. A day later, in the Harsfelt area, elements of the division captured a former 21st Panzer officer leading school students armed with panzerfausts.

To the south General Bayerlein, with LIII Panzer Corps, was ordered by Model on 29 March to try to break out eastwards with the remains of the Panzer Lehr, 9th Panzer, 3rd Panzergrenadier and 3rd Parachute Divisions. This represented the panzers' last major offensive in the West, but by 2 April they were back where they started, driven back by American firepower.

Hodges' US 1st Army broke out of the Remagen bridgehead, then the spearhead of the US 9th and 1st Armies linked up on 2 April at Lippstadt east of the Ruhr. The US 2nd and 3rd Armored Divisions had sealed the Ruhr pocket. The remnants of Model's Army Group B, some nineteen divisions from the 5th Panzer Army and 15th Army along with LXIII Corps from the shattered 1st Parachute Army, were caught in the Ruhr pocket. Hitler grandly dubbed it the 'Ruhr fortress.' The Allies meantime pushed on to meet up with the Red Army on the Elbe. The Ruhr pocket was left to Lieutenant General Leonard T Gerow's specially-created US 15th Army, consisting of eighteen divisions from the US 1st and 9th Armies. The outcome was inevitable.

Surrender

The 9th, 116th and Panzer Lehr Panzer Divisions, who had been unable to contain the American breakout in Normandy but successfully avoided being trapped in the Falaise pocket, surrendered to the Americans in mid-April. Some 36,000 German troops, including 3,000 from 116th Panzer, were rounded up near Brilon. Other elements of the 116th, such as Panzerjäger Abteilung 228 and 9th Panzer, capitulated in the Harz Mountains. On the 21st Generalleutnant Josef Harpe, commanding the 5th Panzer Army, finally surrendered along with 325,000 men, including twenty-nine generals. Model chose death and committed suicide the same day. Within two weeks Nazi Germany had capitulated.

The two remaining Normandy veterans still in the west, who had fought so vainly to halt the American break-out, also laid down their arms. The 2nd Panzer Division, members of which had fought to the last at St Lambert-sur-Dives, had lost almost half its strength in Normandy and since been involved in the Rhine battles, ended the war at Plauen, where it surrendered in May. The ill-prepared 17th SS Panzergrenadier Division, which had been swept away by Operation Cobra yet, nonetheless, escaped Normandy, after taking part in Operation North Wind was pushed back into Bavaria and finally surrendered its weapons in the Achensee area on 7 May 1945. The division was able to muster just two infantry and one transport regiment and three armoured cars.

Chapter 18

The Reckoning in the East

The escape of the Waffen-SS panzer divisions and heavy tank battalions from Normandy also had severe ramifications for the Red Army in the dying days of the Third Reich. While the blow in the west from the reconstituted SS units in the Ardennes had failed, Hitler remained undeterred, planning to launch them in the east. The Soviets received intelligence from the British Military Mission on 12 February 1945 that 6th SS Panzer Army with the 1st SS, 2nd SS, 9th SS and 12th SS Panzer Divisions were on their way. Similarly the troublesome 10th SS, still commanded by SS-Gruppenführer Heinz Harmel, was despatched eastward to Pomerania to help cover the retreating German armies.

The survivors of Schwere SS-Panzer Abteilung 501, (formerly 101), 502 (formerly 102) and 503, having blown up the last of their Tiger tanks in Normandy, were shipped back to Germany. The latter two battalions were destined to fight in Hungary, East Prussia and Berlin in the closing months of the war, while the 501 would be involved in Hitler's last futile offensive in Hungary.

Operation Solstice

While the Soviets claimed it was their winter offensives that saved the Western Allies, there were in fact more German tanks on the Western front at this time. The absence of the 5th and 6th Panzer Armies, committed to Operation Wacht am Rhein (Watch on the Rhine) or Herbstnebel (Autumn Mist), greatly helped the Red Army. At the end of 1944 there were some 2,229 tanks and assault guns committed in the West, compared to just 950 tanks in the East. When the Soviets launched their Vistula offensive, the absence of two of Hitler's most formidable tank armies was a considerable bonus.

In late January 1945 Sepp Dietrich was summoned to Berlin, where he saw Army Chief of Staff, General Heinz Guderian. They both agreed that all available troops, including the 6th SS armour, should be sent to defend the River Oder; the Russians established a bridgehead over the river at Wriezen near Kustrin, just forty-five miles (72km) from Berlin on the 31st. They managed to get 100 tanks across the river before the Germans moved to seal off the bridgehead. Hitler however had other plans for Dietrich and his remaining panzers.

Throughout January the 9th SS conducted a fighting withdrawal to the German border. They were then sent to the Kaufenheim–Mayen area to be re-equipped before being sent to Hungary. The 10th SS, which had also faithfully served II SS Panzer Corps throughout the Normandy campaign, at Arnhem and the Ardennes offensive, was detached from its sister division and sent to the Vistula sector. Its remaining thirty-eight Panzer IVs and fifty-three Panthers would not rejoin the 6th SS Panzer Army for Hitler's forthcoming Hungarian offensive.

Another Normandy veteran, Schwere SS-Panzer Abteilung 502 (formerly 102), was refitted at Sennelager, while the 503's I Kompanie moved to Bentfeld, the II to Eilsen and the III to Hovelhof. Kurt Knispel from the battalion was able to go home one final time. The Panzer Ersatz und Ausbildungs (training and replacement) Abteilung 500 at Paderborn provided much-needed crews and 503 received forty-five new Tiger IIs during 19–22 September 1944. The following month it was shipped to Hungary, subordinated to the Feldhernhalle Panzer Corps and assisted in the futile defence of Budapest.

Panzer Abteilung (Funklenk) 302, which had narrowly missed seeing action in Normandy, was sent to join Army Group Centre on the Eastern Front in August 1944, equipped with three Panzer IVs, forty StuG IIIs and 155 Borgward IVs. By early December there were still thirty-eight StuGs operational, ten of these had been lost by mid-January 1945 and only three were available by March. The unit ended up fighting in Eastern Prussia.

By January 1945 Abteilung 503 was back in Germany to take part in one of Hitler's last ill-fated counterattacks. Split in two, one group was sent to the Arnswalde–Pomerania area and the other to the Landsberg–Küstrin area. In particular, Arnswalde's strategic position of protecting Stargard and the sea port of Stettin meant that there was a strong German garrison defending the town. The first group under Obersturmbannführer Fritz Herzig, along with a panzer support battalion, 1,000 troops and 5,000 civilians, was trapped in Arnswalde on 4 February.

Herzig's Tiger IIs could easily have broken out but that would have meant cruelly abandoning everyone else to their fate at the hands of the Russians. Three days later SS-Untersturmführer Fritz Kauerauf, with three Tiger IIs, set out from Stargard for Arsnwalde via Reetz. Instead he became involved with the 11th SS, trying to stop the Soviet advance to the Baltic.

The Germans decided to relieve Arnswalde and attack in the Landsberg–Küstrin area. The 10th SS, serving with SS-Obergruppenführer Felix Steiner's 11th SS Panzer Army (XXXIX Panzer, III SS Panzer and X SS Corps), was to take part in the counterattack on Marshal Georgi Zhukov's 1st Belorussian Front. In conference with Hitler on 13 February, Guderian, hoping to keep open 2nd Army's lines of communication between East Prussia and Pomerania, along with Dietrich, advocated a pincer movement against the advancing Soviets. Over 1,200 panzers from 3rd Panzer Army were earmarked for the Operation Sonnenwende (Solstice), but there were insufficient trains to move them and little fuel and ammunition.

In the event, just four SS divisions, including the 10th SS and four Army divisions supported by only 250 tanks (barely a division's worth), were thrown into the short-lived attack three days later, between Stargard and Arnswalde. To the displeasure of the SS, the attack was directed by Army General Walther Wenck. Initially they made good progress on the first day, penetrating the Soviet envelopment of Arnswalde and rescuing the German garrison.

Panzer Abteilung 503's Tiger IIs were instrumental in holding the corridor open as the wounded and civilians were evacuated and fresh troops sent in. During the fighting in the Danzig–Gotenhafen area, Tigers of the 503 destroyed sixty-four Soviet tanks. Soviet troops were also expelled from Brallentin and two villages. The Germans then cut into Marshal Bogdanov's 2nd Tank Army to retake Pyritz.

The 10th SS and 503's short-lived success was to swiftly come to a halt. The Tigers could do little once the Soviet 2nd Guards Tank Army brought up heavy Joseph Stalin tanks on the 17th. On the same day, Wenck, returning from Hitler's evening briefing, was injured in a car crash and the momentum of the operation was completely lost.

In reality, this attack constituted little more than a nuisance to the Red Army. Hitler achieved nothing save grinding down those few units that could be relied on to attack. Steiner called off the assault, pulling the III (Germanic) SS Panzer Corps back to Stargard and Stettin on the northern Oder River. The few remaining panzers were moved to the Oder front. By the 19th the Soviets had captured Arnswalde, surrounded Graudenze and destroyed the German base at Stargard. However, the Stargard operations caused enough anxiety in the Soviet headquarters for them to halt the main offensive toward Berlin and lose some six weeks.

Six Tiger IIs from Panzer Abteilung 503 withdrew to Berlin and became the backbone of the defence of the beleaguered government quarter. The delay in the delivery of Tiger IIs to Panzer Abteilung 502, due to heavy air attacks on the Henschel plant in Kassel, meant that the battalion did not move to the Oder between Frankfurt and Küstrin until early March and then with only twenty-nine tanks. Thrown into attack near Sachsenheim, they forced the Soviet armour to fall back and the Tigers soon outstripped the other panzers. On 26/27 March they were involved in the attempt to break through to Küstrin.

Operation Spring Awakening

The crumbling German war effort was threatened with the loss of the vital Hungarian oilfields at Nagykaniza, with the Red Army less than 50 miles (80km) away. These and the Austrian oil fields were providing four fifths of Germany's oil supplies and Hitler convinced himself that they could be saved by a massive panzer counteroffensive that would throw the Soviets back over the Danube and secure Vienna. Even if the plan failed, Hitler hoped it would delay the Soviet offensive against the Austrian capital.

To his generals all this seemed madness. Why defend foreign lands when the Red Army was a mere forty-five miles (72km) from the German capital? The Führer's Hungarian adventure was a final effort that the exhausted German armed forces could ill afford. Perhaps Hitler misguidedly hoped that what 6th SS Panzer Army had so conspicuously failed to achieve in the Ardennes might be pulled off in Hungary, boosting morale on the Eastern Front and on the Rhine.

Sepp Dietrich must have felt a sense of futile *déjà vu*. Rather than withdraw behind the Rhine, Hitler had insisted they fritter away the reconstituted panzers in the Ardennes, leaving 5th Panzer Army once again exhausted. Now, rather than hold the Elbe, it seemed 6th SS Panzer Army was to suffer a similar fate, attacking a relentless and well-equipped enemy. Once again, many of the Normandy generals were to be involved.

On 17 February, to the south, I SS Panzer Corps attacked the Soviet 7th Guards holding the Hron bridgehead with up to 150 tanks and assault guns. Seven days later the Soviets lost their foothold with the bloody loss of 8,800 men and most of their equipment. Nonetheless, this small victory cost the Germans 3,000 casualties and confirmed to the Soviets that a major counteroffensive was looming.

Although I SS Panzer Corps' preliminary attack got off to a good start by destroying the Soviet bridgehead around Estergom, once the Soviets established the attack was being conducted by Hitler's elite Waffen-SS it was obvious what was going on. When Hitler's Operation Spring Awakening commenced two weeks later, the Soviets were already very much awake to the threat.

The 6th SS Panzer Army fielded six panzer, two infantry and two cavalry divisions as well as two heavy tank battalions. General Balck's 6th Army had five panzer and three infantry divisions, and the 3rd Hungarian Army had one tank, two infantry and a cavalry division. On paper, 6th SS Panzer Army was a formidable formation that included four veteran SS panzer divisions. The 1st SS, commanded by SS-Brigadeführer Otto Kumm, and 12th SS, still under SS-Brigadeführer Hugo Kraas, were grouped into the I SS Panzer Corps. The panzer regiment of 1st SS was reinforced with the Tiger IIs of Panzer

Abteilung 501. The 2nd SS, commanded by SS-Standartenführer Rudolf Lehmann, and 9th SS, still under SS-Brigadeführer Sylvester Stadler, formed the II SS Panzer Corps.

In reality, these units had been spent during the Ardennes offensive, but this would not stop them inflicting appalling losses on the Red Army. On the Eastern Front the Wehrmacht enjoyed a local 2:1 superiority in tanks. The Red Army in Hungary was particularly weak in armour, which meant anti-tank guns would be their main defence against the 900 panzers and assault guns about to be thrown at them. Soviet anti-tank gunners were especially contemptuous of the Panzer Mk IV, which they considered old.

On the morning of 6 March 1945, after a thirty-minute artillery bombard-ment supported by air attacks, 6th SS Panzer and 6th Army crashed into the Soviets' well-prepared in-depth defences. As planned, the Germans launched a furious three-pronged attack. 6th SS Panzer Army struck in a southeasterly direction between Lakes Velencze and Balaton; 2nd Panzer Army drove east-ward in the direction of Kaposvar; and Army Group E, in Yugoslavia, attacked northeast from the right bank of the Davra, with the aim of uniting with the 6th SS Panzer Army.

The Hungarian plain between the northern extremity of Lake Balaton and the Danube was not good tank country and was bisected by canals and ditches. The SS-Panzergrenadiers were dropped ten miles (16km) from their jumping off points, ironically, so that the Russians would not alerted by their halftracks. To make matters worse, II SS Panzer Corps found itself in a sea of mud and penetrated the Soviet defences to a depth of just five miles, I SS Panzer Corps made better progress of twenty-five miles (40km).

Dietrich was soon angry with General Wohler, who had maintained that the ground in front of his two panzer corps was passable. The mud claimed 132 panzers and fifteen of Panzer Abteilung 501's Tiger IIs, which sank up to their turrets and had to be abandoned before they had even fired a shot.

General N A Gagen's Soviet 26th Army and elements of the 1st Guards Fortified Area (part of the 4th Guards Army) bore the brunt of the steel storm. In response, an artillery group of 160 field guns and mortars was established to provide 26th Army with massed covering fire. During the opening day General Sudet's Soviet 17th Air Army flew 358 sorties, of which 227 were directed at the exposed panzers. A huge and furious battle followed as each side brought their well-honed tactics to bear.

Lehmann's 2nd SS Panzer Division joined the combat with 250 tanks on 8 March, followed by Stadler's 9th SS the next day, bringing the total number of panzers committed to the battle up to 600. However, the Germans were rapidly running out of time and resources. On 11 March Dietrich contacted

Hitler's headquarters, requesting permission to call off Spring Awakening; he repeated his request three days later knowing full well that his panzer divisions were bleeding to death.

The 6th Panzer Division with 200 tanks and self-propelled guns, Spring Awakening's last reserves, were thrown into a desperate push for the Danube on the 14th. They attacked resolutely for two days and almost reached the Soviet's rear defence line, but Marshal Tolbukin's men held on. By 15 March Dietrich had lost over 500 tanks and assault guns, 300 guns and 40,000 men, battering themselves to death against the Soviets' defences. Using the excuse of defending Vienna, Dietrich retrieved his shattered forces and withdrew.

Whilst Spring Awakening slowed the Soviet drive on Vienna, ultimately it did not greatly affect their plans, although the main axis of their forthcoming offensive was now moved south of the Danube to Tolbukin's command. He was still weak in tanks, which numbered just 200 while the German panzer units could still scrape together some 270 tanks and self-propelled guns. The Soviet 6th Guards Army from Malinovskii's command joined Tolbukin, bringing with them 406 tanks and self-propelled guns. Their job was the final destruction of the remnants of the 6th SS Panzer Army. Two Soviet infantry armies, the 9th and 4th Guards, were assigned the task of cutting the German armour off.

Final defeat

The Soviets launched their counterstroke on 16 March along the entire front west of Budapest and the German spearhead was sheered off. The weight of the attack fell on General Balck's 6th Army and the Hungarian 3rd Army north of Lake Velencze. Soviet armour and lorried infantry poured through a breach, which Kraas' 12th SS Panzer Division was hastily sent to seal. The Soviets swung in a southwesterly direction toward Lake Balaton.

Instead of throwing the Red Army back in disarray, 6th SS Panzer Army and 6th Army now found themselves in danger of being cut off and a huge battle ebbed and flowed around Lake Balaton. Under pressure, 1st SS Panzer gave ground, exposing Balck's flank. Six days after the Soviet counteroffensive commenced, 6th SS Panzer Army, with just a mile-wide escape corridor that was already under heavy enemy fire, was faced with complete encirclement south of Szekesfehervar. Four panzer divisions and an infantry division fought desperately to keep the closing Soviet pincers apart and 6th SS Panzer Army only just managed to escape.

In the meantime, elements of 6th SS Panzer Army and 6th Army attempted to hold the River Raab, south of Vienna, and Lake Neusiedler against Tolbukin's troops. The Soviets crossed on 28 March and brushed aside the exhausted defenders. By the end of the month up to 45,000 German and Hungarian soldiers had surrendered. Vienna now lay open to the Red Army.

Hitler could not believe his Waffen-SS had failed him and raged: 'If we lose the war, it will be his, Dietrich's fault.' In a fit of ingratitude he ordered General Guderian to fly to the front to instruct the exhausted troops to remove their SS cuff bands. Guderian was appalled and pointed out that they were under the jurisdiction of Reichsführer-SS Himmler, not the Wehrmacht. The spineless Himmler sent a message, but Sepp Deitrich was made of sterner stuff.

In the seven months since their defeat at Falaise the panzer divisions had worked wonders for the Führer, but in the end he was simply not grateful. Upon receiving the teletype message Dietrich remarked with bitterness: 'This is thanks for everything.' He summoned his four divisional commanders and threw Hitler's message on the conference table, saying: 'There's your reward for all that you have done the past five years'. Dietrich instructed them not to pass the order on, but word of it quickly spread through the tattered ranks of the SS divisions.

It was rumoured that the German Army deliberately ensured their rivals knew of their final shame. Removal of unit insignia was largely symbolic, as they had already been removed when 6th SS Panzer Army moved secretly into Hungary, but Hitler's order was still seen as an insult by the surviving SS veterans who had shed so much blood for him and their beloved Reich.

Dietrich's response was to inform Berlin that he would rather shoot himself than carry out the order. When he got no reply he reportedly sent all his decorations back to Hitler. Setting Dietrich's war crimes and political beliefs aside, this was appalling ingratitude for a general who had served Nazi Germany so well. It also shows the level of insanity that Hitler and his entourage had reached as the Nazi house of cards collapsed around them.

Dietrich, avoiding censure, was assigned to General von Buenau, Battle Commander of Vienna; both men knew the defence could last little more than a few days. By his own admission, Dietrich's defensive measures round his command post were designed to protect him from the Führer as much as the Soviets. Vienna fell during the second week of April with the loss of 125,000 prisoners and 6th SS Panzer Army's message to Berlin read: 'The garrison of Vienna has ceased to exist. Despite their exhaustion, the troops are fighting with exemplary courage'.

After the fall of the Austrian capital, Dietrich withdrew west to the River Traisen, where 10,000 men gathered from local training units reinforced his forces, and held the Soviets for several more weeks. The Soviets though had shifted their main attention to capturing Brno, an important industrial centre in Czechoslovakia.

The Red Army finally stormed into the shattered rubble of Berlin on 21 April 1945, just as 5th Panzer Army was finally surrendering in the Ruhr pocket. Panzer driver Sturmmann Lothar Tiby witnessed the end of Panzer Abteilung 503 and the final demise of the panzer units that had escaped from Normandy on 2 May. He recorded almost with an air of unreality:

> Attempt to break out from Berlin in a westerly direction with the two last panzers of our *abteilung*. Our vehicle with commander Lippert, the second panzer with the holder of the Knight's Cross Schafer of III Kompanie. The heavy fighting against a vastly superior force lasted all day. There were very high losses of vehicles, infantry, and civilians on our side and very high losses of personnel carriers and infantry on the Russian side due to the action of the two panzers. During a renewed attempt to break through, Schafer's panzer took a direct hit, two men dead, the rest seriously wounded. A further attempt to break out was no longer possible. Our vehicle, the last panzer of the *abteilung*, was destroyed.

By the end of the war, the once-mighty 6th SS Panzer Army had ceased to exist because of Hitler's obsession with Hungary and Budapest. One can only speculate how things might have gone if Guderian and Dietrich had got their own way and kept the 6th SS Panzer Army on the Oder. Sepp Dietrich was taken by the Americans at Kufstein, southeast of Munich.

Surrender

The 21st Panzer Division, which had struggled to counterattack the British on D-Day and had played a key role in stopping Goodwood, after fighting in the Lauban, Görlitz and Cottbus areas was finally overrun by the Soviets in April 1945. Losing command of 21st Panzer in January 1945, General Feuchtinger was arrested and busted to the ranks for his absence from divisional head-quarters on the night of 5/6 June 1944 and transferred to the 20th Panzer-grenadier Division, though he never served with the unit.

The Waffen-SS veterans of Normandy suffered varying fates on the Eastern Front, most seeking to avoid the wrath of the Soviets by retreating westward. The 1st SS Panzer Division, which had come to the rescue of the German defences south of Caen on the Bourguébus Ridge, now totalling just 1,500 men with sixteen tanks, as well as the remnants of the 9th SS, surrendered to American forces at Styer in Austria in May 1945. However, the Russians captured some of the forlorn rearguard of 1st SS.

Survivors from the 2nd SS, which had achieved miracles at Mortain, surrendered to American forces in Slovakia after fighting the Czech insurrection in Prague. The 10th SS, masters of Hill 112, surrendered to the Red Army at Schönau. Panzer Abteilung 502, which had also fought for Hill 112, ended its days trapped with the 9th Army in the Halbe pocket. The 12th SS, Hitler's teenage Nazis who had so bitterly contested Caen and Falaise just eight months earlier, numbering 455 men, also surrendered to the Americans in Austria. The bulk of the division finally gave up their arms to Patton's 65th Infantry Division, near Amstetten in Austria on 8 May. The sole surviving panzer belonging to the 12th SS also surrendered to the Americans that day. Those who had survived Falaise and the Ardennes must have felt bitterly that it had all been for nothing; in many ways they were right.

Eight bloody months

The Western Allies' victory in Normandy may not have been as resounding as they had hoped or planned, their faltering advance on Germany across France, Belgium and the Netherlands in the following months testified to that. Expectations that the war could be over by the autumn of 1944 in the wake of the destruction of the panzers in the Falaise pocket and the Rouen bridgehead, do seem over optimistic and grossly underestimated the Germans' ability and desire to carry on resisting. The defeat at Arnhem and the long drawn-out battle to clear the Scheldt estuary and open Antwerp soon crushed such optimism, resulting in a much broader and unnecessary effort against Germany's defences.

The panzer divisions' escape, fighting withdrawal and Herculean resurrection after the near destruction of Panzergruppe West in August 1944 ultimately prolonged the ugly death throes of Nazi Germany by eight bloody months, even though the Nazi High Command, apart from Hitler, recognised that the strategic initiative had long been lost. If Hitler had not insisted on throwing away his two revitalised panzer armies in the winter of 1944 it is likely the war could have dragged on even longer.

Appendix I

Panzer Division and General Headquarters Panzer Formations Strength in Northern France, June–September 1944

Panzer Division Strength as of June–August 1944

Unit	Personnel	Panzers*
2nd	13,100	175
9th	13,500	166
21st	16,297	135
116th	14,358	183
Panzer Lehr	13,099	237
1st SS	12,800	220
2nd SS	11,195	208
9th SS	16,800	164
10th SS	15,800	77
12th SS	17,000	197
17th SS	16,121	42
Total:	160,070	1,804

Panzer Division Strength as of 1 September 1944

Unit	Personnel	Panzers*
2nd	1,200	5
9th	11,000	0
21st	11,000	10
116th	10,600	15
Panzer Lehr	6,000	20
1st SS	7,800	0
2nd SS	12,357	6
9th SS	6,000	20

Unit	Personnel	Panzers*
10th SS	3,500	10
12th SS	12,000	0
17th SS	16,832	0
Total:	98,289	86

General Headquarters Panzer Formations Strength as of June–August 1944

Unit	Personnel	Panzers*
Panzer Abteilung 100	664	25
Schwere SS-Panzer Abteilung 101	?	45
Schwere SS-Panzer Abteilung 102	?	45
Panzer Abteilung 206	385	46
Sturmpanzer Abteilung 217	?	45
Panzer Abteilung 301 (Funklenk)	200	8
Schwere Panzer Abteilung 503	?	44
Schwere Panzerjäger Abteilung 654	?	33
Panzerjäger Abteilung 657	?	19
Fallschirm Sturmgeschütz Brigade 12	?	31
Sturmgeschütz Brigade 341	?	45
Sturmgeschütz Brigade 394	?	31
Sturmgeschütz Abteilung 902	?	31
Sturmgeschütz Abteilung 1348	122	10
Total:	?	458

General Headquarters Panzer Formations Strength as of 1 September 1944

Unit	Personnel	Panzers*
Panzer Abteilung 100	?	0
Schwere SS-Panzer Abteilung 101	?	0
Schwere SS-Panzer Abteilung 102	?	0
Panzer Abteilung 206	?	0
Sturmpanzer Abteilung 217	700	0

Unit	Personnel	Panzers*
Panzer Abteilung 301 (Funklenk)	?	0
Schwere Panzer Abteilung 503	?	14
Schwere Panzerjäger Abteilung 654	?	8
Panzerjäger Abteilung 657	?	0
Fallschirm Sturmgeschütz Brigade 12	?	0
Sturmgeschütz Brigade 341	434	12
Sturmgeschütz Brigade 394	350	0
Sturmgeschütz Abteilung 902	265	10
Sturmgeschütz Abteilung 1348	?	0
Total:	?	44

* This includes tanks, assault guns and tank destroyers, but not light tanks, self-propelled guns or armoured cars.

Appendix II

German Panzer Divisions in Normandy

Heer Panzer Regiments

2nd Panzer Division
Panzer Regiment 3

9th Panzer Division
Panzer Regiment 33

21st Panzer Division
Panzer Regiment 22

116th Panzer Division *Windhund*
Panzer Regiment 16

Panzer Lehr Division
Panzer Lehr Regiment

Waffen-SS Panzer Regiments

1st SS Panzer Division *Leibstandarte Adolf Hitler*
SS-Panzer Regiment 1

2nd SS Panzer Division *Das Reich*
SS-Panzer Regiment 2

9th SS Panzer Division *Hohenstaufen*
SS-Panzer Regiment 9

10th SS Panzer Division *Frundsberg*
SS-Panzer Regiment 10

12th SS Panzer Division *Hitlerjugend*
SS-Panzer Regiment 12

17th SS Panzergrenadier Division *Götz von Berlichingen*
SS-Panzer Abteilung 17

Independent and Infantry Panzer Units in Normandy

Heavy Tank Battalions
Schwere SS-Panzer Abteilung 101
Schwere SS-Panzer Abteilung 102
Schwere Panzer Abteilung 503

Tank Battalions
Panzer Abteilung 206
Sturmpanzer Abteilung 217
Panzer Abteilung 301 (Funklenk)
(IV Kompanie – assigned to 2nd Panzer Division)
Panzer Abteilung 302 (Funklenk)
(Kompanie 316 (Funklenk) only – assigned to Panzer Lehr Division)

Training Units
Panzer Ersatz un Ausbildungs Abteilung 100
(Assigned to 91st Airlanding Division)

Panzerjäger Battalions
Schwere Panzerjäger Abteilung 654
Panzerjäger Abteilung 657
Panzerjäger Abteilung 668 (towed anti-tanks guns only)

Assault Gun Units
Fallschirm Sturmgeschütz Brigade 12
Strumgeschütz Brigade 341
Sturmgeschütz Brigade 394
Sturmgeschütz Abteilung 902
Sturmgeschütz Abteilung 1348

Infantry Panzerjäger Battalions in Normandy
German infantry divisions' anti-tank battalions largely consisted of towed weapons, but at least six Heer Panzerjäger Battalions were also each equipped with fourteen Marder self-propelled and ten Sturmgeschütz assault guns:

243rd Infantry Division
Panzerjäger Abteilung 243

326th Infantry Division
Panzerjäger Abteilung 326

331st Infantry Division
Panzerjäger Abteilung 331

346th Infantry Division
Panzerjäger Abteilung 346

352nd Infantry Division
Panzerjäger Abteilung 352

353rd Infantry Division
Panzerjäger Abteilung 353

German Order of Battle

German Order of Battle June 1944

It should be noted that the divisional allocations to the various Corps varied considerably throughout the Battle for Normandy. The date in brackets is when the unit deployed to the Normandy theatre of operations or went into action.

Army Group B (Northern France and the Low Countries)

Panzergruppe West

I SS Panzer Corps
Panzer Lehr Panzer Division (went into action 7 June)
1st SS Panzer Division *Liebstandarte Adolf Hitler* (by 30 June)
12th SS Panzer Division *Hitlerjugend* (went into action on 7 June)
17th SS Panzergrenadier Division *Götz von Berlichingen* (8 June)

XLVII (47th) Panzer Corps plus LXVI (66th) Reserve Corps
2nd Panzer Division (mid-June)
11th Panzer Division
19th Panzer Division (returned to the Eastern front in July)
21st Panzer Division (went into action 6 June)
116th Panzer Division *Windhund* (24 July)

LVIII (58th) Reserve Panzer Corps
2nd SS Panzer Division *Das Reich* (mid-June)
9th Panzer Division (6 August)
189th Reserve Infantry Division

Reserve Panzer Divisions
155th Reserve Panzer Division
178th Reserve Panzer Division
179th Reserve Panzer Division
273rd Reserve Panzer Division

7th Army

XXV (25th) Corps (in Brittany)
265th Infantry Division (*kampfgruppe*, 12 June)
275th Infantry Division (*kampfgruppe*, 11 June)
343rd Infantry Division (*kampfgruppe*, 26 June)
353rd Infantry Division (16 June)

LXXIV (74th) Corps
77th Infantry Division (8 June)
266th Infantry Division (*kampfgruppe*, mid-June)

LXXXIV (84th) Corps
319th Infantry Division
352nd Infantry Division
709th Infantry Division
716th Infantry Division

Army Reserve
91st Airlanding Division (from Brittany in May)
243rd Infantry Division

II Parachute Corps
3rd Parachute Division (10 June)
5th Parachute Division (25 June)

15th Army

LXVII (67th) Corps
344th Infantry Division
348th Infantry Division

LXXXI (81st) Corps
17th Luftwaffe Field Division (by mid-August)
245th Infantry Division
711th Infantry Division

LXXXII (82nd) Corps
18th Luftwaffe Field Division
47th Infantry Division
49th Infantry Division

LXXXVIII (88th) Corps (in the Netherlands)
16th Luftwaffe Field Division (mid-June)
347th Infantry Division
719th Infantry Division

LXXXIX (89th) Corps
48th Infantry Division (mid-August)
70th Infantry Division
712th Infantry Division

Army Reserve
19th Luftwaffe Field Division
84th Infantry Division (by 30 July)
85th Infantry Division (5 August)
182nd Reserve Infantry Division
326th Infantry Division (by 30 July)
331st Infantry Division (by 30 July)
346th Infantry Division (7 June)

Army Group G (Southern France)

1st Army

LXXX (80th) Corps
158th Reserve Infantry Division
708th Infantry Division (by 30 July)

LXXXVI (86th) Corps
159th Reserve Infantry Division
276th Infantry Division (mid-June)

19th Army

IV Luftwaffe Field Corps
271st Infantry Division (mid-July)
272nd Infantry Division (mid-July)
277th Infantry Division (29 June)

LXXXV (85th) Corps
338th Infantry Division (mid-August)
244th Infantry Division

LXII (62nd) Reserve Corps
157th Reserve Infantry Division
242nd Infantry Division

From outside France and the Low Countries
9th SS Panzer Division (Russia – 29 June)
10th SS Panzer Division (Russia – 29 June)
2nd Parachute Division (Germany – to Brittany 12 June)
89th Infantry Division (Norway – early August)
363rd Infantry Division (Denmark – by 30 July)

German Order of Battle July–August 1944

Army Group B (Northern France and the Low Countries)

Panzergruppe West (5th Panzer Army)

I SS Panzer Corps
1st SS Panzer Division *Liebstandarte Adolf Hitler*
12th SS Panzer Division *Hitlerjugend*
716th Infantry Division

II SS Panzer Corps
9th SS Panzer Division *Hohenstaufen*
10th SS Panzer Division *Frundsberg*
277th Infantry Division

XLVII (47th) Panzer Corps
2nd Panzer Division
116th Panzer Division *Windhund*
276th Infantry Division
326th Infantry Division
1st SS Panzer Division *Liebstandarte Adolf Hitler* (Mortain counterattack)
2nd SS Panzer Division *Das Reich* (Mortain counterattack)
17th SS Panzergrenadier Division *Götz von Berlichingen* (Mortain counterattack)
275th Infantry Division (Mortain counterattack)

LVIII (58th) Panzer Corps
Panzer Lehr Division (Mortain counterattack)
17th SS Panzergrenadier Division *Götz von Berlichingen* (Mortain counterattack)
2nd Panzer Division (by 9 August)
2nd SS Panzer Division *Das Reich* (10 August)
10th SS Panzer Division (by 9 August, Corps reserve)

III Flak Corps
Flak-Sturm-Regimenter 1 to 4
Flakkampfgruppen 11700, 13300 and 12400

7th Army

II Parachute Corps
3rd Parachute Division
352nd Infantry Division (initially subordinate to LXXXIV Corps)
Fallschirm-Sturmgeschütz Brigade 12

XXV (25th) Corps (stationed in Brittany)
77th Infantry Division
265th Infantry Division

266th Infantry Division
319th Infantry Division (stationed in the Channel Islands)
343rd Infantry Division
2nd Parachute Division

LXXIV (74th) Corps
21st Panzer (transferred from LXXXVI Corps late July)

LXXXI (81st) Corps
9th Panzer Division
Panzer Lehr Panzer Division
331st Infantry Division (*kampfgruppe*)
708th Infantry Division

LXXXIV (84th) Corps
Panzer Lehr Division
2nd SS Panzer Division *Das Reich* (Kampfgruppe Weidinger)
17th SS Panzergrenadier Division *Götz von Berlichingen*
21st Panzer Division (transferred mid-June to LXXXVI Corps)
116th Panzer Division *Windhund* (Kampfgruppe Lueder)
243rd Infantry Division
275th Infantry Division
353rd Infantry Division
5th Luftwaffe Division
91st Airlanding Division

LXXXVI (86th) Corps
21st Panzer Division

Panzergruppe Eberbach (subordinate to 7th Army)

II SS Panzer Corps

XLVII Panzer Corps

LVIII Panzer Corps

Included remnants of 1st SS, 2nd SS, 9th SS, 17th SS, 2nd and 116th Panzer Divisions and 708th Infantry Division

Panzergruppe West and 7th Army Panzer Division Commanders

Heer Panzer Divisions

2nd Panzer

Generalleutnant Vollrath Lübbe	5 Sep 1942–1 Feb 1944
General der Panzertruppen Heinrich Freiherr von Lüttwitz	1 Feb 1944–5 May 1944
Generalleutnant Franz Westhoven	5 May 1944–27 May 1944
General der Panzertruppen Heinrich Freiherr von Lüttwitz	27 May 1944–31 Aug 1944
Generalmajor Henning Schönfeld	31 Aug 1944–15 Dec 1944
Generalmajor Meinrad von Lauchert	15 Dec 1944–20 Mar 1945
Generalmajor Oskar Munze	20 Mar 1945–1 Apr 1945
Oberst Carl Stollbrock	1 Apr 1945–8 May 1945

9th Panzer

Generalleutnant Erwin Jolasse	27 Nov 1943–10 Aug 1944
Oberst Max Sperling	10 Aug 1944–3 Sep 1944
Generalmajor Gerhard Müller	3 Sep 1944–16 Sep 1944
Generalleutnant Harald Freiherr von Elverfeldt	16 Sep 1944–6 Mar 1945
Oberst Helmut Zollenkopf	6 Mar 1945–26 Apr 1945

21st Panzer

Generalleutnant Edgar Feuchtinger	15 May 1943–15 Jan 1944
Generalmajor Oswin Grolig	15 Jan 1944–8 Mar 1944
Generalleutnant Franz Westhoven	8 Mar 1944–8 May 1944
Generalleutnant Edgar Feuchtinger	8 May 1944–25 Jan 1945
Oberst Helmut Zollenkopf	25 Jan 1945–12 Feb 1945
Generalleutnant Werner Marcks	12 Feb 1945–Apr 1945

116th Panzer

Generalmajor Gerhard Müller	28 Mar 1944–1 May 1944
General der Panzertruppen Gerhard Graf von Schwerin	1 May 1944–1 Sep 1944

| Generalmajor Heinrich Voigtsberger | 1 Sep 1944–14 Sep 1944 |
| Generalmajor Siegfried von Waldenburg | 14 Sep 1944–Apr 1945 |

Panzer Lehr

| Generalleutnant Fritz Bayerlein | 10 Jan 1944–20 Jan 1945 |
| Generalmajor Horst Niemack | 20 Jan 1945–Apr 1945 |

Waffen-SS Panzer Divisions

1st SS Leibstandarte Adolf Hitler

SS-Brigadeführer Theodor Wisch	7 Apr 1943–20 Aug 1944
SS-Brigadeführer Wilhelm Mohnke	20 Aug 1944–6 Feb 1945
SS-Brigadeführer Otto Kumm	6 Feb 1945–8 May 1945

2nd SS Das Reich

SS-Gruppenführer Heinz Lammerding	23 Oct 1943–24 July 1944
SS-Standartenführer Christian Tychsen	24 July 1944–28 July 1944
SS-Brigadeführer Otto Baum	28 July 1944–23 Oct 1944
SS-Gruppenführer Heinz Lammerding	23 Oct 1944–20 Jan 1945
SS-Standartenführer Karl Kreutz	20 Jan 1945–29 Jan 1945
SS-Gruppenführer Werner Ostnedorff	29 Jan 1945–9 Mar 1945
SS-Standartenführer Rudolf Lehmann	9 Mar 1945–13 Apr 1945
SS-Standartenführer Karl Kreutz	13 Apr 1945–8 May 1945

9th SS Hohenstaufen

SS-Obergruppenführer Willi Bittrich	15 Feb 1943–29 June 1944
SS-Oberführer Thomas Müller	29 June 1944–10 July 1944
SS-Brigadeführer Sylvester Stadler	10 July 1944–31 July 1944
SS-Oberführer Friedrich-Wilhelm Bock	31 July 1944–29 Aug 1944
SS-Standartenführer Walter Harzer	29 Aug 1944–10 Oct 1944
SS-Brigadeführer Sylvester Stadler	10 Oct 1944–8 May 1945

10th SS Frundsberg

SS-Gruppenführer Karl Fischer von Treuenfeld	15 Nov 1943–27 Apr 1944
SS-Gruppenführer Heinz Harmel	27 Apr 1944–Apr 1945
SS-Obersturmbannführer Franz Roestel	Apr 1945–8 May 1945

12th SS Hitlerjugend

SS-Brigadeführer Fritz Witt	24 June 1943–14 June 1944
SS-Brigadeführer Kurt Meyer	14 June 1944–6 Sep 1944
SS-Obersturmbannführer Hubert Meyer	6 Sep 1944–24 Oct 1944
SS-Brigadeführer Fritz Kraemer	24 Oct 1944–13 Nov 1944
SS-Brigadeführer Hugo Kraas	13 Nov 1944–8 May 1945

Waffen-SS Panzergrenadier Divisions

17th SS Götz von Berlichingen

SS-Gruppenführer Werner Ostendorff	30 Oct 1943–15 June 1944
SS-Standartenführer Otto Binge	17 June 1944–20 June 1944
SS-Brigadeführer Otto Baum	20 June 1944–1 Aug 1944
SS-Standartenführer Otto Binge	1 Aug 1944–29 Aug 1944
SS-Oberführer Dr. Eduard Deisenhofer	30 Aug 1944–Sep 1944
SS-Oberführer Thomas Müller	Sep 1944–Sep 1944
SS-Standartenführer Gustav Mertsch	Sep 1944–Oct 1944
SS-Gruppenführer Werner Ostendorff	21 Oct 1944–Nov 1944
SS-Standartenführer Hans Linger	Nov 1944–Jan 1945
Oberst Gerhard Lindner	15 Jan 1945–21 Jan 1945
SS-Oberführer Fritz Klingenberg	21 Jan 1945–22 Mar 1945
SS-Oberführer Georg Bochmann	Mar 1945–8 May 1945

Heavy Tank Battalions

Schwere Panzer Abteilung 503

Hauptmann Graf Kageneck	May 1943–Feb 1944
Hauptmann Fromme	Feb 1944–Dec 1944
Hauptmann von Diest-Koerber	Dec 1944–Jan 1945

Schwere SS-Panzer Abteilung 101

SS-Obersturmbannführer Leiner	9 Nov 1943–13 Feb 1944
SS-Obersturmbannführer von Westerhagen	13 Feb 1944–20 Mar 1945
SS-Sturmbannführer Kling	20 Mar 1945–8 May 1945

Schwere SS-Panzer Abteilung 102

SS-Sturmbannführer Laackmann	Jan 1944–Mar 1944
SS-Sturmbannführer Weiss	Mar 1944–18 Aug 1944
SS-Sturmbannführer Hartrampf	Aug 1944–May 1945

Principal Allied Codenames

Allied Deception Codenames

BODYGUARD

Overall Allied strategic deception plan for the invasion of France, designed to shield Overlord from German intelligence. This encompassed Operations Fortitude, Quicksilver and Zeppelin.

FORTITUDE (NORTH AND SOUTH)

Allied deception plans designed to convince the Germans that the main invasion in France would occur in the Pas de Calais area and/or Norway.

QUICKSILVER

Part of Fortitude which covered the fictitious US 1st Army Group under General George S Patton in southeast England, poised to strike across the Pas de Calais.

CASCADE

Deception plan designed to mislead the Axis as to the true strength of Allied forces in the Mediterranean; was followed by Operation Zeppelin.

ZEPPELIN

Deception plan designed to convince the Germans that the Allies would attack Crete or Western Greece from the Mediterranean, or Romania via the Black Sea.

Principal Allied Operational Codenames

OVERLORD

6 June 1944: American, British and Canadian seaborne invasion of northern France, conducted on the Normandy coastline between Quineville in the west and Ouistreham to the east.

NEPTUNE

6 June 1944: The naval and assault landing element of Overlord.

PERCH
13–14 June 1944: British attack west of Caen designed to turn the German flank by seizing Villers-Bocage.

EPSOM
25/26 June – 1 July 1944: British offensive west of Caen toward Evrecy, south of the city; intended as a pre-emptive strike to tie up German armour reinforcements.

DAUNTLESS
25 June 1944: Subsidiary attack supporting Epsom, designed to secure the western flank prior to the main operation.

MARTLET
25 June 1944: British operation to capture Fontenay-le-Pesnil as part of Epsom and Dauntless.

CHARNWOOD
7–10 July 1944: Frontal assault launched by the British and Canadians to capture Caen, only succeeded in taking the northern half of the city.

JUPITER
10 July 1944: British attack west of Caen following Charnwood.

GREENLINE
15 July 1944: British attack intended to pin down German armour west of Caen prior to Goodwood.

GOODWOOD
18–21 July 1944: British offensive east of Caen, intended to assist the capture of the city and pin down German forces prior to the American break-out from the Cotentin Peninsula.

ATLANTIC
18–20 July 1944: Launched by the Canadians in conjunction with Operation Goodwood to capture Caen and get over the Orne.

SPRING
24–27 July: Conducted by the Canadians, designed to capture the Bourguébus and Verrières ridges south of Caen to open up the Falaise road. Also tied German forces down during Operation Cobra.

COBRA

25–31 July 1944: Launched by the Americans just west of St Lô to break out from the Normandy bridgehead, enabling them to strike southwest into Brittany and southeast toward Falaise and the River Seine.

BLUECOAT

30 July–7 August 1944: Intended to support Operation Cobra by drawing German forces to the Caen area and capturing Mont Pinçon.

TOTALISE

7–13 August 1944: British, Canadian and Polish attack along the Caen–Falaise Road intended to capture Falaise.

TRACTABLE

14–16 August 1944: Development of Totalise designed to close the neck of the Falaise salient, thereby trapping 5th Panzer Army, Panzergruppe Eberbach and 7th Army.

DRAGOON

15 August 1944: Allied invasion of the south of France between Toulon and Cannes forcing the German evacuation of France.

Appendix VII

Table of Equivalent Ranks

German Army	Waffen-SS	British Army	US Army
Feldmarschall	Reichsführer-SS	Field Marshal	General of the Army
Generaloberst	SS-Oberstgruppenführer	General	General
General der Panzertruppen etc	SS-Obergruppenführer	Lieutenant General	Lieutenant General
Generalleutnant	SS-Gruppenführer	Major General	Major General
Generalmajor	SS-Brigadeführer	Brigadier	Brigadier General
Oberst	SS-Oberführer or SS-Standartenführer	Colonel	Colonel
Oberstleutnant	SS-Obersturmbannführer	Lieutenant Colonel	Lieutenant Colonel
Major	SS-Sturmbannführer	Major	Major
Hauptmann	SS-Hauptsturmführer	Captain	Captain
Oberleutnant	SS-Obersturmführer	Lieutenant	1st Lieutenant
Leutnant	SS-Untersturmführer	2nd Lieutenant	2nd Lieutenant
Stabsfeldwebel	SS-Sturmscharführer	Regimental Sergeant Major	Sergeant Major
Hauptfeldwebel	SS-Hauptscharführer	Sergeant Major	Master Sergeant
N/A	SS-Oberscharführer	N/A	Technical Sergeant
Feldwebel	SS-Scharführer	Staff Sergeant	Staff Sergeant
Unteroffizer	SS-Unterscharführer	Sergeant	Sergeant
Stabsgefreiter	N/A	N/A	Staff Corporal
Obergefreiter	SS-Rottenführer	Corporal	Senior Corporal
Gefreiter	SS-Sturmmann	Lance Corporal	Corporal
Oberschütze	SS-Oberschütze	N/A	Private 1st Class
Schütze	SS-Schütze	Private	Private

Bibliography

Note on Sources

English language published and unpublished literature covering the many aspects of D-Day and the subsequent Normandy campaign is simply quite vast, but little of it deals explicitly with German experiences or indeed that of the panzer divisions. I have referred to, and quoted extensively from, the wide-range of works listed in full in the bibliography. Detailed endnotes, most notably for the quotes, have been deliberately omitted for the sake of brevity.

In preparing this volume I would particularly like to recommend Eric Lefevre's superb *Panzers in Normandy then and now*, Richard Hargreaves' *The Germans in Normandy*, and Niklas Zetterling's *Normandy 1944*. Lefevre's work is by far the best single volume dealing with the panzer regiments role and organisation in Normandy. Zetterling's magisterial study, drawing on primary German sources, provides a comprehensive organisational survey of almost every single German ground unit, including Heer, Waffen-SS and Luftwaffe, committed to the battle.

Also of note is Georges Bernage's *The Panzers and the Battle for Normandy*, though this only covers up to late July 1944, missing out the final stages of the battle, and Jean-Paul Pallud's *Rückmarsh!*, looking at the German retreat to the Seine. In contrast, Paul Carell's *Invasion – They're Coming!*, first published in Germany in 1960, documenting the battle from the German perspetive, has since been discredited as being inaccurate in places.

The postwar debriefs by Generals Eberbach, Fahrmbacher, von Gersdorff, Hausser, von Lüttwitz and von Schweppenburg, edited by David Isby, provide invaluable insight into the deployment of the *panzertruppen* and subsequent bitter squabbles amongst the German commanders about how the battle played out. They do, though, need to be treated with a degree of caution as many of the generals were seeking to exonerate their own performances, whilst blaming others for any perceived shortcomings. The original interviews are held at the US National Archives and the Military History Institute at the US Army War College. Basil Liddel Hart's classic *The Other Side of the Hill*, in which he interviewed many of the senior German generals, provides similar insight into the German High Command.

The German sitreps, or Weekly Situation Reports, also provide a snapshot of the slowly deteriorating situation in Normandy, especially in terms of the Allies mounting pressure on the German defences and the paucity of replacement troops and equipment. The Imperial War Museum, Public Archives of Canada, and the UK and US National Archives are the key depositories for most of the English language primary source material relating to this campaign.

Readers seeking a good overview will not do better than reading Major General David Belchem's perceptive *Victory in Normandy*. He served as head of Montgomery's planning staff and provides a first rate, concise yet comprehensive account. Likewise Max Hasting's *Overlord* has much to recommend it.

The best accounts of the brutal battle for Caen are the works by Henry Maule and Alexander McKee, while the best works on Operation Cobra are James Carafano's very detailed analysis, though this is mainly from the American point of view, and Steven Zaloga's readily accessible volume. There are many works on Falaise. The best known is James Lucas and James Barker's study and the most concise is Ken Ford's, while William Breuer's book verges toward the sensational. Recent detailed battlefield guides include the useful volumes by Stephen Hart and Paul Latawski. The most readily available accounts of 2nd SS Panzer Division's troubled march north are those by Max Hastings and Phil Vickers, both titled *Das Reich*. Notably, many of the earlier published studies consulted are out of print.

Contemporary Sources and Memoirs

Belchem, Major-General D, *Victory in Normandy* (London, 1981).

Butcher, H C, *Three Years with Eisenhower* (London, 1946).

De Guingand, Major-General Sir Francis, *Operation Victory* (London, 1947).

Eisenhower, D D, *Crusade in Europe* (London, 1948).

Fey, W, *Armour Battles of the Waffen-SS 1943–45* (Mechanisburg, PA, 2003).

Guderian, H G, *From Normandy to the Ruhr: With the 116th Panzer Division in World War II* (Bedford, PA, 2001).

Hagen, L, *Arnhem Lift* (Barnsley, 1993).

Harris, Marshal of the RAF Sir Arthur, *Bomber Offensive* (London, 1947).

Horrocks, Lieutenant General Sir Brian, *A Full Life* (London, 1960).

Isby, D C, (ed), Freiherr von Gersdorff, Generaloberst Paul Hausser et al, *Fighting the Breakout: The German Army in Normandy from 'Cobra' to the Falaise Gap* (London/ Mechanicsburg, PA, 2004).

Isby, D C, (ed), Heinz Guderian, Fritz Kraemer, Fritz Ziegelmann, Freiherr von Lüttwitz et al, *Fighting In Normandy:The German Army from D-Day to Villers-Bocage* (London/Mechanicsburg, PA, 2001).

Liddell Hart, B H, (ed), *The Rommel Papers* (London, 1953).

Liddell Hart, B H, *The Other Side of the Hill* (London, 1951).

Luck, Hans von, *Panzer Commander* (New York, 1991).

Montgomery, Field Marshal Bernard Law, *The Memoirs of Field Marshal Montgomery* (London, 1958).

Morrison, A, *Silent Invader* (Shrewsbury, 2002).

Moulton, Major-General J L, *Battle for Antwerp* (London, 1978).

Powell, G, *The Devil's Birthday: The Bridges to Arnhem, 1944* (London, 1984).

Rohmer, Major-General R, *Patton's Gap* (London, 1981).

Trevor-Roper, H R, (ed), *Hitler War Directives 1939–45* (London, 1964).

United States War Department Technical Manual *Handbook on German Military Forces* (15 March 1945).

Urquhart, Major General R E, *Arnhem* (London, 1958).

Warlimont, W, *Inside Hitler's Headquarters 1939–1945* (New York, 1964).

Wilmot, C, *The Struggle for Europe* (London, 1952).

Other Published Sources

Ambrose, S E, *Pegasus Bridge, D-Day: The Daring British Airborne Raid* (London, 2003).

Ambrose, S E, *D-Day June 6, 1944: The Battle for the Normandy Beaches* (London, 2002).

Ambrose, S E, *Citizen Soldiers: From the Beaches of Normandy to the Surrender of Germany* (London, 2002).

Angolia, J R, *On the Field of Honour*, Volumes I and II (San Jose, 1980).

Badsey, S, *Normandy 1944: Allied landings and breakout* (Oxford, 1990).

Baverstock, *Breaking the Panzers: The Bloody Battle for Rauray, Normandy, 1st July 1944* (Stroud, 2002).

Belfield, E, and Essame, H, *The Battle for Normandy* (London, 1983).

Bender, R J, and Odegard, W W, *Uniforms, Organisation and History of the Panzer-truppen* (San Hose, 1980).

Bender, R J, and Taylor, H P, *Uniforms, Organisation and History of the Waffen-SS*, Volumes I–V (Jan Jose 1980).

Bennet, R, *Ultra in the West: The Normandy Campaign* (London 1980).

Bernage, G, *The Panzers and the Battle for Normandy, June 5th–July 20th 1944* (Bayeux Cedex 2000).

Bernage, G, and Cadel, G, *Cobra* (Bayeux 1984).

Bernage, G, and Cadel, G, *Invasion Journal Pictorial* (Bayeux 1984).

Breuer, W B, *Hoodwinking Hitler: The Normandy Deception* (Westport, Connecticut 1993).

Breuer, W B, *The Death of a Nazi Army: The Falaise Pocket* (USA 1985).

Bruce, G, *Second Front Now! The Road To D-Day* (London 1979).

Buckingham, W F, *D-Day The First 72 Hours* (Stroud 2004).

Carafano, J J, *After D-Day Operation Cobra and the Normandy Breakout* (London 2000).

Carell, P, *Invasion – They're Coming!* (London 1963).

Carruthers B, and Trew, S, *The Normandy Battles* (London 2000).

Cawthorne, N, *Fighting them on the Beaches – The D-day Landings June 6, 1944* (London 2002).

Chant, C, *The Encyclopedia of Codenames of World War II* (London 1986).

Chicken, S, *Overlord Coastline: The Major D-Day Locations* (Tunbridge Wells 1993).

Clark, L, *Orne Bridgehead* (Sutton 2004).

Clark, L, *Operation Market Garden Netherlands 17–25 September 1944* (London 2004).

Clark, L, and Hart, Dr S, *The Drive on Caen Northern France 7 June–9 July 1944* (London 2004).

Collet, J M, (ed), *Arromanches 44 The Normandy Invasion* (Brussels 1984).

Collier, R, *Ten Thousand Eyes* (New York 2001).

Culver, B, and Murphy, B, *Panzer Colours*, Volumes I–III (London 1976).

Cross, R, *The Battle of the Bulge 1944 Hitler's Last Hope* (Staplehurst 2002).

Daglish, I, *Operation Goodwood* (Barnsley 2004).

Daugherty, L, *The Battle of the Hedgerows, Bradley's First Army in Normandy, June–July 1944* (Shepperton 2001).

Delaforce, P, *Churchill's Desert Rats, From Normandy to Berlin with the 7th Armoured Division* (London 2001).

D'Este, C, *Eisenhower* (London 2003).

D'Este, C, *Decision in Normandy* (London 1984).

Doherty, R, *Normandy 1944 The Road to Victory* (Staplehurst 2004).

Ellis, C, *21st Panzer Division Rommel's Afrika Korps Spearhead* (Hersham 2001).

Essame, H, *Normandy Bridgehead* (London 1971).

Ford, K, *Falaise 1944 Death of an Army* (Oxford 2005).

Ford, K, *D–Day 1944 Sword Beach and the British Airborne landing* (Oxford 2002).

Ford, R, *Fire From the Forest, The SAS Brigade in France, 1944* (London 2004).

Forty, G, *7th Armoured Division The 'Desert Rats'* (Hersham 2003).

Franks, N, *Typhoon Attack* (London 2003).

Fürbringer, H, *9 SS-Panzer-Division Hohenstaufen* (Bayeux 1984).

Gardiner, J, *D–Day Those Who Were There* (London 1994).

Grant, R, *The 51st Highland Division at War* (London 1977).

Hamilton, N, *Monty Master of the Battlefield 1942–1944* (London 1983).

Hamilton, N, *Monty The Field-Marshal 1944–1976 (London 1986)*.

Hargreaves, R, *The Germans in Normandy* (Barnsley 2006).

Harrison, G A, *United States Army in World War II: European Theatre of Operations 'Cross Channel Attack,'* US Army Dept of Military History (Washington DC 1970).

Hart, S, *The Final Battle for Normandy Northern France 9 July–30 August 1944* (London 2005).

Hart, S, *Road to Falaise* (Stroud 2004).

Hart, S Dr, Hart, R Dr, and Hughes, M Dr, *The German Soldier in World War II* (Staplehurst 2000).

Hastings, M, *Armageddon The Battle for Germany 1944–45* (London 2004).

Hastings, M, *Overlord D–Day and the Battle for Normandy* (London 1984).

Hastings, M, *Das Reich* (London 1981).

Hills, S, *By Tank into Normandy* (London 2003).

Hook, H, *Hohenstaufen 9th SS Panzer Division* (Hersham, 2005).

Howarth, D, *Dawn of D–Day* (London 1959).

Hunt, E, *Mont Pinçon August 1944* (Barnsley 2003).

Hunt, R, and Mason, H, *Camera at War: The Normandy Campaign* (London 1976).

Hunter, R, and Brown, T H C, *Battle Coast: An Illustrated History of D–Day The Sixth of June 1944* (Bourne End 1973).

Irving, D, *The War between the Generals* (London 1981).

Johnson, G, and Dunphie, C, *Brightly Shone The Dawn: Some Experiences of the Normandy Invasion* (London 1980).

Keegan, J, *Six Armies in Normandy* (London 1982).

Latawski, P, *Falaise Pocket* (Stroud 2004).

Lefevre, E, *Panzers in Normandy then and now* (London 1983).

Kershaw, R J, D-*Day Piercing the Atlantic Wall* (Shepperton 1993).

Lehman, R, *Die Leibstandarte*, Volumes IV and V (Osnabruck 1984).

Lewis, J E (ed), *D-Day As They Saw It* (London 2004).

Lucas, J, and Barker, J, *The Killing Ground* (London 1978).

Lucas, J, and Cooper, M, *Hitler's Elite: Leibstandarte SS 1933–45* (London 1975).

MacDonald, C B, *The Battle of the Bulge* (London 1984).

Macksey, K, *Rommel: Battles and Campaigns* (London 1979).

Man, J, *The Penguin Atlas of D-Day and the Normandy Campaign* (London 1944).

Maule, H, *Caen: The Brutal Battle and the Break-out from Normandy* (Newton Abbott 1976).

McCue, P, *SAS Operation Bulbasket: Behind the lines in Occupied France 1944* (London 1996).

McKee, A M, *Caen Anvil of Victory* (London 1964).

Messenger, C, *The D-Day Atlas: Anatomy of the Normandy Campaign* (London 2004).

Messenger, C, *Hitler's Gladiator: The Life and Times of Oberstgruppenführer and Panzer-general-Oberst der Waffen-SS Sepp Dietrich* (London 1988).

Munoz, A, *Iron Fist: A Combat History of the 17 SS Panzergrenadier Division Gotz von Berlichingen* (1999).

Neillands, R, and De Norman, R, *D-Day 1944 Voices from Normandy* (London 2002).

Perrett, B, *The Tiger Tanks* (London 1981).

Pallud, J P, *Rückmarsh! The German Retreat from Normandy* (Old Harlow 2006).

Quarrie, B, *German Airborne Troops* (London 1983).

Ripley, T, *Patton Unleashed: Patton's Third Army and the Breakout from Normandy, August–September 1944* (Staplehurst 2003).

Ryan, C, *The Longest Day June 6 1944* (London 1982).

Ryan, C, *A Bridge Too Far* (London 1974).

Saunders, T, *Hill 112 Battles of the Odon – 1944* (Barnsley 2001).

Saunders, T, *Nijmegen US 82nd Airborne and Guards Armoured Division* (Barnsley 2001).

Seaton, A, *The German Army 1939–45* (London 1982).

Seaton, A, *The Fall of Fortress Europe 1943–1945* (London 1981).

Sharpe, M, and Davis, B L, *Das Reich Waffen-SS Armoured Elite* (Hersham 2003).

Sharpe, M, and Davis, B L, *Leibstandarte Hitler's Elite Bodyguard* (Hersham 2002).

Smith, S, *2nd Armoured Division 'Hell on Wheels'* (Hersham 2003).

Somerville, C, *Our War How the British Commonwealth Fought the Second World War* (London 1998).

Stafford, D, *Ten Days to D-Day – Countdown to the Liberation of Europe* (London 2003).

Stein, G H, *The Waffen-SS* (London 1977).

Steinzer, F, *Die 2 Panzer Division 1933–45* (Freidberg 1980).

Telp, C Dr, *The Advance from the Seine to Antwerp 25 August–30 September 1944* (London 2005).

Thompson, J, *The Imperial War Museum Book of Victory in Europe* (London 1994).

Thompson, R W, *D-Day Spearhead of Invasion* (London 1968).

Tout, K, *Roads to Falaise 'Cobra' and 'Goodwood' Reassessed* (Stroud 2002).

Tout, K, *The Bloody Battle for Tilly, Normandy 1944* (Stroud 2000).

Tout, K, *A Fine Night for Tanks: The Road to Falaise* (Stroud 1998).

Thornton, W, *The Liberation of Paris* (London 1963).

Tucker-Jones, A, *Hitler's Great Panzer Heist, Germany's Foreign Armour in Action 1939–45* (Barnsley 2007).

Turner, J F, *Invasion '44* (Shrewsbury 2002).

Tute, W, Costello, J, and Hughes, T, *D-Day* (London 1975).

Vickers, P, *Das Reich – 2nd SS Panzer Division Das Reich – Drive to Normandy June 1944* (Barnsley 2000).

Warner, P, *The D-Day Landings* (London 1980).

Wellstead, I, *SAS with the Maquis in Action: with the French Resistance June–September 1944* (London 1994).

Whiting, C, *Siegfried The Nazis' Last Stand* (London 2003).

Whiting, C, *West Wall The Battle for Hitler's Siegfried Line September 1944–March 1945* (London 2002).

Whiting, C, *Patton's Last Battle* (Staplehurst 2002).

Whiting, C, *Bounce the Rhine* (London 1985).

Whiting, C, *'44 In Combat on the Western front from Normandy to the Ardennes* (London 1984).

Williams, A, *D-Day to Berlin* (London 2004).

Wilt, A F, *The Atlantic Wall 1941–44 Hitler's Defences for D-Day* (New York 2004).

Wise, T, *D-Day to Berlin* (London 1979).

Wynn, H, and Young, S, *Prelude To Overlord* (Shrewsbury 1983).

Young, Brigadier P, *D-Day* (London 1981).

Zaloga, S J, *Operation Cobra 1944* (Oxford 2001).

Zetterling, N, *Normandy 1944, German Military Organization, Combat Power and Organizational Effectiveness* (Winnipeg, Manitoba 2000).

Index